SECOND HELPINGS OF
ROAST
CHICKEN

By the same author
Roast Chicken and Other Stories

SECOND HELPINGS OF
ROAST
CHICKEN

A Recipe Book
By

SIMON HOPKINSON

ILLUSTRATIONS BY FLO BAYLEY

NEW YORK

For Ann and Franco Taruschio with love and gratitude

First paperback edition published in 2006 by Ebury Publishing,
a division of Random House.

ISBN: 978-1-4013-2332-5

Hyperion books are available for special promotions,
premiums, or corporate training. For details contact Michael
Rentas, Proprietary Markets, Hyperion, 77 West 66th Street,
12th floor, New York, New York 10023, or call 212-456-0133.

First U.S. Edition

10   9   8   7   6   5   4   3   2   1

641.5

CONTENTS

FOREWORD

Simon Hopkinson can be quite peremptory. Which is why we worry about things in our shopping baskets of which he wouldn't approve, or things we do over the stove which he would find sloppy, or things in our pantries which are pre-packed or just packaged. Why can't we all be as autocratic as Simon? Well, I can, so now I'm giving you exact instructions on how to read this book:

1. First read the essay at the start of each section (forty-seven of these). Now you will understand why a very few cookbooks should be read, and the rest just used. These exceptional books enhance your understanding of cooking – and even of life. The rest just enhance a dish or a meal. Thank goodness for them, of course, but they're reference, not reading. Simon's predilections are not just good copy. They are well researched, brilliantly observed, and compulsively readable.

2. Now turn back to the chapters you found most seductive and choose a recipe. The best are so mouthwatering that you will already be preheated to the point where your "oil is almost smoking."

3. Just before you launch into one of these irresistible dishes, spare a thought for this little conundrum:

a) Simon always says you should not decide in advance what to cook. You should go to the market, see what's freshest and best, buy it, and then decide what to do with it. And, of course, he's right if you live in Normandy, or Perigord, or Provence.

b) Simon gives you a recipe so compelling that you've simply got to do it for supper. So you rush out to buy the ingredients. OK, the tarragon is a bit tired and the spring onions aren't exactly sparkling, but how else are you to do what Simon so commandingly says?

4.   Forget the conundrum and get cooking. These are recipes that work. You will not just eat sumptuously, you will also learn how suddenly pears go bad, how tarragon is indispensable, how rice needs real understanding, how suet is not to be disregarded, how mussels are more than *marinières,* and how peas and pears in cans are not to be sneezed at. Since I am invoked in the cocktail chapter I had better be tactful, but you ought to know that I have moved on – to the Cajun Martini, gin wickedly marinated in jalapeño peppers.

You will also find a threnody running through this book, for good things neglected, forgotten, or undervalued. For the woodcock, for the vanished fish markets of our coastal towns, and for moms who once cooked from the land and not from the freezer. Not a sad book, though. Actually rather a sparky one. Cook alongside Simon Hopkinson and life can never be glum for long. And hang on to your own culinary foibles, even if they seem a bit feeble in the face of Simon's magisterial sideswipes at the world of trendy cooking.

Of course since I'm writing this foreword, I've had a privileged preview of this book. So I know that you who are standing in line for second helpings will enjoy your meal more than ever before. Me (although this is strictly not allowed), me, I'm starting the queue for thirds.

Michael Birkett

INTRODUCTION

It took me a very long time to write the first *Roast Chicken and Other Stories* (published by Ebury Press in 1994). Around about five years, in fact, all told. In those days I wrote every single word with a nice and soft 2B pencil and used a yellow American legal pad on which to scribble them – simply because I liked the color and smoothness of the paper's surface. Apart from anything else, I had always enjoyed writing – in the calligraphic sense, that is – and had acquired a particular skill in this respect at an early age. This quietly pleasurable talent has now deteriorated somewhat, mainly due to many years of unnecessarily speed-handwriting the lunch and dinner menus for both Hilaire (the first London restaurant in which I cooked) and, later, Bibendum, and which I constantly think of as a most tragic loss to me.

And with this in mind, if you will permit me, I feel moved to fondly recall my reading and writing master at prep school in the early 1960s, Mr. Hooton (an extremely tall man who had previously been employed by the Cambridge police force), who, although being mildly eccentric – "You, boy, make all speed to the Lord High Pen at Heffers and equip yourself with the finest Osmiroid!" – was possessed of the finest script and also introduced me to *The Hobbit* at eight years old, which he recited in a different voice for each and every character, with his Smaug interpretation being particularly terrifying.

Personally, however, I will forever remember him as K. V. Hooton, as that was how I referred to him in my first letter home: ". . . and we had a reading and writing lesson with K. V. Hooton." For it was as "*Cave* Hooton" that his name first came to be used by my previously informed, roister boistering school chums as he strode along the school corridor, inexorably making his way towards juvenile din and the open classroom door . . .

Roast Chicken was also my first serious attempt at writing anything expansive at all on the subject of food. In fact, if I think back to the late 1980s and early 1990s – that approximately five-year span I spent trying to put *Roast Chicken and Other Stories* together – I did not take the matter seriously at all. After all, I was busy cooking. How on earth would I find time to write a cookbook too? Yes, well, the simple answer, of course, is that someone asked me if I would like to. Oh, hello, ego! But it is really to four people in particular that I wish to give thanks for enabling me to write something about food rather than simply cook it. In chronological order they are Fay Maschler, Anthony Goff, Jill Norman, and Lindsey Bareham.

After having consumed a seemingly enjoyable lunch at Hilaire, circa 1985, Fay Maschler suggested to me that I might like to deputize for her in the "Eating In" column she was then writing for the *Evening Standard,* as she was due to go on holiday a few weeks hence. At the time, the column consisted of a chosen daily recipe accompanied by a brief closing résumé of suggested ingredients to purchase for the following day's recipe. It quickly became clear she would be most grateful if I took on the task: "I think you'd be very good," she said (hello, ego, again). And I would like to point out here that however flattering this generous offer seemed to me at the time – and it really did and I would do it again tomorrow – seventeen years on, it seems that it is now only the visual and in-your-face cookery-related commissions that light up the face and (so often, fraudulently) line the wallet of the unscrupulous.

As a result of this hugely enjoyable deputy service, a letter from someone called Anthony Goff of "David Higham Associates" (and who has remained my literary agent from that day to this) promptly arrived the following week – and on very smart letterhead. He was absurdly suggesting that I might like to write a cookbook. Secretly terrified, I was, nevertheless, absolutely thrilled to bits. I must now admit to being thankful, however, that there was no mention in this letter of the heinous typo where the ingredients for pastry for a cherry and almond tart recipe called for only 2 oz butter to be worked into a whole 1 lb of flour . . .

I thought, but surely I'm just a cook. I only managed five "O" levels, for heaven's sake, *and* failed Eng. lang. to boot (I passed lit., but only just), and felt I wasn't really ready for this. Memories of school, then, still seemed relatively fresh in my mind – particularly my lazy thoughts of all things done at a desk. But soon after this, I also met the editor and publisher Jill Norman, who chose to ask me the very same question: "How about a book?" And then someone else informed me that Jill Norman had, without doubt, become the most important cookbook editor in the land and had further been entirely responsible for gathering together the past writings of Elizabeth David for a book she had recently published under the title *An Omelette and a Glass of Wine* and which, to this day, remains my favorite of all her books. Most importantly, I liked Jill immediately.

And then Elizabeth David herself came to dinner at Hilaire with James Olney (brother to the late Richard Olney) and Valerie Eliot. I recall sending up a small bowl of shrimp consommé that I just happened to have made that very morning – and was particularly proud of – as an extra taste between first and main courses. (I learned later that she had begun to loathe these precocious "show off" intrusions into her chosen meal; and with experienced hindsight, how very right she was.) Gladly, however, although the waiter had gently informed me that the proffered bowl of fish broth was initially met by E.D. with resignation and a slump of the shoulders, twenty minutes later it was to be all Oliver Twist and Mr. Bumble. My scuffed copy of *Omelette* was generously inscribed over coffee and I beamed stupidly.

And then Paul Levy brought Richard Olney to dinner. And then I had lunch with Richard at his home in France. And then I asked Elizabeth David out to lunch. Inspiration had never arrived so richly. K. V. Hooton's order "Off to the Lord High Pen[cil] at Jeffers!" rang memorably in my ears – and get yourself a good dictionary and a thesaurus too, while you're about it, kiddo, I thought. Eventually, after sporadic jottings here and there by me, coupled with the suggestion to Anthony Goff that Jill Norman should most definitely also be my editor, wheels slowly began to grind. It transpired, rather embarrassingly, that not one of those yellow-legal-pad jottings came to be neatly assessed until I had already left Hilaire by three years as I had, by then, become distractedly overcome by pressures of birth of the big and bold Bibendum.

So torturous, worrying, dispiriting and angst-ridden was the putting together of the restaurant that it now occurs to me that those who actually *enjoy* such a pastime are, quite clearly, queer in the head. In fact, the thought of throwing in the towel (a crisp, unused *torchon,* perhaps?) in favor of simply getting on with quietly writing an enormously user-friendly cookbook (it was never going to be a chef's book), which had been expected from me for far too long as it was, very nearly became the more serious option.

But could I get this book done? Could I fish-hooks! (A particular favorite exclamation often used by my late mother and which also remains one of mine to this day.) Enter Lindsey Bareham: "Look here, my dear, if you're finding it impossible to finish this book why don't you let me help you get it done?" And so with a swift exchange of vows over the telephone from the middle of a particularly hectic lunch service at Bibendum to a particularly less-stressed street in Chiswick, the innards of *Roast Chicken and Other Stories* quietly began to ripen and mature.

Twice, sometimes three times a week in leafy Chiswick I would read from my rather crumpled orange-tinged sheets (one can't really say "yellowed," can one, in this instance?) and churn out chat and recipes that would, in turn, appear on the screen of L.B.'s computer thingy. And we also happily compiled data as far away as Abergavenny and Suffolk on two memorable occasions. With regard to the latter location, almost an entire chapter was lost one evening when L.B.'s overexcited dog

Sam suddenly decided to career uncontrollably about the sun lounge detaching wires, plugs, and sockets in his wake. We had chosen the room thinking it might produce some excellent work, bathed as it was in the waning Walberswick sunshine and ideal for sipping chilled glasses of fragrant Trimbach Riesling as we worked. The crab chapter was very nearly lost forever in the smacking of a dog's bottom.

So, then, here I am another seven years later with the follow-up. Somehow, it seems to have taken even longer to write than the first effort – possibly due to there being no L.B. to crack the whip a little this time around. Mind you, it is considerably longer: the chapter count in this volume is forty-seven compared with the forty in *Chicken One*. The system is exactly the same, the illustrator is the same (the illustrious and spinningly lovely Flo Bayley), and each chapter begins with an introduction of some sort (also much lengthier this time) and is then followed by three recipes. The single repetition is the "Chicken" chapter, obviously, but it is brand-new for *Chicken Two*. As too is my long-suffering, endlessly patient, deeply loyal editor, the gorgeous George Morley (sadly not involved in *Chicken One,* but very much so with *The Prawn Cocktail Years* and *Gammon and Spinach)*. And she is a Georgina, by the way, to no one who knows her.

You will note that I have been fairly direct in some of the introductions throughout this book. As it has been thirty years since I made my tentative first step into a professional kitchen, but yet had also been extremely well informed in culinary matters previous to that in the home in which I had grown up, I now feel I have a few very definite things to say about the practice of good cooking. And, I feel emboldened to say, all is not well. Something seems ever so slightly rotten in the state of the home kitchen, just now.

Along with many other like-minded folk, I just sometimes feel that we have all but lost the grasp of how to cook nicely at all – or, perhaps to be a little less brutal, *wish* to cook nice things and take time over doing so. Conversely – and irritatingly and maddeningly – as a nation we Brits now possibly buy more cookbooks per capita than any other country in the world (bar, perhaps, the U.S., but I bet you they cook from them more than we do). We watch endless cooking shows (the primary source of most of those books in the first place) but prefer, finally, to spend lots of money on prepared supermarket meals while idly turning the pages of (spotlessly clean) cookbooks until the microwave pings.

And then there is the kitchen pantry stocked with at least three or four different brands of olive oil (incomprehensibly, *all* of them Italian); four vinegars (balsamic, balsamic, balsamic, and sherry); unopened packages of Arborio, red Camargue and wild rice, Puy lentils, Maldon salt, and dried Spanish Judion beans; and an astonishing number of jars of stale sun-dried tomatoes because some bright spark long ago suggested that they might have now become "a little passé." And there will always be the half-used jar of very good, expensive Dijon mustard that has lived on that warm kitchen shelf forever – and yet is *still* in use. I have been known to throw other people's mustard away before now, when cooking in their kitchen. This simply won't do.

It further seems that no one anymore can even be bothered to pick over a simple lettuce, wash it, drain it, and dry it, to save their very lives. People have also been hoodwinked into thinking that scraping a new potato clean or picking off *both* ends of a green bean is just one more little chore that is no longer necessary. I, for one, am not taken in by those who like to tell me that this recent fancy allows the potato or bean to remain so "natural and healthy-looking." Excuse me? You mean those papery scraps of unwanted spud skin or sharp little green spikes that become neatly lodged between the teeth? Yet, bizarrely, enormous trouble will be taken to peel, seed, and neatly, minutely, *concasser* out-of-season, under-ripe tomatoes, because that is how chefs do it in restaurants and anyway, "it's only there for a little color." And there will be much arugula, but no lettuce. And Parmesan will be shaved, not grated. And it will be called *jus,* not gravy, "Thank you *very* much, Jerry."

This book has nothing to do with any of that at all.

Simon Hopkinson

ALMONDS

Once I realized that I was happily destined for cooking for most of my working life, I very soon became an expensive little show-off in my patient mother's kitchen. Timothy White's and Taylor were regularly plundered for the tiniest bottles of olive oil for mayonnaise (a request then, for "extra-virgin," would have prompted the strangest looks from the starched white uniform behind the wooden counter, staining my mother's reputation as a bona fide grammar school teacher forever), while the weekly cream order also escalated dramatically. Stewing steak became fillet; salted anchovies and bottled capers had to be bought from posh Manchester delicatessens; pepper was not pepper unless it was ground from a mill. Ground almonds, however, became an ingredient I felt should really become a staple. Mum thought different. Almonds in any form in the early 1960s cost a small fortune.

Still, I baked and baked. There was the favorite *dacquoise* (a sort of meringue cake) and an almond and cherry tart. There were endless cookies and a puff-pastry pie called *pithiviers* – which was very French indeed according to the *Cordon Bleu* magazine of that particular week. The delicious Bakewell pudding Mum often made may, perhaps, have relied more on almond extract (or ratafia) than it might have, but if yours truly was to have a go, it was a quarter of ground almonds all the way. (To be truthful, I regularly feel that just a few drops of *good* almond extract always round off the taste of a good almond cake or cookie.)

Anyway, whether nibbed, ground, flaked, whole – either skinned or not – the magic of the exotic almond was the absolute pantry favorite of my culinary formative years. Naturally, I hadn't the faintest idea how they grew, where they came from, or that they were full of a fragrantly rich oil when pressed for it. But the greatest revelation of all occurred many years later while shopping for this and that in the market of Arles in the Provence region of southern France, where I was alerted to this extraordinary pile of furry green lozenges: fresh almonds. Nobody had ever told me they started out as beautiful as this!

Once they were gently cracked with a tap of a wooden mallet, my understanding of the almond was finally complete. I had occasionally read about almond "milk" and how this natural secretion was essential to the fabrication of an almond blancmange. "Hmmm . . . ," I said to myself, "I see what they mean now." Apart from the exquisite creaminess of the fresh kernel – yet crisp too, all at the same time – this milk most evidently seeped out gently once disturbed from its furry casing. I wonder what happens to all this seepage in the bowels of the commercial almond factories of southern Europe? Turned into soap and bath oil, no doubt.

ALMOND AND BLUEBERRY SPONGE CAKE

The sort of pudding my mother used to make without a second thought. In those days, however, we made it with whimberries—which are like small blueberries—and I wish I could confidently suggest them to all, for this recipe here. So vivid and intense is the memory of their smell and stain, and the odor of that cake as it baked in the oven, that I now find myself moved to suggest that if my friend Howard Hodgkin had been there at the time he would most surely have been inspired to paint a picture: *Small Purple Stain,* perhaps as its title?

Serves 4

8 tbsp butter, softened
1½ cups blueberries
½ cup sugar
2 eggs
½ cup ground almonds
1 tbsp Amaretto liqueur
a little extra sugar

Serve with

heavy cream

Preheat the oven to 350°F.

Grease a wide and shallow baking dish with 1 tbsp of the softened butter. Strew with the blueberries but do not crowd them into the dish. Beat together the remaining butter and the sugar until very light and fluffy and then add the eggs, one at a time, beating them in thoroughly before folding in the ground almonds (it is a good idea to sift these into the mixture) and the Amaretto.

Spoon the sponge mixture over the fruit, sprinkle with the extra sugar, and bake in the oven for 40–45 minutes, or until puffed up and gently firm to the touch. Leave to cool for 10–15 minutes before eating with very cold heavy cream.

ALMOND BLANCMANGE

A recipe from the late, great Richard Olney. This man was so in tune with raw materials and ingredients, how to prepare them, how to cook them, and how to *serve* them (so often overlooked in these days of obsessive presentation; who said *la nouvelle cuisine* was dead?), that it is a constant source of angry irritation to me how his enormous influence has been so absurdly overlooked and by so many.

Well, of course, it hasn't been overlooked at all by those of us who choose to search out and embrace the writings of such a passionate scholar – and, almost above all, Olney was as passionate about his chosen oeuvre as it is possible to be. A stickler for detail, an obsessive over the provenance of an original dish, and forever ready to give credit where credit was due (sadly – and famously – on more than one occasion this was not reciprocated when the source turned out to be his), he was also the most generous teacher, regularly offering advice and insight to those receptive to his strict principles and abundant knowledge of when something was "just right." So, if you are interested, please read the following quote taken from his preface to *The French Menu Cookbook*:

> Emphasis throughout the book has been placed on the importance of tactile sense, which I consider to be a sort of convergence of all the senses, an awareness through touching but also through smelling, hearing, seeing, and tasting that something is "just right" – to know by seeing the progression from the light, swelling foam of an initial boil to a flat surface punctuated by tiny bubbles, by hearing the same progression from a soft, cottony, slurring sound to a series of sharp, staccato explosions, by judging from the degree of syrupiness or the smooth, enveloping consistency on a wooden spoon when a reduction has arrived at the point a few seconds before which it is too thin, a few seconds after which it may break or burn; to know by pinching and judging the resilience of a chop or a roast when to remove it from the heat; to recognise the perfect amber of a caramel moments before it turns burnt and bitter; to feel the right liquid flow of a crêpe batter and the point of light but contained airiness in a mousseline forcemeat that, having absorbed a maximum of cream to be perfect, would risk collapsing through any further addition . . .

One need only open this book and read it from cover to cover to learn how to cook. It has nothing to do with television or the Internet, it is simply something to use when you walk into the kitchen wishing only to make something extremely good to eat. It also suggests that you might work a little bit too, to achieve the best results you can, so that you too may be able to get things "just right." Here is his immaculate *blanc-manger* taken, almost verbatim, from *The French Menu Cookbook*.

Serves 4

9 oz whole almonds
(briefly blanched in boiling water,
then ruffled together in the folds of a dish towel with your hands,
so removing their brown skins)
3 bitter almonds (If unavailable, substitute a dash of almond extract.

Note: The French brand labelled "*Malilé — Amande amère*"
is the very best I have yet found.)
⅔ cup water
1¼ cups light cream
4 gelatin leaves, soaked in cold water until soft
5 tbsp sugar
½ cup heavy cream
a little almond oil

Pound the almonds in a stone mortar, adding a spoonful of the water each time the paste becomes too resistant to work easily. When half the water has been used, put the rest aside and continue pounding and turning, adding the light cream in small quantities at a time, until it has all been added. This should be done slowly and thoroughly to produce the finest possible purée.

Place a sieve over a mixing bowl. Dip a strong linen towel in cold water and wring it out well. Line the sieve with it. Pour in the almond mixture, gather together the edges of the towel in one hand, and begin twisting. Relax your hold from time to time to mix up the almond paste and then twist again, as tightly as possible, continuing until all the almond milk possible has been wrung from the paste.

Add the soaked gelatin to the remaining water and gently heat until it has dissolved. Add the sugar and stir in until it too has also dissolved. Leave until almost cool, stir it into the almond milk, and then place the bowl in a larger container filled with cracked ice. Stir steadily with a wooden spoon until it begins to take, whip the cream until it is only loosely stiffened, fold it into the almond mixture, and pour the mixture into a 1 quart mold that has been lightly oiled with almond oil. Embed the mold in cracked ice, place a plate over the top, and keep it in the refrigerator for at least 4–5 hours. Unmold only just before serving, first dipping the mold for a couple of seconds into hot water and wiping it dry.

POMMES AMANDINES

Charles Fontaine used to cook these for most of the 1980s at the London restaurant Le Caprice, where he was chef. They usually accompanied a grilled spatchcocked poussin chicken, which also came with the finest buttered spinach leaves. Almost without exception, whenever I ate there during that time, this was the dish I ordered. One of the most perfect plates of food I can ever recall. I wish they still did it.

Serves 4

1 lb potatoes, peeled and cut into chunks

For the choux paste

½ cup water
2 tbsp butter
salt and freshly ground white pepper
scant ½ cup all-purpose flour
2 eggs
1 egg yolk

For finishing

flour and beaten egg
2–3 handfuls of flaked almonds
oil, for deep-frying

Steam the potatoes until tender and then pass them through a vegetable mill onto a sheet of wax paper or a tray. Leave to cool in the air until dry. Meanwhile, make the choux paste. Boil together the water, butter, and seasoning in a saucepan. Then, while it is still hot, tip in the flour all at once and using a stout wooden spoon or stiff whisk beat together with gusto until thoroughly combined and very smooth. One by one, start to beat in the eggs and egg yolk, making sure that each egg has been fully incorporated before introducing the next one. The final result should be a glossy, yellow paste. Beat this thoroughly into the dry potato until smooth. Spread into a shallow dish, cover with plastic wrap, and put in the fridge to firm up.

Using floured hands, take small amounts of the mixture and form into balls the size of an oversized walnut. Roll them in flour and put on a tray. Have ready the flaked almonds, spread out on a tray. Now pass each potato ball through the beaten egg and then roll it through the flaked almonds, making sure of a good covering.

Heat the oil in the deep fryer to 325°F. and cook the *pommes amandines* in two or three batches for about 3–4 minutes, until crisp and golden. Keep warm in a low oven, on crumpled paper towel, while you continue with the next batch.

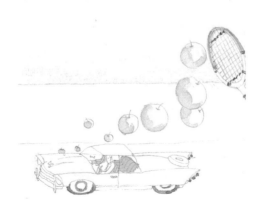

APPLES

I am lucky enough to have grown up in a house with a big garden, with five apple trees in it and a swing. Dowry Cottage was situated by a moderately busy main road – busy, that is, for the late 1950s and early '60s; say, seven Wolseleys, four Austin Cambridges, and a Jowett Javelin puttering by every half an hour: but in retrospect, I suppose my Lancastrian childhood enjoyed an insulated and carefree lifestyle.

However, though I am somewhat embarrassed to admit it, those five poor apple trees, when in fruit, used to get quite a hammering when Robert, Douglas, and Nigel Barden came round to play during the school holidays. Battered old tennis rackets were retrieved from a dark storeroom, gripped in surprisingly strong fists and, with remarkable accuracy, employed to project as much fruit as possible into the next-door garden, across the road (at cars if they happened to be passing, although cyclists were easier), and occasionally through some of our own open windows, raised only just enough for that most accurate of thwacks.

Finally, we were all caught red-handed one late summer afternoon by both Mum and Auntie Pat Barden (childhood friends' mothers were only referred to as "auntie" until they offered you your first gin and tonic), they having returned early from a disappointing shopping trip to Manchester. I will never forget that gorgeous scenario of my livid mother saying it was all *my* fault, alongside the spluttering gushes of the other mother insisting that, no, it was most definitely *her* boys who had been the wicked influence and were fully to blame. Of course it had been my idea. It was my garden, for heaven's sake!

But the thing that upset Mum most was that we had taken the trouble to climb the trees and use freshly picked apples rather than windfalls for our tennis practice. Excuse me! Any fool knows that a nice and hard under-ripe apple makes a much more satisfying projectile than a semi-decayed, wasp-ridden brown lump in the grass. I don't know about the Barden boys, but I recall being given a bit of a smack from Dad when he came home, swiftly - and absurdly - followed by the usual delicious supper and apple pie and cream for dessert. Wrath was always followed by good food in our house.

Mum was a demon when it came to housekeeping. Several years later, when I first began to be excited by the cooking thing, I had a go at baking an angel cake, which was an utter disaster. The prima donna in me chucked it in the trash without a second's thought, promptly followed by the alma mater fetching it out. "Just *do* something with it!" she scolded. Meanwhile, Mum had quietly gone upstairs to the spare room, rummaged under the spare bed, collected a handful of apples, and made another of those apple pies or a crumble, just in case. I have, ever since, thought that all spare bedrooms should smell of apples.

TARTE FINE AUX POMMES

Before *la tarte des demoiselles Tatin* (to give it its full, unexpurgated title) became all the rage – that's fashionably, not historically, and long before all its little mango nephews and endive or onion nieces were born – *la tarte fine aux pommes* was *the* apple tart to end all apple tarts. Strictly speaking, it should be called *la tarte fine aux pommes à la minute* – in other words "cooked at the last minute," which is why this particular tart always tastes so fresh, so fragrant, so good.

Serves 4

8–9 oz best-quality puff pastry
8 dessert apples, peeled, cut in half
lengthways, and cored
juice of ½ a lemon
1 tbsp butter, melted
2–3 tbsp sugar

Serve with

very cold vanilla-flavored crème Chantilly

Preheat the oven to 425°F.

Divide the pastry into four. Flour a surface and very thinly roll each one out to form a square of about 8 in. Now take a plate that measures approx. 7½ in in diameter, lay it carefully on a square, and cut around it in a circle. Repeat with the other 3 pieces of pastry. Roll up all the off-cuts, put in a plastic bag, and store in the freezer for another time.

Generously prick the surface of each pastry disc and lay on a lightly greased baking sheet (you may have to use two). Put in the fridge for 30 minutes. Meanwhile, thinly slice the apple halves, put them in a roomy bowl, and sprinkle with the lemon juice. Take the pastry discs from the fridge and carefully arrange and cover each one with the apple slices in the form of concentric circles, but making sure that you leave a gap of about ½ in around the edges. (This allows the pastry to attractively puff up and form a crusted border as it cooks.)

You may find that you do not use all the apple slices, particularly the knobbly end bits of each half. Now, with a pastry brush, coat each tart thoroughly with the butter and replace in the fridge until ready to cook. Once the oven is up to temperature, whip the tarts out of the fridge, dredge with the sugar, and place on the top shelf of the oven. Bake for 20 minutes or so, until the edges of the apples are lightly scorched and the tarts are well puffed around their edges. Serve with very cold vanilla-flavored crème Chantilly.

Note: Depending on the size of your oven, you may not be able to cook all four tarts in one go, on one shelf. If it is convection-assisted then it will probably be OK on two shelves. But in a conventional oven, using two shelves, the topmost tarts are going to cook quicker than the ones underneath. And puff pastry needs a quick, hot heat to cook evenly. Try changing each tray around halfway through the cooking, so that each pair of tarts gets an equal blast on the top shelf.

STEWED APPLES

This is as simple as dessert gets, but none the worse for that. I have tried making the dish with Coxs, Granny Smiths, and Red Delicious too, but, I'm afraid, it's Golden Delicious apples that perform best for this one; all the others fluffed and broke up during the cooking process. Mind you, as these apples are stewed to within an inch of their lives, the fragrance of any particular variety will have been simmered away, smothered by the taste of the sugar and vanilla.

Serves 4

1¼ cups water
¾ cup + 1 tbsp golden granulated sugar
1½–1¾ lb Golden Delicious apples,
peeled and lightly cored at each end
1 vanilla bean, broken into bits

Serve with

extra-cold heavy cream

Mix together the water and sugar in a pan that will also later hold the apples snugly, in one layer, and bring to a boil. Put in the apples (the syrup *should just* cover them) and distribute the vanilla bean amongst them. Simmer gently, turning them over from time to time, until the sugar, water, and apple juices have become golden and syrupy, but not sticky. The apples themselves should be a wonderful shade of pinky-gold, their flesh within wondrously fondant and very, very sweet. The cooking time should not be much longer than about 50 minutes. Serve warm, with extra-cold cream.

PAIN PERDU AUX POMMES

I first ate this astonishingly fine apple dessert at Marc Meneau's restaurant, L'Esperance, in northern Burgundy. Until a few years ago, M. Meneau held three Michelin stars, but he was then, inexplicably, demoted to just the two. This I cannot understand, as it is here, perhaps more than anywhere in France, that I have eaten some of the finest dishes of my life. I have adapted the following recipe from his book *La Cuisine en Fêtes* (Robert Laffont, 1986). Essentially, it is French toast with apples.

Serves 4

For the custard

1 cup milk
½ a vanilla bean, split lengthways
4 egg yolks
2 tbsp sugar

For the caramel sauce

4 tbsp butter
5 tbsp sugar
6 tbsp whipping cream
2 egg yolks

For the apples

4 tbsp butter
4 thick slices of good baguette (a touch stale, if possible), cut on the diagonal
4 Granny Smith apples, peeled, halved, cored, and cut into wedges

First make the custard. Scald the milk, with the vanilla bean, in a heavy-bottomed saucepan and leave to infuse for 10 minutes. Remove the vanilla bean, rinse out, dry, and store in a jar of granulated sugar, so flavoring the sugar for further confections. Briefly beat together the egg yolks and sugar and then strain the hot milk over them, whisking as you go. Return to the saucepan and cook over a very low heat (with a heat-diffuser pad if possible) until limpid and lightly thickened. When you think it is just about ready, give a final vigorous whisk and pour into a bowl. Cover and allow to cool. *Note:* If you are unlucky enough to split the custard, a blast in a blender will usually rescue it.

Make a caramel sauce by melting the butter with half the sugar in a small pan until golden brown. Add half the whipping cream (it will splutter slightly) and stir together until well amalgamated; it should be the color of butterscotch. Keep warm. Mix the egg yolks with the remaining sugar and whipping cream in a shallow soup bowl, or similar. Set aside.

Lightly color the apples in half of the butter using a small frying pan, but do not cook through. Then transfer to the caramel sauce and finish cooking them in this, until tender. Keep warm. Melt the remaining butter in a large frying pan, briefly soak the bread slices in the egg yolk/sugar/cream mixture and then fry over a fairly high heat until golden on both sides and puffed up. Drain on paper towel.

To assemble, place 1 piece of bread on each plate, arrange the apples along their length while spooning over the caramel sauce as you proceed, then finally dribble some of the custard all around.

BEANS

Dad, without fail, always has a couple of cans of lima beans in the kitchen cupboard. They may sit there for months at a time, but eventually they will be consumed at the moment when he mutters . . . "Hmmm, yes, some lima beans would do very nicely indeed." Forthwith: can opener and small pan at the ready, a moderate heat, and usually a couple of Welsh lamb chops all ready to grill. Dinner. Quite perfect, really. I'd have some mint jelly too, probably, made by the excellent Wiltshire Tracklement people.

No one need ever feel lacking in culinary expertise when taking the easy option of opening a can of beans. And that is not simply Heinz baked beans, of course – although I am immensely partial to these on toast, from time to time – but something such as those mentioned above. All beans and myriad other legumes lose their quality not one jot when processed under pressure, enclosed by tin. Haricot beans, red kidney beans, pale green flageolet beans, cranberry beans, chickpeas, ordinary peas (but only when canned by the French), lentils, and so on are all excellent products and ought to – along with an equal supply of their dried alternatives – take up most of the shelf space within the cupboard of the enterprising and intelligent cook.

I have often made the most delicious instant soup using the simple process of heating up a pan of good, homemade chicken stock (pork, beef, veal, and, of course, ham are every bit as serviceable here) with a little chopped carrot, celery, and leek, a bouquet garni, and a splash of white wine, and then upending a can of legumes into it once the aromatics have done their work. A fifteen-minute simmer to amalgamate everything and then a quick whiz in the blender. Once sieved and enriched with a light cream, reheated and seasoning rectified, here is a soup of the utmost luxury and finesse. A hefty addition of freshly chopped parsley stirred in and the offer of a dish of small and buttery croutons on the side are an optional — though, for me, an essential — toothsome flourish.

As far as I can recall, the only time I was forced to eat something I truly hated was while I was at prep school. It was a summer Sunday supper and the plate of food in question was a sort of salad thing which included some huge, cold and gray, wrinkled and leathery fava beans. I was not partial to fava beans at all and, in fact, had recently grown to loathe them. These particular specimens, however, were the very worst of their kind. I just knew they would make me sick on the spot if I were so much as to even attempt to put one in my mouth.

Enter Matron. Ah, Matron . . . So vociferously did she insist that either I ate them or did without ice cream to follow (once a week as a Sunday treat, a very small yellow square of it, still with its little bit of wax paper attached to the upper surface) — as if! — that I ate one, chewed it for a bit, and promptly threw up all over Miss Fletcher's deep blue shiny nylon apron. Not surprisingly, I still didn't get my ice cream. What a vile cow she truly was.

I quite like fava beans now, but would enjoy them even more were it not for the fact that E. Fletcher's heavily powdered mug looms up in my memory on each and every occasion. Mum always reckoned it was "In Love," by Norman Hartnell, that Matron used to grout her extensive wrinkles. "I've never liked the pong of that talc," opined Mum. "If ever anyone gives it to me it goes straight into the church jumble." Not forgetting Matron with it, I remember thinking at the time.

ALMOST INSTANT CREAMED BEAN SOUP WITH ROSEMARY AND ANCHOVY BUTTER

This soup could also be made with haricot, cannellini, or pale green flageolet beans – or even chickpeas, I guess.

Serves 4

6 tbsp butter
2 large onions, peeled and sliced
3 sticks celery, chopped
2 sprigs of rosemary
2 x 14 oz cans of lima beans (Spanish ones are particularly good)
3 cups chicken stock
salt and pepper
⅔ cup whipping cream

For the rosemary and anchovy butter

9 tbsp unsalted butter, softened
2 sprigs of rosemary, leaves only
1 clove garlic, peeled and crushed
a 2 oz can anchovies
juice of ½ a small lemon
pepper

Serve with

croutons

In a roomy pan, melt the butter and fry the onions and celery until lightly colored. Add the rosemary, stir around, and allow the aroma to lift. Tip in the beans, juice and all, add the stock, and bring up to a boil. Remove any scum that forms and then allow to gently simmer for 20–30 minutes or until the beans are all but falling apart. Add plenty of pepper and check for salt – but don't add too much, as the butter will be fairly salty from the anchovies.

Meanwhile, make the rosemary and anchovy butter by combining all the ingredients together in a food processor until very smooth. Pass through a small sieve to remove any spiky rosemary bits. Tip into a small bowl and leave at room temperature until the soup is to be served. Lift out the rosemary sprigs and then put the beans, vegetables, and liquor into a blender and process until very smooth. Pour through a sieve into a clean pan, stir in the cream, and gently reheat without boiling.

The consistency should not be too thick; if it is, add a little water or maybe some milk. To serve, pour into large soup plates or bowls, drop a spoonful of the rosemary and anchovy butter into each, and serve with croutons.

RED KIDNEY BEANS BAKED WITH CHORIZO, CHILLI, GARLIC, AND OLIVE OIL

Here is one of those comforting, cold-weather bean stews so beloved of Spain and also of the southwest of France; think of cassoulet. We don't utilize the humble dried bean enough in Britain, I feel. The very fact that the superlative, large Spanish dried bean known as Judion is a costly item – in bean terms, at least – confirms just how much esteem is placed upon them. Humble here they are not. One might almost be moved to say that the Spaniards have a finger on the pulse in these matters.

Serves 3–4

7 oz dried red kidney beans, soaked in
cold water overnight
5 tbsp olive oil
2 onions, peeled and chopped
4 cloves garlic, peeled and chopped
7 oz dried chorizo sausage, thinly sliced
½–1 tsp dried chilli flakes
¼ cup dry sherry
¾ cup well-flavored stock
2 tbsp freshly chopped mint

Drain the beans, wash them well, and cover with fresh water. Bring up to a boil, drain once more, and refresh under cold water. Re-cover with fresh water, *do not add salt* (this can toughen their skins), and simmer for 1–1½ hours or until tender. Leave in the water to cool.

In a large pan heat 3 tbsp of the olive oil and fry the onions and garlic until lightly colored. Add the chorizo sausage and stir around until its paprika-infused oil starts to run. Stir in the chilli flakes, the sherry, and the stock. Bring to a simmer. Drain the beans in a colander suspended over another pan. Add the beans to the simmering ingredients and add enough of their drained cooking water to achieve a sloppy and soupy mixture. Adjust the seasoning, but do not over-salt. Stir in the mint. Tip into a shallow brown earthenware pot (a *cazuela,* in Spanish). Spoon over the remaining olive oil. Place in the oven, uncovered, and bake for about 1 hour, or until most of the liquid has evaporated or absorbed itself into the beans.

A meal in itself, but a crisp green salad might also be welcome.

BLACK BEAN SOUP

This soup was first cooked for me several years ago by my sous chef at the time, Henry Harris. He adapted it from a Jeremiah Tower recipe, added a few of his own ideas and we put it on the menu. It is now called Henry's Black Bean Soup forever more and is delicious. The recipe that follows is a mixture of his and the original. Please buy fresh spices before you make this soup as it makes all the difference. Tired old spices at the back of the cupboard will not do it justice.

Serves 6–8

1 lb dried black beans, soaked overnight
2 large red onions, peeled and chopped
1 large carrot, peeled and chopped
3 sticks celery, peeled of strings and chopped
6 cloves garlic, peeled and bashed
2 bay leaves
an 8 oz piece of smoked bacon (Italian flat pancetta is ideal), skin intact
4–6 cups of stock – ham (favorite), chicken, or beef, but good flavor is paramount
1 tbsp ground cumin (made from fresh cumin seeds dry-roasted in a small frying pan until fragrant and toasted)
1 tbsp chilli powder (This is *not* cayenne pepper, rather it is a chilli powder mix; it has "Chilli Powder" on the label and is dark red in color.)
4 tbsp sour cream, loosened with a little milk to a pouring consistency

For the salsa

6 ripe tomatoes, skinned, seeded, and coarsely chopped
1 small red onion, peeled and finely chopped
½ a bunch of cilantro, leaves only,
coarsely chopped
juice of 2 limes
2 green chillies, seeded and chopped
¼ tsp sugar
salt

Drain the beans, rinse, and put them in a large pot with the vegetables, bay leaves, bacon, and enough stock to cover by 2 in or so. (Add more stock, or water, later on if there seems to be insufficient liquid.) Simmer ever so slowly for 1½ hours or so, skimming off any scum that is generated and stirring from the bottom on occasion, to check that none of the beans are sticking.

Meanwhile, make the salsa. Mix all the ingredients together in a bowl. Cover with a plate or plastic wrap, and leave at room temperature for 30 minutes before using.

When the beans are tender, lift out the bacon and allow it to cool. You can either chop it into small pieces and add to the soup later, or you can slice it thinly, and use in sandwiches for instance, spread with some fiery mustard. Now put the soup through a mouli-légumes (vegetable mill) on a fine setting. Do not be tempted to blend in a blender, as the soup can become gloopy. Stir in the cumin and chilli. Reheat the soup and add stock or water until the consistency is thin porridge. Serve in shallow soup plates dressed with swirls of sour cream and the salsa.

BEETS

The late Joyce Grenfell neatly epitomized the very Englishness of beets in one of her memorable monologues. The scene took place in the sort of teashop that was in reality not much more than a cafe. Joyce Grenfell's character was that of a gauche young Cockney girl on a first date with her timid young man. Towards the end of their difficult "tea," and around about the time that her stumbling suitor attempted to lean across the table to place a peck upon her cheek, the impeccable Grenfell delivered the following immortal line: ". . . and as Brian stretches across the table I see his tie go in the beet salad, but I don't say nuffin."

Well, that, at least, is how I roughly remember the gist of it even though my script may not be word perfect. But one has surely been informed here that beet was not exactly seen as one of our most exotic or sophisticated ingredients. To be frank, it was something that, along with fish paste, jellied eels, and cans of corned beef, had long been looked upon as a joke among British fare. That is, until now.

Beets are enjoying a renaissance like no other vegetable in recent times. I think part of this new love affair can be attributed to their color. Some chefs use the beet for this reason alone even though it might be totally unsuitable within the dish in question, but then this sort of carrying on is nothing new. An influx of cooking literature imported from the west coast of America, where beets (both red *and* yellow) have been seen as a creditable root vegetable in their own right for ages, might well have been a further nudge in the right direction. However, it may simply be because other vegetables have been cast aside as boring, as part of this incessant search we have lately (misguidedly) adopted to impatiently experience yet another fashionable ingredient. Curious and interested cooks have never been biased when it comes to one ingredient over another. Ingredients just are. A beet just is.

Naturally, most detractors of the British way with beets still think of it as thick ruby slices sitting in a pool of malt vinegar, the leached juices staining the resultant liquid crimson, which, as so neatly observed by the aforementioned Joyce Grenfell, will stain and ruin a nice gentleman's tie for ever more – silk, wool, or nylon, it makes not a ha'p'orth o' difference. Beet-blotched clothing is a stain for life – and with the vinegar to help, it sticks nice and fast.

There is nothing wrong at all with this traditional, sharp preparation per se, as home-cooked fresh beets, carefully peeled, sliced, and moistened with a fine red-wine vinegar, can be one of the nicest, freshest, and perkiest salads it is possible to eat. Eat it naked in the bath if you generally shop in Knightsbridge or Bond Street.

BEET, EGG, AND HERRING SALAD

A colorful, intensely savory, and substantial salad here. If you find those sweet-cured herrings a tad too sweet, feel free to use the saltier Dutch *matjes* herrings instead. Once made, do not keep the salad hanging around for too long as the beets tend to bleed into the other ingredients and then it will all begin to look rather a mess.

Serves 4

For the dressing

1 tbsp smooth Dijon mustard
1 tbsp red wine vinegar
salt and pepper
a little lukewarm water
⅔–¾ cup peanut oil

For the salad

3 large eggs
4 medium-sized raw beets, washed, then boiled
in salted water for 40 minutes or so, until tender
1 small onion, preferably white-skinned,
peeled and very thinly sliced into rings
12 pieces of sweet-cured herring fillets, cut in half
1 tbsp capers, drained and squeezed of their juice a little
the leaves from 4–5 sprigs of flat-leaf parsley, coarsely chopped
Maldon sea salt and freshly ground black pepper

To make the dressing, put the mustard, vinegar, seasoning, and a couple of tablespoons of water in a blender or food processor. Process until smooth and then start adding the oil in a thin stream. When the consistency is creamy white, have a taste. If you think it is too thick, add a little more water; the consistency should be that of mayonnaise-based dressing. Decant into a bowl and set aside.

Boil the eggs for precisely 7 minutes and run under cold running water for at least 5 minutes. Shell, put into a bowl, and set aside. Peel and slice the beets thinly and lay out to cover a handsome white platter. Distribute the onion rings over them and then spoon over a little of the dressing, but don't swamp the dish. Slice the eggs (if you have one of those dinky egg slicers, by all means use it; such a clever little kitchen toy) and carefully lay them over too. Tuck in the herring pieces here and there and scatter the capers over. Spoon over some more dressing (you may not need to use it all, but it keeps well in the fridge), sprinkle with parsley, and add seasoning.

JELLIED BEET CONSOMMÉ WITH SOUR CREAM, CHIVES, AND CAVIAR

This is a glorious cold soup. Its color is quite magnificent and it should always be served in pristine white soup plates for the most dramatic effect. For the liquid, beef broth is the traditional Russian flavor; duck stock can be particularly fine too, the perfect use for a leftover carcass from a roast, but any well-made and tasty stock will do just fine. I have also made a very passable borscht using canned beef consommé.

You might think that this whole recipe is a real fuss. You might well be right. But just wait until you taste the result.

Serves 6

2 tbsp vegetable oil
1 lb chicken wings, chopped up a bit
1 large carrot, peeled and chopped
2 sticks celery, chopped
2 leeks, cleaned and sliced
1 onion, peeled and stuck with 3 cloves
2 cloves garlic, bashed
a little salt
a few black peppercorns
2 sprigs of fresh thyme
2 bay leaves
2 quarts good stock

For the clarification

4 large raw beets, peeled and grated
2 wineglasses ruby port
2 egg whites, beaten
5 oz lean ground beef

For the consommé

2 leaves gelatin, previously soaked in cold water until soft
3 cooked beets, peeled and grated
2 tsp red wine vinegar
⅔ cup sour cream, thinned with a little milk
4 demitasse spoons Sevruga caviar
snipped chives

Serve with

rye bread
vodka

In the base of a large, heavy-bottomed stew pan, heat the oil until smoking. Put in the wings and fry for a couple of minutes until lightly browned. Tip the pan up and spoon out any excess fat. Put in all the vegetables, seasoning, and herbs. Fill with stock. Bring to a boil, skim off any scum on the surface, and put to simmer for 1 hour on a very low heat, uncovered. Strain through a roomy colander and allow to drip for 10 minutes or so, then sieve the broth into a large, clean stainless-steel or enameled pan. Remove any fat from the surface with several sheets of paper towel. Leave to cool until lukewarm.

In a roomy bowl, mulch together with your hands the raw beets, port, egg whites, and ground beef. Tip into the stock and whisk together. Put back onto a moderate heat and return to the merest simmer. During this stage, make sure that this mulched mixture does not stick to the bottom of the pan; feel around with a wooden spoon perhaps, but try not to disturb the crust that has formed upon the surface. Simmer gently for 40 minutes.

What occurs now is the clarification process: the mixture of the egg whites and natural albumen in the meat is collecting into itself all the impurities in the stock, whilst the meat, grated beets, and port are also flavoring it. As the stock gently blips through the crust, it should be clear and ruby red. After the 40 minutes is up, make a hole in the crust with a spoon and lift some of it away. Now take a ladle and transfer, through a damp muslin-lined sieve (or an old thin dish towel; it will forever be stained by the beets, remember), the clear liquid that lies beneath into a clean pan. Collect all you can. Discard the crust; it has done its work.

Stir the softened gelatin into the hot, clear, beet-flavored stock (consommé) together with the grated cooked beets and the vinegar. Gently stir together. Cover and leave to infuse for 1 hour. Drain for the last time, once more through muslin, into a clean bowl.

Put the beet consommé into the fridge and allow to set to a jellied consistency. When cold, just jellied and wobbly, spoon out into chilled soup plates, decorate with a thick slurry of sour cream, and place a spoonful of caviar on the cream. Sprinkle with chives. Serve with buttered rye bread and a glass of iced vodka.

BEET DUMPLINGS WITH HORSERADISH CREAM

A bit of a mad-looking dish this, all pink-and-cream-colored; the kind of dish Barbara Cartland would have "simply adored." I suppose, therefore, and with that lovely loony lady in mind, I look upon these as an Anglicized version of the Italian gnocchi. Memorial Barbara Cartland Dumplings coming on menus soon in restaurants up and down the land, I'll be bound. Roll up, roll up!

Serves 4, as a first course

1 lb small raw beets, washed and scrubbed
salt
12 oz peeled potatoes, cut into large chunks
2 tbsp butter
4 tbsp cream cheese
1 egg
pepper
¾–1 cup all-purpose flour

For the horseradish cream

7 oz crème fraîche
5 oz piece of fresh horseradish root, peeled and freshly grated
1 tsp sugar
salt and white pepper
a squeeze of lemon juice
snipped chives

Preheat the oven to 375°F.

Put the beets onto a sheet of foil, sprinkle over a little salt and roll them in it, wrap up loosely but securely, and place in a baking pan. Bake for 1 hour or until fully tender. Meanwhile, steam the potatoes until also very tender. Pass these through a vegetable mill (mouli-légumes) directly onto a dish towel laid on a tray, sprinkle with a little salt, and allow to dry out.

Once the beets are cooked, unwrap the foil and leave them to cool until you are able to handle them comfortably (switch off the oven as normal, but you will require its waning heat later on). Melt the butter in a wide pan and then coarsely grate the beets directly into it. Cook very, very gently over a mere thread of heat, stirring from time to time until all excess moisture has been driven off and the mixture is good and dry. Tip out onto a plate and leave to cool.

Place the beets in a food processor together with the cream cheese, egg, and a little salt and pepper, then purée until smooth. Tip the dried-out mashed potato onto a generously floured surface (taken from the given amount) and add the beets to it. Put a large pan of salted water on to boil.

Now, little by little, sift over some of the flour (you will certainly need the full ¾ cup, but maybe a little more), working it into the beet and potato mixture with your fingers using a gentle kneading movement, until the mixture feels like biscuit dough with a trace of stickiness and is a uniform pink color throughout; lurid it may now look, but, fear not, it is delicious once cooked and eaten. Tear off large pieces and roll each into a long sausage shape, about the thickness of a chipolata. Cut off small pieces with a sharp knife and put aside.

Now make the horseradish cream. Scald the crème fraîche in a small saucepan and then whisk in the horseradish, sugar, and seasoning while it is still hot. Leave to infuse for 10–15 minutes, then strain through a sieve into a clean pan, pushing hard on the horseradish debris using the back of a small ladle to extract as much flavor as possible. Discard the debris and put this sauce to one side.

Drop the dumplings into a pan of gently boiling water, a dozen or so at a time. Once they float to the surface, allow them to poach for a further 30 seconds or so, lift out with a slotted spoon, and put on a large hot plate adorned with a double fold of paper towel. Keep warm in the waning heat of the oven while you cook the rest.

To serve, slide the dumplings onto a heated serving dish, gently reheat the sauce, and sharpen with a little lemon juice. Pour over the dumplings and sprinkle with the chives.

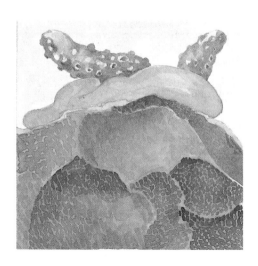

BRISKET

I don't recall ever eating brisket as a cut of beef during my childhood. I remember bits called chuck, shoulder, rib, rump, and skirt, but on all the numerous occasions that I accompanied either Mum or Dad to the butcher's (at any opportunity: I was always there and have loved the lingering sweet odor of raw meat ever since) I cannot for the life of me recollect master butcher John Pendlebury ever deftly wrapping up a piece of brisket within ripped pages of the previous day's *Daily Sketch*. It wasn't until I arrived in London, many years later, that I first became familiar with the cut of beef known as brisket.

I guess it must have been in 1978 or thereabouts that the jovial and passionately well-informed David Wolfe (whom I met while employed as an Egon Ronay inspector at the same time that Wolfe was engaged as Ronay's assessor of restaurant wine lists) first alerted me to the joys of Jewish salt beef. And, in particular, he insisted, those of the salt brisket served up at the Nosh Bar, Great Windmill Street, just a short stroll off Shaftesbury Avenue in London's celebrated West End. This joint was David's absolute favorite.

So, my eager taste buds were thus further pleasured by yet another new gustatory sensation. Those few thin, fatty, warm slices of succulent pink brisket sandwiched between two pieces of rye bread (with caraway seeds in them), a viscous smear of nose-runningly pungent mustard, a fat gherkin or two on the side, and a cup of lemon tea still remain in my memory as one of the most delicious combinations I have ever put in my mouth. One might say I used to wolf it down . . . But not for long, sadly.

Surprise, surprise, the Nosh Bar no longer exists. Rumor has it that it fell prey to rapacious local rent increases, a bullying local vice ring, and – possibly more of a reason than anything underhand or vicious – the simple fact that filthy kebab shops, dreadful pizza vendors, and a plethora of pretentious cafes had suddenly become, astonishingly, the preferred places of frequent and transient nourishment to the masses. The British surely have only themselves to blame for allowing such places as the Nosh Bar to disappear without trace. If such a tragedy as this were to occur to something such as the Carnegie Deli in New York City there would be a national outcry. Why, oh why, have we simply ceased to care about such things?

And, with this in mind, what on earth has become of the Cockney tradition, boiled beef and carrots? Although I never watch *EastEnders* I feel sure this local speciality is not something that might be found listed as a lunchtime favorite on the bar menu of the Queen Vic (I wait to be corrected). I do have a feeling, however, that the cut of salted beef used in boiled beef and carrots was generally silverside rather than deliciously fatty brisket. But no matter.

Although silverside is a leaner cut and not as naturally lubricated or succulent as those rosy Nosh Bar carvings, the poignant fact remains that a plate of nourishing boiled beef and carrots is now verging on extinction. Now then, does it not speak volumes that the Parisian bistro *plat du jour, bœuf aux carottes* (simply *bœuf carottes,* to regulars chez Lipp) continues to delight and sustain those who consider such things part of everyday life? The recipe might bear little relation to the English equivalent (the French beef is *non-salé* and is, in effect, a slow braise), yet it is surely a comfort to know that somewhere, not too far away, convention remains a finer thing than fashion, perceived expediency, and, above all, complacency on the part of the consumer.

BOILED BEEF AND CARROTS, WITH PARSLEY DUMPLINGS AND *CHRAIN*

Original it may not be but the following recipe is, at least, a thoughtful one and hugely scrumptious. Also, there is a bit of cross-culture going on here too: the purée of beet and horseradish (*chrain*) is, essentially, a favorite relish of Jewish people around the time of Passover, but so delicious is it that I feel sure it is often consumed outside this particular festival too. Personally, I could eat it almost every day.

The dumplings, of course, are a perennial English favorite with any boiled food at any time and should, I feel, be much more in evidence in these tiresome days of overgrown arugula hedges, lava-flows of polenta, and so much chopped cilantro all over the kitchen that this particular herb will, very soon, I suspect, finally replace parsley as our national herb. And if and when that culinary Armageddon comes to pass, I will be off.

Serves 4

2.2 lb salt brisket (nice and fatty)
12 small carrots, peeled and split lengthways
8 small onions, peeled and each one
stuck with 1 clove
4 celery hearts, trimmed and their outside ribs peeled

For the dumplings

¾ cup self-rising flour
2 oz suet
salt and pepper
2 tbsp chopped parsley

For the *chrain* (beetroot and horseradish purée)

4–5 medium-sized beets, cooked and
peeled and cut into chunks
a 6 oz piece of fresh horseradish root,
peeled and freshly grated
1 tbsp balsamic vinegar
2 tbsp sugar
salt to taste

Put the beef in a large pan and just cover with cold water. Bring up to a simmer and catch any scum that forms along the way. Once the water looks clear, turn down to the merest simmer and cover. Check from time to time that the water is not simmering too fast; the secret of good salt beef is its gentle cooking, which ensures soft and tender meat. Simmer for about 1 hour, or until there remains a modicum of resistance when poked right through with a skewer. Now add the vegetables and mingle around the beef with a spoon. Return to a simmer and further cook until all the vegetables are tender (about 40–50 minutes) and the beef is fully fondant and exceptionally tender.

Meanwhile, make the dumplings and the *chrain*.

First, mix together the ingredients for the dumplings in a roomy bowl. Using a knife, stir and flick them together while also incorporating hesitant splashes of ice-cold water until this crumbly collection easily coheres into a not-too-sticky mass. Bring it together with your hands, tip out of the bowl onto a surface, and knead together until fully amalgamated. Slip into a plastic bag and chill in the fridge until ready to cook.

The *chrain* is very easy to prepare. Simply blend all the ingredients in a food processor until coarsely puréed and decant into a pretty bowl.

Lift the beef and vegetables out of the pot using, respectively, a spatula and slotted spoon and attractively arrange on a heated serving platter. Loosely cover with foil and keep warm in a very low oven. Form the dumpling dough into small balls the size of a walnut. (It's *always* a walnut, isn't it? Well, thank heavens for walnuts is all I can say, even though they happen to be my least favorite of all nuts. Dimensions here, therefore, are of vital importance, with texture and flavor discarded almost without a second's thought.) Bring the beef-cooking liquor to a gentle rolling boil and pop in the dumplings. Simmer for 15–20 minutes or until they have visibly swelled and are all gathered on the surface.

To serve the beef, cut into thin slices, lay on a handsome platter, and surround with the vegetables and the dumplings. Spoon over a little of the cooking liquor to give everything a shine, and hand the *chrain* separately.

BRISKET AND POTATO PIE

This is a giant, family-sized version of the oh-so-delicious looking – and smelling! – individual meat and 'tatie pies that I used to salivate over as a child. They appeared on various stalls throughout Bury market and I would plaintively point these out to Mum while accompanying her (aged about seven or eight years) on regular shopping trips there. I never got to eat one, though.

I have always felt that Mum was a bit snooty about actually being seen to be buying meat and 'tatie pies, just in case she saw someone she knew who might just think she couldn't make her own. Which, of course, she could – and most deliciously so. This pie is based upon hers, although this one has a bottom as well as a top, just like those in the market.

You will need a loose-bottomed pastry pan measuring approx. 2 in deep by 9 in wide, lightly buttered, and a flat oven pan, which should be put in the oven in advance, to heat up, so that the base of the pie will also cook through evenly from beneath.

Serves 6

For the pastry

7 oz dripping or lard, very cold from the fridge
and cut into small pieces
3 cups flour
pinch of salt
7–8 tbsp ice-cold water

For the filling

1¼ lb brisket (make sure it has bits of fat and sinew in it),
cut into small pieces
1¾ cups chopped onion
1 large peeled potato, diced
salt and plenty of freshly ground white pepper
1 tbsp all-purpose flour
¾–1 cup water
a little milk

Serve with

malt vinegar
piccalilli or tomato ketchup

To make the pastry, rub together the fat, flour, and salt until it resembles coarse bread crumbs. Quickly mix in the water and work together until a coherent mass. Knead lightly and put in a plastic bag. Leave to rest in the fridge until the filling has been prepared.

Preheat the oven to 400°F., and put the baking pan onto the middle shelf.

Put all the ingredients for the filling (except the water and milk) into a roomy bowl and mix together well with your hands. Divide the pastry into two-thirds and one-third sized pieces. Roll the larger into a circle about ¼ in thick – it does not want to be too thin. Line the pan, leaving the overhang intact. Roll out the pastry for the lid and set aside. Pile the filling in right to the top (all of it should go in, so don't fret) and carefully pour in the water until it *just* reaches the surface. Brush the edge of the overhanging pastry with water and put on the lid. Press the edges together at the rim of the pan and then slice off the excess pastry with a knife.

Brush the surface with the milk and then decorate and further press the edges together with the tines of a fork. Make 2 generous incisions in the center of the pie and place in the oven. Cook for 25 minutes, and then turn the temperature down to 325°F. Bake for a further 1½ hours, checking from time to time that the pastry is not browning too much. If it is, then turn the oven down a little more and loosely cover the surface with a sheet of foil. Remove from the oven and leave to cool for 20–30 minutes or so before unmolding and sliding onto a plate.

What makes this sort of pie so very special is the long, slow cooking, with all the elements cooking together as one. To be truly authentic, eat with a splash of malt vinegar and some piccalilli or tomato ketchup – Heinz, of course.

BRAISED FRESH BRISKET IN STOUT, WITH ONIONS

The meat in this stew emerges melting and very tender. As the meat is better cooked as two whole pieces and on the bone, it is pleasing to know that all that is further needed is a spoon to break it up into manageable pieces once it is ready to be served. Do not be alarmed over the quantity of onions; they should be looked upon almost as a vegetable here in their own right, as well as being an integral part of the braise.

Serves 4

2 × 1 lb pieces fresh beef brisket
salt and pepper
3 tbsp flour
2 tbsp beef dripping or lard
8 tbsp butter
3⅓ lb onions, peeled and sliced
3–4 tbsp red wine vinegar
1 tbsp mushroom ketchup
1 tbsp anchovy paste
1 cup stout
1 cup beef stock
2 bay leaves
2 tbsp chopped parsley

Serve with

boiled or creamed potatoes

Preheat the oven to 275°F.

Season the beef all over with salt and pepper then dredge with flour. Melt the dripping or lard in a deep cast-iron lidded casserole dish until very hot. Sear the meat on all surfaces and remove to a plate. Pour off all of the fat and then add the butter; I know there is a lot of it, but this is necessary to cope with the large amount of onions. Allow the butter to become fully melted and turn frothy and toasty-smelling before carefully tipping in the onions. Stir them around thoroughly in the butter until well coated and *do not add any salt* (this can prevent the onions from browning). Gently sweat over a very low heat with the lid on, stirring from time to time, until they have flopped down into the bottom of the pan as a slippery muddle; this can take anything up to 30–40 minutes or so.

Turn the heat up a little now and, stirring more frequently, allow the onions to color to a deep, rich, golden brown. Add the vinegar, allow it to bubble furiously, and drive most of it off over full heat until the onions are dry and buttery once more. Stir in the mushroom ketchup, anchovy paste, stout, beef stock, and bay leaves. Bring up to a simmer and remove any scum that forms on the surface with a ladle. Slip the beef back into the pot and bury it under the onions and liquid. Cover with a sheet of wax paper cut to fit the dimensions of the pot and press gently down upon the surface. Put on the lid and cook in the oven for 1½–2 hours, or until completely tender when poked with a skewer. Check for seasoning, stir in some of the parsley, and sprinkle the rest over the surface. Serve directly from the pot in deep soup plates, and accompany by either plainly boiled or creamed potatoes.

BUTTER AND DRIPPING

I have noticed in recent years that when a lubricant of some sort is specified to sear, seal, sauté, sweat, or even prosaically fry a piece of fish, fowl, or meat, it is always, but always, olive oil. We didn't used to do this before. Well, I say before, but what actually *was* "before"? For me to be quite content cooking things in good dripping or nice yellow butter, is what "before" was. These are the indigenous fats, lubricants, and grease that we have felt perfectly happy and familiar with for centuries.

Beef dripping used to be made by every single butcher as a matter of daily routine at the rear of his shop, where suet and flare fat from every single carcass were carefully rendered down, collected, strained, and decanted into tall, slightly tapering, wax-paper cartons. In turn, this regular purchase was used to lubricate all roast meats and fry the morning egg and bacon, and was sometimes cut with flour to make pastry – in every domestic kitchen throughout the land.

After each use it was collected and poured back into the dripping bowl, the flavor becoming richer each time. The memory of this vintage spread, scraped across a thick slice of toast as a late-night snack (making sure that one always managed to scrape a bit of brown goo from beneath when no one was watching), almost brings a tear to the eye of those long deprived of such a treat.

I remember noticing a few years ago, while judging a chefs' competition at Birmingham's excellent catering college, a curious machine in the corner of one of the practical classrooms. Initially, I was more drawn by the smell emanating from it than by its aesthetic qualities: cream-enameled and looking like something straight out of the kitchen of my grammar school canteen.

It was a sort of box affair standing on four legs, with a circular lid on top and a wide spout that protruded from below. "Whatever it is that's in there," I said to the director of the college, "it certainly smells pretty good." Well, would you believe, this little metal box turned out to be a contraption solely designed for the manufacture of beef dripping. Each and every scrap of gristle, sinew, fat, and suet of beef that could not be used by students in everyday curricular recipes was simply thrown into that simmering hot-box. Imagine the goo that settled in its bottom! Almost immediately, I wanted to ask him where the toaster lived.

It seems that no one does dripping anymore. Well, I do, my dad still does, and maybe half a dozen other diehards still do, but in the average middle-class British kitchen today the opposite is most definitely the case, for the dripping pot's comfortable position next to the stove has been usurped by the neat and tidy bottle of extra-virgin. I view this as an extremely sad state of affairs. I enjoy the flavor, uses, and versatility of olive oil as much as anyone, but it is not, nor ever has been, a suitable replacement for the dripping pot – or, for that matter, the butter pot.

Really sad folk – by which I mean those cooks who haven't the first clue as to how to carefully fry an egg – now advocate the use of lashings of extra-virgin olive oil in almost every single recipe; they actually fry with it, make dreadful risotto with it, drizzle it over everything in sight, and probably even use it as bath oil. No one in their right mind would heat up an expensive slug of extra-virgin, in which to fry, say, a dreary chicken breast, but they surely do, these equally dreary people.

I would guess that the average, thrifty southern Italian housewife might only choose to buy a single bottle of extra-virgin once a year, for use in rare moments during the hot summer months: poured over cool slices of fresh, milky mozzarella or lubricating seasonal vegetables such as fennel, artichokes, peppers, and a glut of ripe, red tomatoes. Otherwise, her staple supply of olive oil will be nothing more than the stuff simply known as "pure." She will fry with this, use it for roasting, make sauces with it, and dress an everyday salad with it. She will also buy it in a large can, cheaply and without the slightest concern over which particular grove harvested her oil's original olives or who pressed them.

In the north of Italy, however, it is butter all the way. Once again, it seems that most recipes I now read for the making of the sublime risotto of Piedmont, Lombardy, and the Veneto, stipulate the use of olive oil in which to fry the essential chopped onion (never shallots) before the rice is first introduced to the pan. It's butter! Butter, butter, butter, and more butter beaten into the rice at its very completion. Even the River Café girls use olive oil at that initial stage. I just don't get it. What's it for? Is it not possible to fry the onions in butter alone? Well, I do. I also cook all manner of things in butter, all the time, mainly because I simply see this as both obvious and sympathetic to the traditional British kitchen.

ROAST POTATOES IN BEEF DRIPPING

There is nothing quite as difficult as turning out perfect roast potatoes and yet there really could not be anything simpler too. I think it *does* take a little practice, to be truthful, and a great deal of that is knowing your oven inside out and back to front. Some of the most successful roasties I remember were those cooked in a battered old Baby Belling – and in France, no less.

By the way, the very best variety of spud I have ever used for roast potatoes – and for fried too – is the one known as Wilja.

Serves 4

2¼ lb Wilja, red-skinned, all-purpose, or thin-skinned white all-purpose potatoes
peeled and chopped into medium-sized chunks and then very well washed
4–5 tbsp beef dripping, the more it has been previously used the better
salt

Preheat the oven to 425°F.

Salt then steam the potatoes until almost fully tender. Lift off the steaming basket and leave to cool for 10–15 minutes. Have a solid-bottomed roasting pan ready over a medium heat. Now gently shake the potatoes around a little to help roughen their edges (the secret to a good crust). Add the dripping to the roasting pan, turn up the heat, and allow it to become good and hot. Deftly tip in the potatoes and spread them out – it matters not one jot that the odd one or two collapse or break a little; these are the very ones that always go first. Tip up the dish diagonally, collect drippings from the corner with a serving spoon, and generously baste the tops of the potatoes. Place on the top shelf of the oven for 10 minutes. Do not even think of touching them. Remove from the oven and pour off all but the merest dribble of dripping. Replace in the oven and turn the heat down to 375°F. Continue roasting for a further half hour. Remove once more and turn the potatoes over with the help of a spatula, forcing it under their crusty bottoms (oo-er, Matron) to release them. Another 20–25 minutes in the oven should now do them to a turn. *Note:* If the very bottom of your oven generates a great deal of heat, then this can often be just the right spot to achieve a great crust underneath. And that's right on the very bottom, not simply on the bottom shelf.

BUTTERY RISOTTO WITH VERMOUTH, HERBS, AND SPRING ONIONS

A particularly fragrant and savory risotto, this one. Yet it is also uncomplicated, pure, and – if you use vegetable stock – as nice a risotto for vegetarian folk as I can think

of. And, incidentally, for vegetarians, instant vegetable stock is most acceptable here –
but then any self-respecting vegetarian must know this already.

Serves 4

10 tbsp butter
5¼ cups lightly flavored chicken stock;
you may not need all of this
2 bunches of spring onions, trimmed and thickly sliced
1⅓ cups Carnaroli rice
leaves from 4–5 sprigs of fresh tarragon
a bunch of chives
leaves from a small bunch of flat parsley
a generous slug of dry vermouth
salt and white pepper
5 tbsp freshly grated Parmesan

Melt 8 tbsp of the butter in a heavy-bottomed pot that is not too wide: the narrower
and higher-sided the vessel, the more intense and compact the stirring will be, which
helps to release starch from the rice and make it creamy. Have the stock sitting close
by, at a low simmer. Add the spring onions to the butter and cook slowly, until soft
and translucent. Tip in the rice and turn up the heat. Stir the rice around with the
onion until glistened by the butter before adding the first ladle of hot stock.

This will immediately cause a satisfying seethe, whereupon the stock will almost
immediately be absorbed by the rice as you stir vigorously. Now add the second
ladleful, continuing to stir energetically, until this too has been absorbed. As you
continue this process, each additional ladle of stock will take longer to be absorbed as
the rice finds its work more arduous, its starchy coating being continually eroded by
the efficiency of your sturdy spoon. Do also ensure that you keep the heat high under
the risotto during the entire process.

Soon after two-thirds of the stock has been incorporated, it is time to have the odd
nibble at a grain of rice. Along with checking on pasta, this is clearly the obvious way to
find out when rice is on the way to being ready. Once the texture of the rice is almost
firm to the teeth – or almost *al dente* (which never means, under any circumstances, "still
a little chalky in the middle") – now is the time to add the last ladle of stock.

Once that last ladleful has been added and incorporated, also stir in the herbs and
vermouth. Stir and cook for a couple of minutes more. Finally, add the remaining
butter, check for seasoning, switch off the heat, and tightly cover the pan. Leave the
risotto alone for 5 minutes now, to allow the rice to enjoy a final, quiet swell. For a
last-minute, fail-safe indication that the rice is cooked, eat a bit after this; the swollen
grains should now give nicely to the bite, sort of fudgy yet melting. Reheat the risotto
briefly, and vigorously stir it for the last time. As you so do, sprinkle in 2–3 tbsp of
Parmesan and incorporate fully, until the whole mass is sleek and glossy. Serve straight
from the pan and hand the remaining cheese at table.

ARNHEM BISCUITS [COOKIES]

A short distance from the bookshop there is a patisserie called Hagdorn at 14 Grote Oord, and while I was still signing away, the proprietor sent in to me a present, a small box of his own special biscuits called *Arnhemse Meisjes*. While my right hand kept signing, my left hand idly opened the box and fished out one of the biscuits. It was flat and thin and oval, and crystals of sugar were embedded in the top of it. I took a nibble. I took another nibble. I savoured it slowly. I took a big bite and chewed it. The taste and texture were unbelievable. This, I told myself, is the best biscuit I've ever eaten in my life. I ate another and another, and each one I ate only strengthened my opinion. They were simply marvellous. I cannot quite tell you why, but everything about them, the crispness, the flavour, the way they melted away down your throat made it so you couldn't stop eating them. The lady who owned the bookshop was standing beside me. "They're wonderful," I said.

That evocative quote comes from the late Roald Dahl and is taken from *Roald Dahl's Cookbook* (Penguin, 1996), which he wrote with his wife, Liccy. The quote was taken from almost two pages of a story concerning these cookies. They truly are quite wonderful.

This is a treasure of a book. Not only is it full of terrific recipes, it is also a joy simply to read, filled as it is with tributes to cooks and friends, endearing anecdotes of family ups and downs, and many vociferous opinions on all aspects of how very important it is that every single meal eaten should be nothing less than special. There are wine stories, gambling stories, festive stories, sad and happy stories, and, of course, just the odd chocolate story or two . . . I love this cookbook. It goes without saying that you should use the best butter you can buy.

Makes about 35–40 bisquits

"The dough is best left overnight for ease of handling.

1⅓ cups all-purpose flour

½ cup milk

4 drops lemon juice (more later if necessary)

¼ oz fresh yeast

a pinch of salt, only if using unsalted butter

4 oz unsalted butter (divided equally
into 5 pieces of approx. ¾ oz each)

rock sugar is used instead of a floured
surface [I used sugar cubes that I
lightly crushed with a rolling pin]

"Mix together the flour, milk, lemon juice, and yeast, adding a pinch of salt if necessary. With an electric beater on high speed, beat 1 piece of butter into the mixture for about 2 minutes. Continue in the same way for the remaining butter pieces. Wrap the dough in cling film [plastic wrap] and refrigerate overnight so that it is easier to handle.

"Preheat the oven to 275°F.

"Line your baking sheet with non-stick baking paper [parchment paper]. Dredge your rolling surface with the rock sugar [crushed sugar cubes], then roll out the dough over the sugar, sprinkling it with some more crushed sugar and continue to roll until very thin.

"With a biscuit cutter, cut out the dough. [Ovals are the traditional shape.] Place the biscuits on the lined baking sheets and sprinkle with more sugar. Bake for 30–45 minutes or until crisp and lightly golden."

Note: I noticed that when the biscuits had turned "lightly golden" they were not exactly "crisp." But then this is the case with all biscuits: they do not fully crisp up until left to cool. I only point this out so that you do not feel tempted to cook further (to a darker color, which ruins them) just so that they turn crisp while still in the oven.

CABBAGE

I cannot recall ever disliking cabbage, even as a nipper. It certainly never caused me the interminable grief that it appeared to inflict upon several unfortunate childhood chums. They were the norm; the overdeveloped childhood palate that was mine, I now know, was an unusually receptive one. I guess to have also been a perpetually hungry adolescent (no perceptible shift, forty years on) helped a bit, but I really did enjoy my cabbage, wolfing it down along with everything else on the plate as a matter of course.

Rarely were the words "If you don't eat your greens there won't be any dessert!" directed towards this one, though I recall my brother Jerry being a touch more contrary. Of course, he is a much, much better boy now: a grown-up doting daddy himself, who now eats up *all* his greens. Jerry recently hinted to me that his teenage son Carl has occasional moments of fussiness with certain foods: "What do you think, Simon? Is it something to do with the relentless fast-food opportunities, constantly bombarding the mind of the easily corrupted teenager with their jargon at any opportunity, day in, day out? You know, McDonald's, Burger King, deep-pan pizzas, all that sort of thing?" Hmmm . . . more like a chip off the old block, I thought.

I even like plainly boiled cabbage. As long as this is cooked in plenty of salted boiling water, very well drained, and then generously buttered and peppered (freshly ground white corns, for preference) this simplest of methods can be the very essence of cabbage in its purest form. Slowly stewing it raw in plenty of butter with no liquid at all is a further option, but this method then takes on the distinctive characteristics of a braise. Delicious in itself but here the butter's flavor and emollient qualities alter slightly, becoming oily as it stews the cabbage and with the greens also taking on a more pungent, sulfurous quality. In other words, a windy night ahead.

I believe it was John Tovey who first alerted me to braising cabbage with white wine and juniper. This is a fine recipe. Gentle slow cooking is the key here, allowing the cabbage to soak up lots of lovely butter while quietly taking on the fragrance of its old friend juniper in the process. The white wine adds a welcome acidity to the brew, mimicking, I guess, the sharp fermented qualities of the Alsatian choucroute, something which could well have been the inspiration of this dish in the first place, what with dozens of little juniper berry punctuations all through it and so on. Frankly, the magisterial choucroute is something that is lost on me, though more than anything else it is the very enormity of the dish that repels me the very minute it is set upon the table. I am instantly full simply by looking at it.

My favorite cabbage of all is the small, very slightly oval, semi-hard green one. This is the best choice when doing the plain boiling and buttering thing. The huge great white football of a cabbage is ideal for making coleslaw and is also the one fermented for spooky old choucroute. Spring greens are a frivolous, light and floppy variety that take little time to cook. So much so, in fact, that it is this particular brassica above all that would move me to simply sweat it in much butter until limp and lovely. Savoy cabbage is deep of flavor but can also develop a bitter edge if not carefully attended to. It is also the favorite of the confused cook who only really uses its verdant green – almost blue, in fact – outer leaves for wrapping up curious, divers items and baking them in a terrine.

BRAISED WILD RABBIT WITH CABBAGE, GARLIC, AND BACON

I have decided to go into great detail on how to go about cutting up a rabbit here. I feel it is time you learned a thing or two concerning simple domestic dissection. The satisfaction of doing it yourself is considerable; not only for your own peace of mind, but also to impress your butcher or game dealer no end. A French housewife would rather die than request her *beau lapin* to be prepared anywhere else than in her own kitchen. Have your knives good and sharp.

Serves 5–6

2 wild rabbits, skinned
½ cup plus 2 tbsp white wine
¾ cup plus 2 tbsp good chicken stock
salt and pepper
a little flour
2 tbsp butter
2 tbsp olive oil
12 large cloves garlic, peeled
a generous slosh of Madeira or sherry
3–4 sprigs of fresh thyme
2 bay leaves
1 Savoy cabbage, divested of the tougher
outer leaves, then cored and quartered
1 small pig's foot, split (optional, but it will add succulence, which is
especially missing in a wild rabbit)
6–8 thick slices of very fat bacon, rind intact if possible

Serve with

boiled potatoes

If the head of the rabbit is still attached, remove it with a hefty blow from a heavy knife. Now cut off each of the shoulders, and chop off the tiny, spindly extreme joint from each one. Cut straight through the rib cage, about halfway along, around about the point where the meaty saddle part nearest to the (now decapitated) head is tapering off; this is quite clear if you look closely and feel around. Chop the rib cage, neck part, and the two tiny shoulder joints into small pieces (it is easily done with that same heavy knife), put into a pan, and add the wine and chicken stock, together with a modicum of seasoning. Simmer together for 30–40 minutes, or longer; this can only improve the flavor of your dish, and is the sort of thing a committed cook does without a second thought. You can add the head to this too if you wish, but hew it in two and wash it well first.

Now then, turning to the leg end and with the rabbit's back uppermost, make an incision around the curved part of each leg, revealing as you so do a sort of pointy and bony central extremity. As you carefully cut down and against this to remove each leg, a neat and obvious ball-and-socket joint will soon show up on either side. Cut through these to detach each leg. Now, once again, with a heavy blow from the knife, remove the pointy bone (its pelvic bone, I guess) where this other end of the saddle meat stops, but more abruptly this time. (If it helps, just think of that area immediately above your buttocks where you place your hands of a morning while having a good stretch, soon after getting out of bed.)

We're getting there. Chop that severed pointy bit up too and add it to the simmering stock. Now remove the membrane that adheres to the saddle using a small sharp knife, lifting it off in thin strips but without cutting into the meat itself: sort of pierce, lift, and separate, if you like. This takes a little practice, but you should get the hang of it quite quickly. So now we have two shoulders, two legs, and a whole saddle. To complete the correct portion distribution, it is now necessary to divide the saddle into three pieces, across the joint, with three equidistant, swift chops of the knife. The final count will be fourteen pieces of rabbit. Now do the same with the other rabbit.

Preheat the oven to 275°F. – or even less in my kitchen. It depends on how volatile your oven is at low temperatures; you wish for the thing to merely blip and murmur.

Season the rabbit pieces with salt and pepper and roll in the flour. Heat the butter and oil together in a large lidded cast-iron pot (a Le Creuset pot is the one I always use here) until a bit frothy. Add the rabbit in manageable amounts and in 2 batches. Cook gently on all sides until golden. Remove to a dish when all done and tip in the garlic. (Incidentally, isn't it nice when onions are not used, for once?) Push these against the crusty bits in the bottom of the pot, hoping vaguely to pick up scraps of residue in the process, until they have also taken on a little golden tinge themselves. Remove and put with the rabbit. Pour off all the residual fats and pour in the Madeira or sherry. Using a stiff whisk, scrape up all the remaining bits and then strain over the rabbit stock. Bring to the boil and reduce by half.

Reintroduce the rabbit and tuck in the thyme, bay leaves, and pieces of cabbage. If you want to use the pig's foot include this now, pushing each half down into the pot amongst the pieces of rabbit. Do not be alarmed if you think there is not enough liquid at this point, as much will exude from the rabbit and pig's foot as they cook.

Lay the bacon, overlapping, all over the surface and let the stew gently rise to a simmer. Cut a piece of wax paper a little larger than the inside of the pot (a *cartouche),* so that it comes up the sides a little; a few snips around the edge with a pair of scissors helps the thing to fall into place. I used to think this contraption a waste of time, but I don't now, as it really does add a secondary muffle to the proceedings in addition to the lid. (This is a similar operation to the one employed inside a kiln, for when wanting a subdued firing; my mother used to teach pottery.) Now put the lid on and put it in the oven for about 2 hours.

Some fat will be floating on the surface once the rabbit is cooked; lift off any excess that offends you with paper towel. Dish up directly from the pot onto hot plates. For those who request some, break up the pig's foot – which will now be deliciously flobby – with the serving spoon and distribute along with everything else. Serve with a large dish of plainly boiled potatoes, nothing more.

SIMPLE BOILED CABBAGE, BUTTER, AND WHITE PEPPER

For this recipe use that small football-shaped pale green cabbage. Of course, this is not mandatory, but, for me, it gives the best results. Otherwise, I think I would rather use spring greens here.

Serves 4

2 cabbages, well trimmed of tough outer leaves
sea salt
plenty of best butter
white pepper

Bring a large pan of water to the boil and add a little salt. Cut each cabbage into 4, lengthways. (Do not remove the core from each quarter now, as this will help the cabbage remain in one piece while it cooks.) Plunge into the water and cook until very tender when pierced with a skewer. Drain well in a colander. Remove the cores with a small sharp knife. Put as much butter as you wish into the empty pan and melt it. Return the drained cabbage, season with a little more salt, and grind over much white pepper. Turn the cabbage carefully through the butter and put on the lid. Simmer very quietly indeed for 3–4 minutes and then lift out into a hot serving dish. If the buttery residue is at all watery, reduce it over a high heat until most of the liquid has been driven off. Spoon the result over the cabbage and serve at once.

STEWED WHITE CABBAGE WITH WHITE WINE, THYME, AND JUNIPER

In essence, bland and naked choucroute.

Serves 4

2 onions, peeled and thinly sliced
1 clove garlic, peeled and chopped
6 tbsp butter
1 medium-sized hard white cabbage, trimmed,
cut into 4, and cored
salt and white pepper
1 tsp juniper berries, bruised flat with the back of a knife
1 large glass of white wine (a Riesling, or similar, would be just perfect here)
½ tsp fresh thyme leaves

Using a large pan, gently sweat the onions and garlic in the butter until softened but not colored. Add the cabbage, season, stir around, and set over the merest flame. Put on the lid and allow the cabbage to flop down in its own steam, for 10–15 minutes. Add the juniper berries, stir again, and continue to stew for a further 10 minutes. Turn up the heat and add the wine. Allow to bubble, turn the heat down once more, and finally stew for a further 15 minutes, uncovered, until very tender. Stir in the thyme leaves, put on the lid, and leave for 5 minutes to infuse.

CELERY

I am of the humble opinion that celery makes one of the finest cream soups of all. Not so Terence Conran when we were about to open Bibendum in the late 1980s. "Oh, I'm not so sure about that celery soup, Simon. It smacks so much of boarding houses of the 1950s."

I'm not quite sure how many boardinghouses young Terence stayed in during that decade to enable him to make such a sweeping comment, but then, I guess, most bowls of soup in a 1950s boardinghouse must have been fairly dire.

So, on reflection, I think I saw a little of his point of view. (I do *always* try to see just a little of it.) There was always a certain pong emanating from the kitchen of a dreary B&B or "Country Inn" in those days and you can bet your life it would be either a mushroom, tomato, leek, chicken, or celery soup that was the cause of it. The thing is, they all smelled roughly the same anyway, having either come out of a package or jumbo catering-sized can. I could just about pick out the tomato as a kid, but then Heinz tomato does have a most particular whiff. But all the others simply smelled like hotel – or boardinghouse – soup.

(I hasten to add that my uneducated palate never failed to be seduced by this whiff and always looked forward to some for supper with a squashy white roll, and butter that I scraped out from my very own, individually foil-wrapped portion. Adams Best Butter, I think it was, which you just don't see anymore, do you?)

After Terence's remark, I remained more determined than ever to make the finest celery soup possible. It was going to be the smoothest, creamiest, most savory bowlful in the land. And it was. Mind you, it wasn't the greatest seller. I suppose most people coming to dine at this wonderful new restaurant in South Kensington wanted to eat something a bit more "sophisticated" than celery soup; perhaps they had all been to the same boardinghouses as Terence. Anyway, I liked it and seem to remember eating quite a lot of it for my supper each night. Well, someone had to.

Now pay attention. There is one simple imperative with celery that almost all cooks ignore, but for which, if someone did it for you, you would be eternally grateful and notice how nice it was that they had bothered. And that is always to peel your celery. (This is unnecessary when making soup, of course, assuming that you will carefully push the result through a fine sieve once pureed.) A stalk stuck into a Bloody Mary, or sliced up into a well-made Waldorf salad or even neat hearts of the vegetable gently braised to go with a traditional roast duckling: celery should always, but always, be peeled. Just why is this so rarely done?

BRAISED CELERY HEARTS WITH CREAM AND CÈPES

The celery hearts found in cellophane packages from supermarkets are ideal here. Caution: do watch out for salt when cooking celery as for some strange reason excess salt often appears from absolutely nowhere.

Serves 4

1¼ cups hot chicken stock (or, for a purely vegetarian option,
instant vegetable bouillon is very good indeed)
½ oz dried cèpes
4 tbsp butter
4 celery hearts, outer stalks ruthlessly peeled and bases trimmed
1 tbsp white wine vinegar
1 small clove garlic, bruised
¼ cup Madeira or Amontillado sherry
1 tbsp chopped fresh tarragon
a tiny pinch of celery salt (optional)
freshly milled white pepper
4–5 tbsp heavy cream

Preheat the oven to 325°F.

Pour the stock over the dried cèpes and leave to soak for 15 minutes. Melt the butter in an ovenproof cast-iron dish. Gently stew the celery in the butter, coloring it lightly, and then add the vinegar. Allow to bubble and reduce to almost nothing before adding the stock and swollen cèpes. Bring to a boil and slip in the clove of garlic, together with the Madeira or sherry, tarragon, and seasoning. Cover with foil (or put on a lid if there is one) and place in the oven for 40 minutes to 1 hour, turning the celery over halfway through. Check from time to time that there is still a sufficient amount of braising liquid, and turn down the temperature and add a little more stock if the dish is beginning to look at all dry. To finish the dish, add the cream, swirl it around the celery (do not mess around with the celery as it will be very tender by now), and reduce swiftly over an open flame until slightly thickened and unctuous.

CREAM OF CELERY SOUP

Serves 5–6

4 tbsp butter
12 oz celery, cleaned and chopped
2 small onions, peeled and chopped
½ tsp celery salt
1 large potato, peeled and chopped
1 qt good chicken stock
⅔ cup whipping cream
freshly ground white pepper

Serve with

croutons

Melt the butter in a roomy pan and gently cook the celery and onions in it for 20 minutes or so until soft but not colored. Add the celery salt. Put in the potato and add the stock. Bring to a boil, check the seasoning to see if any further salt (plain) is needed, skim off any scum, and simmer for 30–40 minutes. Now puree the mixture well, for at least a minute or so for each couple of ladles, as this will accentuate the eventual creamed quality of the soup. Finally, push through a fine sieve into a clean pan, stir in the cream and pepper, and gently reheat without boiling. Serve with tiny, buttery croutons.

A GOOD WALDORF SALAD

Apparently – and who am I to doubt it – the original Waldorf salad was created just prior to the turn of the last century by one Oscar Tschirky, the chef of the Waldorf Astoria Hotel, New York City. Unfortunately, and with great respect to the late chef Tschirky, *my* most vivid and recent memory of a Waldorf salad is that particular one requested of Basil Fawlty by an irate American guest, who simply wished to eat it for a late supper. As if.

Tradition demands that there should be walnuts in a Waldorf salad, but as I don't particularly like them, I have substituted almonds here. (Naturally, you can use walnuts if you prefer.) Also, I quite like the idea of the look of the thing being all the one bland, beige hue. *Note:* Use only tender celery hearts.

Serves 4

4 oz celery, peeled and thinly sliced
4 oz Granny Smith apples, peeled, cored, and sliced into matchsticks
juice of ½ a lemon
2 oz whole almonds, blanched in boiling water for a few seconds, drained, and
then sliced lengthways
2 oz sultanas, plumped up in boiling water for 5 minutes, then drained
about ½ cup mayonnaise (*not* made with
olive oil)

Carefully tumble together the celery and apple with the lemon juice and leave to macerate for 5 minutes. Mix together with all the other ingredients.

CHICKEN

My local butcher Sid recently had a gorgeous-looking chicken in his shop window. "It's from Belgium, Simon," he said with a rueful grin, "a sample, in fact. Here, have it as a gift. Nobody round here is going to buy it anyway, as I'd have to charge about fifteen quid for it!" So I carried it home with many thanks and pathetic protestations – you know, all those "Are you sures?" and "Why doesn't Rosie [Sid's sister] roast it for dinner tonight?" – and not really meaning a single word of it. But Olympia Butchers, Hammersmith, truly is one of a dying breed of proper family butchers. Sid, his sister Rose, and his father Michael are kind to *everyone* as a matter of course. Come the day they finally retire, I, and many others, will feel more bereft than we can possibly imagine.

While putting that terrible thought far to the back of my mind for a moment, I cannot tell you how magnificent that *poulet de Belge* turned out to be. It was ample for four and as fine a family fowl for the weekend as ever it used to be. "A nice chicken for the weekend, Mrs. Hopkinson? Allow me to find you a really nice one," John Pendlebury, our local butcher in Lancashire, used to say. Incidentally, Sid does the "really nice one" thing too. It's a tradition, I know, and is supposed to make everyone feel just a bit special. But where do they keep all the "really horrible ones"? That's what I want to know. And who gets them?

But this is an interesting point: if the average housewife, shopper, and self-satisfied *gourmet de nos jours* possessed just a soupçon of the knowledge of their forebears, they would know perfectly well which was a "nice one" in the first place. Many say that the appreciation and understanding of good food have improved immeasurably over the past few years, but most shoppers now don't have the slightest idea when it comes to knowing the difference between a piece of chuck and a lump of top rump, or what happens to it while it cooks. I find this a very sad state of affairs. Your average granny knows a good chicken when she sees one, but would probably keel over and expire if she knew the price of that Belgian bird.

Oh, pathetic, average British chicken! Oh, pathetic, arrogantly complacent British consumer! How on earth did we manage to allow something so easy to get right to become so very, very wrong? Well, as usual, we only have ourselves to blame. For as the factory farming of chickens became notably easier (read cheaper) to produce, we simply jumped in, rejoicing at the good fortune that brought affordable poultry for all. Beef was elbowed off the carving board in no time at all, in favor of the budget bird. As beef was actually cheaper at the time, pound for pound, there were also moments of gorgeous British snobbery for a while too. "A nice piece of rolled rib for Sunday, Mrs. Hesketh?" John Pendlebury would say with a smile. "No, thank you, John" – eyebrows raised – "just our *usual* chicken, please." Oh, the looks in the queue!

I am from that generation that remembers when that roast chicken truly was a treat. As a little one, once or possibly twice a month we would have chicken for Sunday lunch, or jointed into a dead-exotic pot of *coq au vin* on a Saturday night when Dad would marinate, mulch, and master one of these deep red-wine brews, then allow it all to gently blip of an afternoon in the oven; I guess from about the end of the wrestling till just before *The Morecambe & Wise Show* began. And when I say "blip," I mean only 2 or 3 of these slack eruptions every 15 minutes or so. Sort of Leonard Cohen–type blips.

SOUTHERN-STYLE FRIED CHICKEN THIGHS
WITH GARLIC CREAM

This is the way of frying things in the southern states of America. The only significant preparation known to us Limeys, of course, is Chicken Maryland, with its garnish of fried banana and sweetcorn fritters – never, ever heard of in the U.S., and particularly not by Marylanders.

The best thing of all about fried chicken is its crusted coating. Traditionally, it is hog fat that is the preferred frying medium. Paul McIlhenny, of the Tabasco-making family, once told me that he deep-fries his Thanksgiving turkey whole, in hog fat, and very proud he is at the result. If you try this at home, you will need an old, well-scrubbed oil drum, a very large camp stove, a spacious backyard, strong arms . . .

Serves 4

8 large chicken thighs, skinned
seasoned flour (celery salt, cayenne pepper, paprika, and white pepper)
2 small eggs, beaten
½ cup butter
⅔ cup pure olive oil
lemon wedges

For the garlic puree

3 plump heads of garlic, peeled
salt
2 tbsp virgin olive oil
1 large tub of crème fraîche
a few shakes of Tabasco

Roll the thighs in the flour and shake off any excess. Coat thoroughly with the egg and lay on a cooling rack for a minute or so. Dip again into the flour and once more into the beaten egg. Return to the rack and finally dip into the flour. Set aside on the rack until ready to cook. This seemingly excessive dipping and flouring does, I assure you, provide a good crust, however messy it sounds.

Using a large, shallow pan, melt together the butter and olive oil on a medium heat until the fat starts to sizzle somewhat; drop a small piece of bread into it and if it sizzles nicely, then the temperature should be just about fine. Slide the chicken thighs into the fat and gently shallow-fry (the depth should not be more than ¾–1¼ in) for 15–20 minutes, turning halfway through, until golden brown and crusted all over. Remove from the pan and lay on a double fold of paper towel. Sprinkle with salt and serve without delay. *Note:* You might like to strain the fat into a small bowl and keep in the fridge for further southern-frying excursions.

To make the puree, simmer the garlic cloves in water with a little salt, until just tender. Drain. Puree in a food processor with the olive oil, but leave it a little bit coarse. Tip into a bowl and cool. Add the crème fraîche and beat with a whisk until thick. Add more salt if necessary and the Tabasco. Serve at room temperature, with the chicken, and with lemon wedges.

ROAST CHICKEN WITH BREAD SAUCE, BEST GRAVY, AND SAUSAGE AND BACON ROLLS

A little further worked upon over the last seven years, but still the same old favorite. The addition of the chicken wings to the roast truly does produce excellent gravy. (Some chopped breast of lamb around a roast leg, or chunks of belly under a pork joint will produce an equally fine lotion.) So for just a few pennies more you can produce something that really *is* gravy rather than relying on tasteless, grease-imbued supermarket cartons and a splash of vegetable water.

Serves 4, with second helpings

8 chicken wings, roughly chopped
½ cup softened butter
4 lb (approx.) free-range chicken
salt and pepper
juice of 1 lemon
several sprigs of fresh thyme
1 small glass of dry sherry
4 tbsp chicken stock

For the bread sauce

2 cups milk
6 tbsp butter
8 cloves
2 large bay leaves, crumbled
a good pinch of salt
1 small onion, peeled and finely chopped
3 tbsp heavy cream
about ½ cup fresh white bread crumbs
freshly ground white pepper

For the sausage and bacon rolls

12 best-quality chipolata sausages

12 slices of very thinly cut bacon

Serve with

Roast Potatoes in Beef Dripping (see page 35)

Simple Boiled Cabbage, Butter, and

White Pepper (see page 43)

Preheat the oven to 450°F.

Strew the chicken wings over the base of a solid-bottomed roasting pan. Smear the butter all over the chicken, season well, and position on top of the wings. Squeeze the lemon all over the chicken, then push the exhausted halves and the thyme inside the chicken cavity. Pour in the sherry and stock. Roast in the oven for about 10–15 minutes, then turn the temperature down to 350°F. Continue roasting for a further 1–1¼ hours. (Using this "wet roasting" method, it is inadvisable to baste the chicken, as the liquid can cause the skin to become soggy.)

When the skin is crisp and a rich golden color, skewer the thigh and look for the clear juices that show it's done. Lift out the chicken and pour out its interior juices, thyme, and lemon halves into the roasting pan. Put the bird on a serving plate. Keep warm in the oven (switched off), with the door ajar. Allow to rest for at least 10 minutes before carving.

In the meantime, start to make the bread sauce. (Think about making this at least 30 minutes in advance; in fact, if I am serving bread sauce for dinner, I often infuse the milk with the aromatics that morning.) Heat together the first 6 ingredients until just bubbling, below a simmer. Leave like this for 5 minutes or so, cover, and infuse off the heat. Strain through a fine sieve into a clean pan and press down on the solids to extract all their flavors. Reheat gently with the cream until hot, but do not boil. Whisk in the bread crumbs in batches (until you are personally happy with the consistency) along with some pepper, then leave for a few moments to allow the crumbs to swell. Check for salt and add the pepper. Pour into a bowl, cover with a plate, and keep warm over a pan of hot (not boiling) water.

To make the sausage and bacon rolls, first remove the skin from the sausages, then wrap each up in a slice of bacon (employ a spiraling motion so as to enclose the entire sausage) and lay them out in a roasting pan. Bake in the oven alongside the chicken, coinciding with its final 20–25 minutes of cooking time.

Now begin to make the gravy. Squash the lemon halves around the roasting dish to extract any remaining flavor, then discard. Put the dish directly on the heat and dislodge and incorporate any clingy browned particles from the bottom of the roasting pan with a wooden spoon (mostly deposited by the – still present – nuggety wings) into the bubbling juices. These, by the way, should not necessarily be homogeneous; more of a buttery mingle of sherry, lemon juice, and stock. Now simmer for several more minutes and then strain through a sieve into a small pan. Discard the wing bits. Whisk together, finally check for seasoning – although, curiously, this always seems to be spot on – heat through, and pour into a pitcher or sauce boat. *Note:* If you think there is huge excess of fat, leave the gravy to settle in the pan and then spoon some of the fat away.

CHICKEN PIE

I adore this pie: all creamy and soft pieces of chicken, bouncy little mushrooms, and gorgeous, slightly soggy, pastry. A modicum of toil is involved, but then not everything, after all, is "simplicity itself." And, my, how I loathe that particular phrase.

Serves 4–5

For the pastry

¾ cup dripping or lard, very cold from the
fridge and cut into small pieces
2½ cups all-purpose flour
pinch of salt
6 tbsp ice-cold water
1 egg, beaten

For the filling

1½ lb leeks
2 small onions, peeled and quartered
1 medium carrot, peeled and roughly chopped
2 sticks celery, roughly chopped
a 3 lb (approx.) free-range chicken
a few sprigs of tarragon and flat-leaf parsley
2 cloves
4 tbsp softened butter
juice of 1 small lemon
salt and white pepper
1 cup water
¼ cup all-purpose flour
1 cup milk
8 oz button mushrooms, thickly sliced
⅔ cup heavy cream

To make the pastry, rub together the fat, flour, and salt until it resembles coarse bread crumbs. Quickly mix in the water and work together until a coherent mass. Knead lightly and put into a plastic bag. Leave to rest in the fridge until the filling has been prepared.

Remove the green tops of the leeks and wash thoroughly. Reserve the white parts, slice into thickish rounds, and put on one side. Put the washed green parts into the base of a deep, preferably cast-iron, lidded casserole dish, together with the onions, carrot, and celery. Push the chicken in amongst them (breast side uppermost), tuck in the tarragon and parsley sprigs, and pop in the cloves. Smear the butter over the chicken, pour over the lemon juice, and season. Add the water and put on a medium heat. Once the water starts to bubble underneath, turn the heat down to very low indeed, cover, and simmer for 45 minutes to 1 hour, turning the chicken over halfway through the cooking process. Preheat the oven to 350°F. and also put a shallow baking pan into the oven to heat up.

Lift the chicken from the pot, pouring out any juices from the inside of the bird, and place on a plate to cool. Strain the juices into another pan, discard the vegetables, and allow the juices to settle. With a tablespoon lift off the excess fat and place it in a small pan. Heat until sizzling slightly and stir in the flour to form a roux. Pour in the milk slowly, whisk together, and cook gently for several minutes until thickened, as for a basic white sauce. Put to one side. Simmer the reserved white leeks and the mushrooms in the strained stock until tender. Lift out with a slotted spoon and place in a large bowl. Remove the skin from the chicken and discard. Cut the meat from the carcass and legs, chop into bite-sized pieces, and loosely mix with the leeks and mushrooms.

Now reduce the strained stock by half, add to the white sauce, and whisk together. Simmer very gently until smooth and unctuous, then whisk in the cream and cook for a further 5 minutes. Pour over the chicken, mushrooms, and leeks, mix together, season, and allow the mixture to cool thoroughly.

Take two-thirds of the pastry, roll it out to a thickness of not more than ¼ in, and use it to line an 8 x 1½ in (approx.) loose-bottomed tart pan, making sure to leave a small amount of pastry overlapping the rim. Tip in the cooled chicken mixture and then roll out the remaining third of the pastry into a circle of similar thickness to the base. Brush a little of the beaten egg on the overlapping pastry edge and then lay the second circle of pastry over the filling, pressing both edges together with your fingertips. Now, using a small, sharp knife, slice through the two, keeping the knife well up against the edge of the pan. Remove and discard these trimmings. Brush the whole surface with eggwash, make two little incisions in the middle to allow steam to escape, and decorate the pastry in whichever way you feel is appropriate; I like to press the edges further together with the tines of a fork.

Put the pie on the preheated pan and bake for about 1–1¼ hours, or until the pastry is golden brown and the very smell of the thing indicates all is ready. Remove and allow to cool slightly for about 10 minutes before serving.

CHILLIES

We Brits presently remain extremely proud fumblers when it comes to dealing with chilli peppers. This is hardly surprising. Exactly how long has a supreme freshness of all hues and shapes, lengths and strengths, names and strains of some of the world's chillies been readily available to us in Britain? About eight and a half years, perhaps? Yet, curiously, it seems that almost everyone has now become the all-time expert: "Nah, you don't want those long thin green ones. They're crap! You 'ave to get yourself a nice bag o' 'Bird's Eyes', or yer little 'Serraaanos.' Them'll make the tears run all down your pretty cheeks!"

I actually picked up on this particular conversation in a Thai restaurant near to me in west London, a few years ago now. I guess it was the next stage up from the conversation that might previously have attached itself to the delights of that essential Friday night vindaloo. Though clearly this is a delight now long discarded by the aforementioned chilli expert.

To illustrate my point more clearly, I recall a deeply embarrassing moment during a broadcast of a BBC food program (1999) called *Really Good Food*. (The simple title *Good Food* clearly deemed just *not* enough.) Here were two middle-aged English dudes who had been coaxed into cooking a dish from a recently published recipe book by the celebrity chef Jean-Christophe Novelli. One competitor seemed to do reasonably well, while the other messed up big time – not helped, perhaps, by a healthy disregard for the recipe itself. But you know what this sad person used to "doctor" his pathetic mess? The best part of a quarter-bottle of Thai fish sauce. "Oh yeah, this'll fix it. Wonderful stuff. Put it in everything. Never fails!" – or some such garbage. I wouldn't be surprised if he used it as deodorant.

What is it about the average British male that deems anything "hot 'n' spicy" to be, most firmly, part of his domain? It's never meringues, fish pie, dressing a salad, chicken casseroles, or making pastry, but if there is the merest hint of chilli in something somewhere in the Saturday night dinner party, he's right in there, loudly pontificating: "That's never enough! Needs much more than that! Look, Beverly, when it comes to cooking with chillies, just ask the expert. I've eaten whole ones in the back streets of Singapore that just about blew my head off. Just ask Ron. Ron'll tell you, won't you, Ron?"

So what I am really trying to say is that in this mildly spiced country of ours, we still know next to nothing about fresh chillies, their varying uses, strengths, and subtleties. I, for one, am regularly bewildered. But they have been around for years, if you cared to look for them. How do you think thousands of (mostly) Bangladeshi families have coped over the last forty-odd years? And have all the restaurants they have since made their own simply relied upon a package of powder? You only have to walk up and down Southall High Street (a mere Boeing's roar away from Heathrow) to know that here is a thoroughfare dedicated to the daily needs of the Asian kitchen. Well, it's a little easier to get to than the back streets of Singapore.

And now it's all Thai. And Mexican too. How multitalented the British cook has suddenly become! Jim is a whiz at his green chicken curry while his chum Ron can turn an authentic Mexican salsa out of his Braun food processor in a matter of seconds. The saddest outcome of all, however, is that Jim's and Ron's wives now only grill tuna steaks, sear chicken breasts, and cut open packages of pre-washed salad. The kids continue to be happy with pizza, twirly pasta in sauce, and the odd tray of chicken tikka masala as a treat. Jim's wife is, naturally, in charge of the rice for both the children's tikka and Jim's "best ever green chicken curry." This presents no problem for Beverly, as she can now buy it ready-cooked from the supermarket: "It's always yellow, but it goes with everything!"

I don't suppose that Mrs. Patel of Southall would be particularly proficient at making meringues, shortcrust pastry, fish pie, or dressing a green salad. But she would be just the bee's knees at knowing exactly the right amount of green chilli to add to her fresh masala paste. Just why is it that the British have become more and more obsessed with the taste of things they haven't a clue how to cook, yet have grown increasingly bored with the things they can?

RASAM

Having searched through endless Indian cookbooks in search of this elusive recipe, I eventually found a version in David Burton's excellent book *Savouring the East* (Faber and Faber, 1996), where it turned up as number three recipe: South Indian Tomato Rasam. I tasted my first rasam in a vegetarian restaurant in Tooting, south London, many years ago now, and have never forgotten its sweet and sour, fragrant allure. This particular rendition is every bit as memorable.

Serves 4

8 small very ripe tomatoes
2 tbsp dried tamarind pulp
1 tbsp oil
½ tsp black mustard seeds
1 medium onion, finely chopped
10 cloves garlic
1 small red chilli
1 tsp ground cumin
½ tsp ground black pepper
3 tbsp fresh cilantro, chopped

"Place the tomatoes in a large pot with 1 qt of water and boil until the tomatoes burst. Pick out the skins and discard then mash the tomatoes into the water.

"Meanwhile break the dried tamarind into small pieces and soak in 1 cup of boiling water for 5 minutes. Massage the pieces to release the tamarind juice, then strain the liquid into the pot containing the tomato and water.

"Heat the oil in a pan, add the mustard seeds, cover, and cook over a high heat until the mustard seeds pop. Add the onion and sauté until cooked. Add to the rasam [tomato/tamarind/water mix].

"Pulverize the cloves of garlic and the chilli [using a pestle and mortar or by pulsing in a food processor]. Add to the soup along with the cumin and black pepper. Boil for a few minutes longer. Sprinkle with the freshly chopped cilantro just before serving. Quite delicious spooned over servings of freshly cooked basmati rice or as a soup, just as it is."

Note: There is also a tradition where the soup's liquid is made from the water in which dahl (split peas) has been cooked. And it is the murky remains which, in this particular case, add quite another dimension to it.

MARINATED TUNA WITH AVOCADO, CHILLI, AND CUCUMBER

Based upon the South American favorite ceviche; in other words, raw fish "cooked" by being soaked in lemon or lime juice until slightly stiffened and opaque. I find such preparations immensely addictive in warm weather as they are, all at once, refreshing, piquant, vibrant of flavor, and as colorful as an entire trellis of sweet peas. Eat with buttered rye bread or a bowl of tiny, scrupulously scraped, hot new potatoes.

Serves 4, as a first course

a 12 oz piece of finest-quality tuna fillet
1 tsp sea salt
juice of 2 limes
1 small red onion, peeled and finely chopped
1–2 green or red chillies, finely chopped
(seeds removed or not, as you prefer)
3 plum tomatoes, peeled, cored, and thinly sliced
¼ cucumber, peeled and sliced
1 large avocado, halved, peeled, and sliced
2–3 tbsp freshly chopped cilantro leaves
2 tbsp olive oil

Serve with

⅔ cup sour cream

Slice the tuna thinly and place in a large shallow serving dish. Sprinkle with salt and cover with the lime juice. Leave to marinate for 40 minutes, turning the fish over once. Lift out the fish (which should now look opaque from being "cooked" by the lime juice) and put on a plate. Pour the resultant juices into a small bowl. Return the tuna to the dish in a presentable manner. Scatter over the onion and chillies. Arrange the tomatoes, cucumber, and avocado over the top. Sprinkle the cilantro leaves over the surface and finish with the olive oil.

Finally, return the collected juices to the dish using a spoon, taking particular care to fully anoint each and every piece of avocado, so preventing any discoloration. Cover and chill for a further 40 minutes or so before serving. Hand round a dish of sour cream at table.

CRUNCHY-FRIED GARLIC AND RED CHILLIES

It is difficult, in this particular case, to suggest a serving amount, as the recipe given here is more of a useful garnish than an actual dish in itself. Nevertheless, it can be employed in myriad ways: as a sprinkling over an Oriental noodle salad, offered around as bowlfuls at a barbecue where marinated pork bellies, ribs, or chicken drumsticks are a feature – a nibble here, a nibble there – or as an addition to a sloppy and comforting dish of Indian dahl, stirred in at the last minute, so retaining its crunch. Once you have perfected the process – and it *does* take a little practice - you will soon find endless other uses for this intensely savory mixture.

oil for frying – peanut, for preference,
but *not* olive oil, please
12 large cloves garlic, peeled and sliced
6–7 large red chillies, seeded and sliced
salt

Pour enough oil into a wok or deep frying pan to come to a depth of about ½ in. Put on a moderate flame, and heat up. Add the garlic and chillies to the hot oil. Quietly fry, constantly stirring, until they slowly begin to crisp and turn golden. Once they look as if they have no further use for their frying medium – in other words, they seem to be aimlessly lingering in their unagitated oil – upend the contents of the pan into a colander suspended over another pan so as to drain off all excess oil.

Once the chillies and garlic are now looking correctly dry, and easily rustle when shaken, transfer to a plate that has been lined with a double fold of paper towel. Generously sprinkle with salt and use as needed.

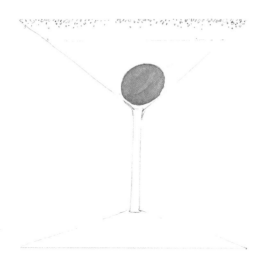

COCKTAILS

Although I have long been an enthusiastic sniffer, taster, drinker, and, eventually, spasmodic collector of a wide variety of interesting bottles of wine it would never, in a Methusalem of Mondays, occur to me to write about any of them "professionally." I mean, you would not find the limpidly lovely Jancis Robinson offering a detailed explanation of how to prepare a pot of braised tripe with pig's heart, celery, garlic, and sherry vinegar in her regular *FT* column when the latest Burgundy vintage requires attention. Enthusiasm is one thing, knowledge and expertise quite another. However, I do know how to make a good drink.

My father's generation, forty years ago, delighted in the drink called Gin and French. This was an abomination to my tender, unaccustomed nostrils between the ages of, say, seven and seventeen (I sniffed it occasionally just to reassure me of its filthiness) and, what's more, remains so to this very day. Simply, it was a smallish glass (always exactly the same one) half-filled with Gordon's gin and topped up with an equal quantity of Noilly Prat (dry vermouth). It seemed critical for Dad, his parents, their relations, friends, and sundry acquaintances that the drink should always be served at room temperature which, in most cases, meant tepid. No ice, no lemon. Just the gin. And the French. Absolute filth. And as far away from the Dry Martini cocktail I now think it was possibly meant to replicate, as it could possibly ever be.

There were two further derivative drinks related to the G&F: Gin and It, and Gin and Mixed. The former constituted a similar measure of Gordon's gin – and it was always, but always, Gordon's – with Martini Rosso (sweet red vermouth), whereas the latter, the most vile brew of all, required the gin to be mixed with both Noilly Prat *and* Martini Rosso; both potions also served at something approaching blood heat, naturally.

I also seem to recall that some of the more jolly (not surprisingly) wives of husbands that were friends of Mum and Dad would occasionally partake of a Gin and It too, but it seemed that it was only a handful of Dad's roister-doister bachelor chums that would regularly imbibe the lethal Gin and Mixed. At grown-ups' parties viewed from halfway down the stairs in jim-jams it was always the G&Ms who were completely legless long before anyone else.

Over the years I have striven to encourage myself to be particular in all things that please the creative side of me and I do not, therefore, necessarily crave an endless choice, as I feel this can often dilute the quality of the selection offered. The ridiculous range of cocktails (a gross misnomer, most of the time) now available to all in trendy bars up and down the country – but particularly in the capital – causes one to ponder that all is not well in the state of Denmark, Finland, Norway, or – come to think of it – even Sweden. Absolutely not!

Personally speaking, if a barman anywhere in the world can make me a good Bloody Mary or a Dry Martini then he is a friend for life; more than any other flippant remark in similar vein, this one rings true the most – and not just in the movies. I am also occasionally tempted by a pink gin or a traditional champagne cocktail if expertly made. (The very finest example of which is that dispensed by the barman of the Oustau de Baumanière, Les Baux de Provence, of which the recipe follows.)

Although I understand that each and every experienced bartender has a particular version of my two most favorite drinks, all I ask is that a bartender not try to reinvent them or introduce absurd additions while still offering them under their original title. I find behavior such as this disrespectful and crass. I mean, even my dad never mucked around with his Gin and French: filth it may well have been, but at least it was exactly the same filth each and every time.

APÉRITIF MAISON "BAUMANIÈRE"

There is an *"apéritif maison"* offered by each and every two- and three-star restaurant throughout all France. Some of them are jolly good, some nothing special, and some . . . well, some are downright disgusting; I would sooner down one of Dad's Gin and Frenches, to be honest, albeit very quickly.

The exception to the rule is this one (a champagne cocktail, in essence) from the fabled Oustau de Baumanière in Provence: a restaurant and hotel set into the bauxite cliffs at one end of the Val d'Enfer and situated directly at the foot of the ancient, mountaintop village of Les Baux. While once staying in the region with my friend Bill Baker and family, of an early evening he and I often (actually, each and every day) suggested that we needed to nip out to do some last-minute shopping in the local village.

After having bought our half cucumber, seven shallots, and a lemon, we would quickly whiz up the winding road to the Baumanière and quietly indulge in two each of these gorgeous drinks – together with a few of their delicious *amuse-bouches*. A clandestine routine of the very finest, we both felt. Towards the end of the week, of course, Bill's wife Katie had finally twigged: "Nice cocktail at the Baumanière, boys?" Must have been Bill's orange and brandy breath that gave the game away. Anyway, here is the cocktail. I can taste it now . . .

Take 1 overlarge chilled wineglass (tulip-shaped for preference, with its rim slightly splayed out) and in it deposit 1 small sugar cube. Douse it with 3 drops of Angostura Bitters. Add ⅔ oz of triple sec, ⅔ oz of good cognac, and 5 oz champagne – once again, as good as you can afford: not vintage, but certainly not cheap rubbish or "sparkling wine." Plop in 3–4 ice cubes and float a thin slice of orange on the surface. Using a long and slender teaspoon (think ice-cream sundae spoons), stir everything together. Serve complete with spoon so that guests may lightly press the juice from the orange into the apéritif as they drink it. At the Baumanière, they also pop in a strawberry or raspberry for added color and frivolity, but this is entirely a matter for you.

BLOODY MARY

A good Bloody should never be too thick with tomato juice. The perfect end result should be one of cool limpidity rather than some kind of chilled tomato soup. And incidentally, the bottle of Bloody Mary mix manufactured by the Tabasco company is one of the finest I have yet come across. It produces just the right consistency time after time: extra spicy, flavored with horseradish (the grated bits sensibly strained out), sharp, fresh, and . . . well, you know, just sam-frantastic! Unfortunately, I have never seen it for sale in the UK. If you happen to come by some in the United States, feel free to send it over.

For 4 large glasses

5 large measures vodka (pepper vodka
made by Absolut is excellent)
1 large measure dry sherry
4–5 hearty shakes of Worcestershire sauce
8 shakes, or more, of Tabasco
juice of 1 juicy lime
¼ tsp celery salt
2½ cups tomato juice
about 20 ice cubes
salt and black pepper, to taste

Mix everything together in a large pitcher and leave for 10 minutes to become really cold. Strain into chilled glasses and, if you like, insert a stick of *freshly peeled* celery.

THE DRY MARTINI

Let's be quite clear about this, I do not like my Martini mucked about with; I guess, in exactly the same way that Dad did not want ice or lemon peel in his Gin and French. Traditional and unmoved to the last, I despise change when something – to my eyes, at least – is pretty close to perfection. But there are now some truly vile so-called Martinis being mixed out there by unscrupulous and, frankly, damaged folk (they have been renamed "mixologists"; I ask you, what exactly is wrong with the title "barman" or "bartender"?) who are endlessly thinking up novel (nasty) things to do to this unique drink. And what makes it worse is that there are plenty of cretins out there who quietly sit on bar stools and order them.

I remain convinced that the Martini should be stirred over plenty of ice, and that that ice should also have been freshly frozen. Excuse me? Well, it is simply that trays of ice that have been sitting in the freezer compartment for days or even weeks (we are talking made-at-home drinks here) are bound to have taken on fugitive flavors from other items stored around them: a couple of containers of old stew; a half-open bag of shrimp; the children's fish sticks; coffee – that sort of thing. Make no mistake, these unassuming impostors will taint the finished drink. You see, I do believe that just that modicum of melted ice which seeps into the gin as it is stirred helps to "soften" it, so removing stridency and strength. Some may say the latter quality is the entire point, but I beg to differ.

I will, however, but only just and very recently, take a Dry Martini cocktail or two from my friend Michael Birkett – who does not go along with the stirring thing. He simply pours one measure of vermouth into an empty bottle (gin, vodka, whiskey, or what he will, just so long as it has been well washed out) and then tops it up with a new, full bottle of gin. He then pops the whole thing directly into the freezer. What I want to know is just what does he do with the remaining measure of gin that doesn't quite fit in the bottle? (I reckon he secretly retires to a previously unknown bathroom, surreptitiously stirs the surplus over ice, and downs it while no one is watching.)

He also prefers to remove the zest from his lemon using one of those "channeling" implements, whereby the skin emerges as one long snakelike spiral. His mild dislike of my "scroll" (see later) is that it "occasionally slips into the mouth as an uninvited tongue" – a more accurate and winsome description I have yet to hear and, sod it, he's absolutely right! But I remain solidly, doggedly, unmoved. Merely ruffled, here is how I like mine.

Have 2 of your favorite Martini glasses ready: 1 in the freezer, 1 to hand. Fill a glass pitcher half-full with fresh ice and pour a good splash of vermouth over it. Stir briefly and strain out all traces of liquid. Fill the Martini glass that's to hand with gin and pour it over the ice. Stir briskly for 20 seconds and strain into the chilled glass. Using a (well-scrubbed) potato peeler, remove a generous piece of zest from an unwaxed lemon and, using your thumb and forefinger, tweak (not twist) it over the surface of the drink. Discard. Remove another piece of zest, repeat, then curl it into a tiny scroll and drop it in. Absolute perfection.

I occasionally favor 3 tiny cocktail onions threaded onto a stick and immersed in the drink too. This is called a Gibson. Traditionally, this does not include lemon zest, but I prefer it with. I guess the terminal purist would now tell me that this was a "mucked-about" Gibson. And I guess he would be right.

COCOA

I love the very feel of cocoa powder. Yet — and I am always tickled by this — whenever I stick my finger in a new package, the feeling almost suggests that there is actually nothing there. So super-fine can be the texture of the best, the very best, cocoa powder that its elusive texture never fails to move me — gastronomically speaking — as I digitally fondle it. The surface of a freshly cut fillet steak and the inside of a recently emptied fava bean pod can also bring about the occasional swoon. Well, yes . . . each to their own, I hear you say.

Apart from the feel of it, you can also tell when cocoa powder is good by virtue of its unique hue: that of dried blood. All cocoa is brown, of course, but premium powders are noticeably tinged with this beautiful sanguine pigment. Genuinely good cocoa smells fantastic too.

Now here's another thing that continually perplexes me. How on earth do you describe the smell of something that smells unlike anything else at all? Although, curiously, some rare and fine clarets can (I assure you this is so) smell of cocoa or its further fabrication, chocolate, it is impossible to say that cocoa smells of anything other than, well, cocoa. I am endlessly fascinated by this. I mean, how do you describe the taste of a carrot to someone who has never tasted a carrot before?

Although a lick of neat cocoa is disgusting it is essential as a coating to the surface of a perfectly made chocolate truffle. Spookily, as I write, I just happen to have a box of Sally Clarke's impeccable chocolate truffles sitting in my fridge. Sally — who also has a restaurant, bakery, and food shop in west London — makes the very finest truffles in the whole world: big, heavy, perfectly round, crisply coated with the thinnest layer of chocolate, and finally rolled in the best cocoa money can buy. My, are they good! That initial hit of bitter cocoa just before the teeth crunch into that brittle chocolate shell is, as far as I am concerned, the epitome of bittersweet bliss. Whenever I am in Paris I feel cheated if I have not managed at least one visit to the Café Angelina before returning home. This traditional *salon de thé* in the rue de Rivoli is world famous for its hot chocolate alone – although their Mont Blanc confection is almost as good a reason for going there. Thick and smooth with rich cocoa butter, a small cup of Angelina's brew is as exquisite as a hot beverage gets. In fact, now I come to think about it, it is the equivalent of half a dozen of Sally Clarke's truffles left to melt in the midday sun. The following recipe is as near as I can get to emulating Angelina's hot chocolate.

HOT CHOCOLATE

If you would like to embellish the following recipe one step further, a teaspoon or two of crème de cacao stirred in at the last minute is a nice idea. And, should you further wish to gild the lily and enjoy the flavor of mint with chocolate, then stir in the same amount of white crème de menthe.

Makes enough for 2 servings

1¼ cups whole milk
4½ oz bitter dark chocolate, broken into bits
3 tsp best-quality cocoa
a tiny pinch of salt
2–3 drops pure vanilla extract

Serve with

whipped cream (optional)

Scald the milk. Remove from the heat and stir in all the other ingredients. Leave for a few moments so that the chocolate melts, then return to the heat and gently whisk to blend everything together. Bring back to a gentle simmer, whisk vigorously, and then decant into previously heated mugs or traditional Continental chocolate bowls. Serve with a bowl of whipped cream on the side, for spooning in, if so desired. I, for one, desire it greatly.

BITTER CHOCOLATE ICE CREAM

Along with a fine vanilla ice cream I rate a great chocolate one as being truly gorgeous. This particular version is almost black, so rich is it in chocolate and cocoa. Interestingly, there is no cream involved here; if there were it would lose that pure and bitter edge. The caramel is important, so do be brave and try and get it really dark, though if you happen to take it too far and it starts to burn, you have no option but to start again; it is only 2 tbsp of sugar, after all, and burned sugar makes burned ice cream.

Serves 4

2 cups plus 2 tbsp whole milk
4 oz best bitter chocolate
4 large egg yolks
7 tbsp sugar

⅓ cup cocoa

2 tbsp water

Bring the milk to the boil and switch off the heat. Put the chocolate into a bowl suspended over a pan of boiled water. Leave to melt. Beat together the egg yolks and 5 tbsp of sugar in a large bowl until light and pale yellow, forming ribbons. Slowly pour in the hot milk, continuing to beat until well amalgamated, then mix in the chocolate and cocoa, blending everything together until luxuriously smooth.

Pour everything back into the milk pan. Now take a small, heavy-based pan and put in it the remaining sugar and the water. Put on a high heat and allow the sugar to melt. When it comes to a boil, turn the heat down a little and start to watch carefully as the sugar starts to caramelize. It will turn pale golden first, then dark golden, and eventually become the color of a shiny chestnut. Holding the metal handle of the pan with a cloth – it will have become very hot – quickly pour it into the chocolate pan, whisking all the time. It may well turn lumpy, but as you are about to give the chocolate mixture a final cooking over heat, these sugar lumps will dissolve.

So, placing the pan onto a low heat, stir with a wooden spoon constantly and cook until slightly thickened, but do not let it come anywhere *near* a boil. Pour back into the bowl, whisk thoroughly, and allow to cool completely before churning the mixture in an ice-cream machine until really thick.

MARQUISE AU CHOCOLAT "TAILLEVENT," SAUCE À LA PISTACHE

I was knocked sideways the first time I ate Taillevent's *marquise au chocolat,* some twenty years ago now. So fudgy and rich was it, and so subtle and limpid the sauce, that I knew this was the best chocolate dessert I had yet eaten. Thanks must go to Patricia Wells, who persuaded Jean-Claude Vrinat to allow her to publish the recipe in her excellent *Food Lovers' Guide to Paris,* and from whose book this is taken.

8–10 servings

For the marquise

10 oz dark chocolate

¾ cup confectioners' sugar, sifted

12 tbsp unsalted butter, softened

5 eggs, separated

a pinch of salt

For the pistachio paste

1 generous cup shelled pistachios (unsalted!) (ask for split nuts that have been
both shelled *and* skinned)
⅔ cup sugar
2 small egg whites

for the sauce

⅓ cup pistachio paste
1 qt milk
8 egg yolks
1¼ cups sugar

To make the marquise, first gently melt the chocolate in a double boiler. Now add, in this order, mixing well after each addition: ½ cup plus 1 tbsp of the confectioners' sugar, all the butter, and the egg yolks. Remove from the heat. Beat the egg whites in another bowl until stiff, then add the remaining confectioners' sugar and beat until glossy. Add one-third of this to the chocolate mixture to loosen it, folding it in carefully but thoroughly. Now add the rest, using the same action. Rinse a large terrine mold with water and fill with the mixture. Cover with plastic wrap and chill for 24 hours. To serve, cut thin slices from the marquise (use a thin, sharp knife dipped into hot water), arrange on chilled plates, and spoon the pistachio sauce around.

To make the paste, simply grind the pistachios in a food processor until as smooth as possible, then add the sugar and egg white until it forms a paste. Store in a screw-top jar and keep in the fridge, where it will last for a week at least.

To make the sauce, put the paste and milk in a saucepan and bring to a boil. Remove from the heat and leave to infuse for at least 5 minutes. Whisk together the egg yolks and sugar until thick and then combine with the warm milk. Cook gently over moderate heat, stirring constantly until lightly thickened – a custard, in other words. Strain through a fine sieve into a bowl and chill.

CUCUMBER

The fragrant waft from a small bowl of peeled, freshly sliced cucumber remains, for me, the epitome of an English summer's day and one of the quintessential smells of my childhood summer, along with a newly mown lawn, Dad's occasional glass of Pimm's, next door's elderflower pollen, popped pea-pods, mint in the new potatoes, linseed on my brother's cricket bat, sweet peas, and the occasional oily whiff of my mother's Ambre Solaire drifting over from around her deck chair in our Lancashire garden (rather than from a damp beach towel in the Seychelles). Warm summer odors then, even in the north of England, were vibrant and memorable.

Whatever impression you may have gleaned from that introductory paragraph, I feel it is important to say here that we weren't remotely a "cucumber sandwich" family. In fact, come to think of it, we weren't really sandwich people, full stop. The only sandwiches that made occasional appearances were those made from banana and tomato – though not together, you understand. And, anyway, it was usually only Mum who ate the tomato sandwich, but only if she was feeling a little off color; even then, it had to be a pretty well perfect assembly: sliced white bread (no butter), thinly sliced tomatoes, and – most importantly – plenty of salt. All nice and damp and eaten in bed. There were, of course, turkey sandwiches at Christmas, but that's a different story entirely. More a case of wrapping up and packaging than a sandwich, don't you think?

Ah, yes, cucumber (sandwiches demand an entire chapter to themselves). But, do you know, that fragrant bowl of lightly vinegared cucumber was always made with malt vinegar? *Malt vinegar!* I can see visions of crossed fingers and hisses all round from a few shocked folk who have just read this, as if Count Dracula had just swept in through the kitchen door with a bottle of Sarson's clamped between his teeth.

Memory may often play naughty tricks upon us but I often think that Dad's cucumber salad has never tasted quite so good when made with the posher stuff.

Never underestimate the beguiling nuance of cucumber within a dish: a proper Greek salad would be nothing without it (by the end of the Patmos holiday, however, to be without Greek salad at all might be most welcome); *panzanella*, the now ubiquitous Italian bread salad, needs, I feel, the cucumber as much as anything else, save the essential stale bread – and cucumber is not exactly seen as a top ingredient in an Italian salad in the first place; a plate of seasonal poached salmon, whether served hot or cold, is, for me, quite unthinkable without the option of a few slivers of mildly pickled cucumber on the side. And last but not least, as the primary player in a bowl of chilled summer soup it has no rival.

CHILLED CUCUMBER SOUP WITH SHRIMP

I have been cooking – or rather preparing, as this does not actually require cooking – this soup for over twenty years now, summer in, summer out. It has the most fragrant combination of flavors, which just demands to be sipped out of doors as a prelude to a weekend cold lunch. Follow with cold poached salmon and mayonnaise, hot, buttery new potatoes, and, of course, raspberries and cream to finish.

Serves 4

1 cucumber, peeled, seeded, and diced small
1 tsp salt
1⅔ cups cold chicken stock
(curious as this may sound, I have found, over the years,
that stock made from a bouillon cube gives a better flavor to the
finished soup than true chicken stock)
⅔ cup good-quality tomato juice
1 cup plain natural yogurt
a few dashes of Tabasco
⅔ cup light cream
7 oz head-and-shell-on shrimp, cooked,
peeled, and de-headed to give about 3 oz shrimp meat
10–12 mint leaves, finely chopped
cayenne pepper

Put the cucumber in a colander or sieve and sprinkle with the salt. Mix around with your hands and leave to drain on a plate for 30 minutes. Meanwhile, whisk together the chicken stock, tomato juice, yogurt, Tabasco, and cream until smooth and thoroughly blended.

Once the cucumber has finished draining, add it to the soup mixture and stir in. Leave to infuse for 20 minutes. Remove any froth that may have settled on the surface and check for seasoning; it may require more seasoning, on top of the salt already used to disgorge the cucumber.

Ladle the soup into bowls and garnish with the shrimp, divided equally between each serving. Sprinkle with the mint and dust sparingly with cayenne pepper. *Note:* Always chill soup bowls in the fridge or freezer before using for cold soups.

FILLETS OF LEMON SOLE WITH DILL, CUCUMBER, AND BUTTER SAUCE

A very simple dish, but with lovely clean flavors. Cucumber and dill are made for each other; think of gravlax with pickled cucumber salad, and dill and mustard sauce, for instance. There is no reason why these flavors cannot be used in a hot fish dish, and sole is perfect here with its delicate flavor. To enhance the aniseed flavor in the dill I always add a splash of Pernod to the buttery juices.

Serves 4

4 medium-sized lemon soles
(approx. 1¼–1½ lb each), filleted and skinned
4 tbsp butter, softened
6 sprigs of dill
salt and pepper
½ a large cucumber, peeled, deseeded, and diced
1 tbsp Pernod
1 glass dry white wine
juice of ½ a lemon
4 tbsp butter, chopped into small pieces
½ tbsp freshly chopped dill

Preheat the oven to 375°F.

With the fleshy side underneath, take each sole fillet and fold the ends to the middle to form a neat parcel. Now turn them over. Smear an ovenproof dish with the softened butter, strew with the dill, and lay the sole parcels on top, with a little room to spare between them. Season lightly and sprinkle over the diced cucumber evenly. Heat together the Pernod and wine in a small stainless-steel pan, and flame with a match. Once the flames have subsided, pour over the fish and add the lemon juice. Cover with foil and cook in the oven for 15–20 minutes, or until the fish is just firm to the touch.

Remove the foil, lift out the fish onto a warmed serving dish, and keep warm. Discard the sprigs of dill from the fish juices and cucumber; pour them back into the stainless-steel pan. Simmer this until lightly syrupy, then whisk in the butter a piece at a time until glossy and thickened. Finally stir in the chopped dill and pour over the fish. Serve at once, with fresh leaf spinach perhaps.

SPICED CUCUMBER SALAD

This is a very simple and effective salad. It is at its best served with grilled oily fish such as salmon, mackerel fillets, or herring. The combination of hot fish and cool spiced cucumber is very pleasing, particularly when eaten on a hot day out of doors, with the fish having been cooked over some glowing embers.

Serves 4

1 large cucumber, peeled and not too thinly sliced
2 tsp coarse salt

For the dressing

1 tbsp finely chopped cilantro leaves
10 mint leaves, finely chopped
½ a garlic clove, peeled and finely chopped
¼ tsp ground cumin
1 tsp sugar
1 demitasse spoon lime juice
2 small green chillies, seeds removed, finely chopped
2 tbsp plain yogurt
cayenne pepper

Mix the cucumber and salt together with your hands, in a colander. Leave to macerate for 1 hour. Rinse lightly under cold water and dry in a dish towel. Whisk all the dressing ingredients together in a bowl and combine with the cucumber. Turn out onto a dish and dust with a little cayenne pepper.

CURRY

It curiously transpired that it was a certain Iris Pringle, the Anglo-Indian cook of a Continental restaurant in the town of Knutsford, Cheshire, who first taught me how to make a real curry. Incidentally, one would now possibly refer to the description "Continental" as meaning "eclectic," but then the thoughtful classification of any restaurant's "style" of cooking thirty-odd years ago would have been seen as pretentious, to say the least.

Apart from the odd Chinese and Indian joints that were only then just beginning to burgeon, a good local restaurant was simply seen as somewhere more interesting to be than sitting at the dining-room table at home. And, furthermore, it usually had better wine, waiters (servants), and someone else to do the washing up, all fully inclusive. Most often paid fully in cash too, which pleased both parties *hugely* . . .

Having now attempted to explain how things were then – and which is, perhaps, a view mainly for those of an age who might not quite get my drift here – although Mrs. Pringle's excellent and authentic curries were seen as, how shall we say, "Continental with a nice little touch of the Raj" ("Jolly nice too, don't you think, Margery? What!") many singularly failed to see that these dishes were, at the time, "actually, rather top-hole." Well, pootle that pomposity in the crushing of a thousand poppadoms, for they were quite superb! – as were many of the other carefully cooked, more close-to-home dishes on offer.

The year was 1973, I was aged eighteen and ensconced in my second job happily working for Joan and Arthur Stirling in the kitchens of this, their highly individual restaurant, the Hat and Feather. At the time, the Hat – as it was known by local patrons – had recently become one of the most highly thought of restaurants in all the land. More precisely, so rare was the quality of the cooking here that Raymond Postgate, then editor (and founder) of *The Good Food Guide,* had been moved to rate it as one of only eighteen restaurants in Great Britain to especially receive his coveted personal distinction.

This was an accolade looked on at the time as having much integrity and only bestowed upon those who displayed a natural talent as true restaurateurs and good hosts. Which is to say, folk who were simply very good at cooking and providing a well-chosen list of wines, were generously given to being nice to people, naturally generated a feeling of ease and comfort as a matter of course, presented a neatly laid table, and offered a truly genuine welcome. There wasn't the merest hint of the now familiar Spice Girl lookalike greeter demanding to know whether you had booked or not before so much as even inquiring whether your evening was good. Nor were there the specially designed chair and ashtray, incessantly talkative waiter/waitress, and a selection of fifty wines available by the glass.

The Stirlings' soup of the day was handsomely ladled at table rather than frothed in individual bowls and stinkingly slicked with the now ubiquitous, seemingly essential truffle oil. Moreover, that tiresome wiggle of a tagliatelle tower on every single plate would then have been perceived as something straight out of Swelter's Gormenghast-dungeon kitchen. Pasta was a course, as a matter of course . . . You see, it seemed to me that it was simply a benevolently interested clientele that came to eat at the Hat, content only to know that here was something very good indeed. And with a passionately well-honed belief, I vociferously insist that it was in those days, those halcyon days, that British restauration manifested itself in its most characteristic manner.

Yes, well, very interesting all of that is, I hear you say. But what of your experiences with all that Cheshire curry carry-on? Well, I rolled out fresh chapatis which all stuck together. I turned out both brinjal (eggplant) and fresh lemon pickles. And I learned to make each of those regular curries: the mild beef koftas and the hotter chicken one. I also discovered packages of Mapleton's creamed coconut for the first time, a brand I still use to this day (Dunn's River brand, if pushed). All of this, in Knutsford, Cheshire, in 1973. I mean, wouldn't any aspiring cook worth his or her Maldon sea salt have found all of this gear absolutely fascinating, twenty-seven years ago, aged eighteen? Froth on a soup simply indicated that it had gone off, then.

Naturally, as Iris Pringle's fascinated disciple, I have since read everything there is to read about fine Indian cooking: Madhur Jaffrey, Camellia Panjabi, E. P. Veeraswamy, to name but three sources of inspiration. I have enjoyed quality time loitering in and around the streets of Southall, far-west London. The truly excellent southern Indian vegetarian cooking of a few places dotted in and around Drummond Street, anonymously tucked away behind Euston Station, have also further contributed to my happy, autodidactic education.

At the time, in those early 1970s, it would never have occurred to Iris Pringle to tell me about the strictness of those who eat meat and those who do not, with relation to the people of her homeland. Simply, this was not an issue, in Knutsford or anywhere else: one ate both, thinking nothing more about it. But now . . . now that things are so illuminatingly different, if ever I suddenly became so moved towards the vegetarian persuasion, I would ponder, quite seriously, over whether to make London NW1 my postal code of choice. For a more ideal vegetarian diet I would find it difficult to contemplate than one entirely provided by the kitchens of the Diwana Bhel-Poori House, at 121 Drummond Street.

Once, here, many years ago, I overheard the conversation of two particularly unhappy and dissatisfied, clearly recently converted vegetarians talking to one of the waiters. "Hmmm, yes, it all looks really very nice. But is there actually anything you can especially do for us? You see, we're vegetarians." Thankfully, over the years, there has been a modicum of improvement in our understanding of the way of the chapati – and even mine don't stick together now.

MRS. PRINGLE'S KOFTA CURRY

This kofta curry is a delicious fragrant preparation, mildly spiced and deeply savory. The perfect TV dinner, really; only a fork is necessary and, perhaps, a cold glass of beer or two. It is based upon the one that I originally learned to make from Mrs. Pringle, but I too have also learned a little bit more since then; let's just say that it is a happy mingle of an eager apprenticeship, some enlightened reading, and over the past twenty-odd years, eating quite a lot of someone else's Indian cooking.

Serves 4

4 onions, peeled and finely chopped
6 cloves garlic, peeled and finely chopped
4 tbsp vegetable oil
1½ lb ground lamb
2 tbsp coriander seeds and
1 tbsp cumin seeds, dry-roasted together in a frying pan
until fragrant, then ground in a pestle and mortar, or coffee grinder
2 tsp ground turmeric
1 tbsp garam masala
½ tsp chilli powder
1 tsp freshly ground black pepper
1 tsp salt
1 tbsp finely chopped mint
1 small egg, beaten
flour
4 tbsp butter
½ stick cinnamon
4 cloves
4 cardamom pods
4 ripe tomatoes, peeled and chopped
juice of 1 lemon or 2 limes
a dozen or so mint leaves, coarsely chopped
1⅔ cups coconut milk

Serve with

boiled rice
poppadoms
pickles

Fry the onions and garlic in the oil until golden brown. Cool on a plate. Mix the lamb together with the spices, pepper, salt, mint, and egg. Form into balls the size of walnuts, roll in the flour, and quietly fry in the butter in a roomy, shallow pan, until golden brown all over. Put in the cinnamon, cloves, and cardamom pods and fry for a minute or so with the koftas. Now tip in the tomatoes and allow to sweat and wilt for 10 minutes, until softened and pulpy. Add the lemon or lime juice, coarsely chopped mint, and the coconut milk. Slowly bring up to a simmer and stew for 20–25 minutes, by which time the coconut milk should have thickened somewhat. Taste for salt. Serve with plainly boiled rice, poppadoms, and pickles. *Note:* Do not be alarmed over the slightly separated, oily look to this curry; this, as far as I am concerned, is a sure sign of its authenticity.

CONSTANCE SPRY'S ORIGINAL CORONATION CHICKEN SALAD DRESSING

Once you have made the "curry essence" for this time honored Anglo-Indian salad dressing, I am sure you will agree with me that it is essential to its success. (Those cowboys who continue to think that bottled curry paste mixed with mayonnaise is in any way at all a reasonable substitute here need a good slap with a cold chapati.) Do you know, the weirdest thing happened when I used my spell-check for "chapati." All it could throw up was "teapot." What a hoot! ("cha": tea?)

You might like to make larger quantities of the essence, in fact, storing it in a screw-top jar in the fridge for when you need it. Useful stuff to have around, and it will keep there for a couple of weeks or so, if not longer.

I have used it (mixed to taste with mayonnaise) to dress shrimp and crabmeat before now, mixed with firm chunks of avocado and cucumber. Curiously, it also has a sort of mad affinity with pieces of melon when partnered with the aforementioned shrimp – very 1970s, but surprisingly refreshing and truly delicious. (See "Lobster" chapter, page 130.)

Serves 6

¼ cup chopped onion
1 tbsp sunflower oil
1 demitasse spoon good-quality (and freshly purchased) Madras curry powder
1 tsp tomato puree
⅔ cup red wine
½ cup water
1 bay leaf
salt
a little sugar

a touch of pepper
a slice or two of lemon plus a good
squeeze of juice, possibly more
1⅔ cups mayonnaise
1–2 tbsp apricot puree (sieved apricot jam or
mango chutney is also eminently suitable)
3–4 tbsp lightly whipped heavy cream

Gently stew the onion in the oil until transparent. Add the curry powder and cook for a few minutes longer. Add the tomato puree, wine, water, and bay leaf. Bring to a simmer and add salt, sugar, pepper, and the lemon slices and juice. Simmer for a further 5–10 minutes. Strain through a fine sieve, pushing down on the solids with a small ladle, and cool. Add by degrees to the mayonnaise with the apricot puree (or jam or chutney) to taste, followed by the whipped cream.

Generously combine slivers of carefully cooked chicken with the dressing. Traditionally this is served with an imaginatively composed rice salad. Or what you will. Apparently it has recently also been used as a sandwich filling. I can only think, what would Connie have said?

SPINACH AND COCONUT DHAL

Sloppy, warming, comforting, and astonishingly delicious. Also, extremely gassy. Time to tether the duvet to the bedposts.

Serves 4

9 oz onions, peeled and finely chopped
6 tbsp butter
1½ tsp whole cumin seeds, roasted
1 tsp whole black mustard seeds, roasted
4 cloves
4 cloves garlic, peeled and thinly sliced
2 tsp ground turmeric
½ tsp chilli powder
¾ cup plus 2 tbsp split red lentils
1⅔ cups water
1⅔ cups coconut milk
3–4 thick slices of fresh ginger, unpeeled
1 lb fresh ripe tomatoes, peeled and roughly chopped
9 oz fresh leaf spinach, washed, trimmed,
and roughly chopped

plenty of freshly ground black pepper
juice of 1 large lime
1 tbsp freshly chopped cilantro
2 tbsp freshly chopped mint
1 tsp salt

Serve with

naan or pita bread

Fry the onions in 4 tbsp of the butter until pale golden. Add the whole spices and half the garlic and continue to cook gently for a further 5 minutes. Stir in the turmeric and chilli powder until well blended, and cook for a couple of minutes. Tip in the lentils and the water, coconut milk, ginger, tomatoes, and spinach. Bring up to a simmer, add the pepper, and cook very gently, stirring occasionally, for about 30–40 minutes, or until the lentils are tender and have all but dissolved into the liquid.

Remove the pan from the heat. Melt the remaining butter. When it starts to froth, throw in the rest of the sliced garlic and stir around vigorously until it starts to take on a little color, and the butter starts to smell nutty. Immediately tip into the lentils and stir in. (There will be spluttering, so watch out.) Add the lime juice, the cilantro, mint, and salt to taste. Cover with a lid and leave to mellow for 10 minutes before serving, remembering to remove the slices of ginger before you do so. Eat with hot and fresh flat bread, such as naan or, failing that, pita bread.

DUCK

N ow, here's a thing. Aylesbury duck. Part of a television program transmitted at the beginning of 2000 was an interesting interview with a duck farmer from the town of Chesham, in Buckinghamshire, just a few miles from Aylesbury itself. Apparently, he is what is now known as an "accredited" Aylesbury duck farmer. And do you know what this actually means? Well, it transpires that, by some potty EU directive, he may only sell his ducks locally. Not in London. Not in Kidderminster. Not in Norwich. Not nowhere but in and around Aylesbury. A *caneton de Challans,* a leg of Spanish *jamon jabugo,* or even the recently interloping - of the very nicest kind, it has to be said – Gressingham duck may all happily be eaten anywhere from Dungeness to Dundee. So that's the thing. And how very English a thing it is too.

So why is it that the Bucks duck, the most famous of all English ducks, the very duck for which the Bramley apple was grown at all, suddenly found itself singled out for such strictures of distribution? Protection of its origins and fear of cowboy companies calling any old duck an "Aylesbury" seem, at the very least, to be woolly words over the matter. Now this self-preservation theory may be all well and good, but surely if the French can manage to regulate all regions that surround the town of Bresse by the strict numbering, labeling, and tight quality control of their unique chickens, why cannot the burghers of Aylesbury initiate a similar undertaking?

So perhaps it comes as no surprise, once you pause a moment to think about it, that you have immense trouble recalling the last time you noticed Roast Aylesbury Duckling – and that's simply "roast," by the way, rather than the recently absurd use of the description "roasted" (now bizarrely applied to such things as figs, squid, carrots, and strawberries) – on a restaurant or hotel dining room menu anywhere in England. The prefix Norfolk still exists here and there but nobody really takes much notice and, anyway, I believe it is only the *county* of Norfolk where such a duck might have its origins (where it actually lives), whereas the Aylesbury duck truly is a unique breed.

The crunch, however (and the word is crucial in this context), is not the question of whether the roast duckling is Aylesbury, Norfolk, Gressingham, or even Trelough (the latest darling ducky, also very good), it is the rarity of finding a simple, traditional roast duckling offered on any British restaurant or hotel menu anywhere. Period. Now this is a tragedy, but it is also absolutely typical.

For the majority of keen young cooks today have never, ever at any time at all during their (all too often absurdly brief) apprenticeships been taught how to properly roast a duck in the English fashion. Sadly, as far as duck is concerned for these unfortunate fellows, duck menu-speak is either "duck breast" or "duck confit." An entire cooked duck no longer exists. It has become a fallacy. "Can't be done, Chef. Boned 'em all out before you got 'ere! Stock's on already – them bones'll make a loverly *jus* by lunchtime!" . . . "Aylesbury? Wot's that, Chef? A new goat's cheese?"

ROASTING A DUCK

I wonder whether over the years, like me, you have sometimes had one of those unfortunate ducks in your oven that just will not crisp. However much you primp it with sharp knife points, pour boiling water over it, dry it out overnight (or with hair dryers) as I like to do to the festive goose, there remains that devastatingly sad moment when the eagerly awaited roasted duck skin more resembles blotting paper than sandpaper.

There was a certain Mrs. Hogg of the Haven, Gressingham (a small and most individual restaurant in north Lancashire), who once cooked the finest roast ducks in the land. The story goes that she would put her ducks into the oven at around about four thirty in the afternoon, to be served up to guests at eight that night. The birds were slowly roasted on specially tilted racks, so allowing the fat to drip out into trays underneath. (It was rumored that the resourceful Mrs. Hogg would then have soap made from this collected grease.) I tried this method once and with great success. Here is how I went about it.

Serves 2

Preheat the oven to 325°F.

At about 4:30 P.M. have the duck at room temperature and lightly rubbed with salt inside and out. Put the middle rack of the oven on a severe slant (i.e., from the top right slot across to the bottom left slot), and place the duck directly on the oven rack with parson's nose in dive position. Arrange a large roasting pan underneath to catch the drips from the nose. Roast the duck for 3 hours, turning the temperature down somewhat towards the end and removing fat occasionally from the pan. (Note the meaty drippings congealed on the base of the pan in lumps, perfect for making gravy later using a little vegetable and potato water, sherry, and the merest dusting of flour for thickening; a slug of mushroom ketchup may be necessary, even a tentative drip of gravy browning, but there's good English duck gravy for you.)

The skin begins to rumple and puff itself to a definite crispness fairly early on. An hour later, you will clearly see the subcutaneous layer of fat through the skin, melting and bubbling on its way out of the duck into the growing bath of fat below. When the duck is carved there will be that telltale good sign: a generous gap between soft and tender meat and a dry and parchmentlike skin. Serve with your favorite stuffing and homemade apple sauce. (For this I usually stew peeled and sliced apples with sugar, a splash of water, and a few cloves, until reduced to a mush – and I always prefer it served cold, not hot.)

DUCK AND ORANGE SOUP

What better way to utilize the leftover carcass of the roasted duck? If you are able to find some duck giblets add these to the stock too, for extra flavor.

Serves 4

2 tbsp duck fat
4 thick slices bacon, cut into slivers
2 onions, chopped
2 carrots, peeled and chopped
3 sticks celery, washed and chopped
3 flat black mushrooms, chopped
2 cloves garlic, peeled and crushed
salt and pepper
a thick squirt of tomato puree
1 tbsp flour
1 small glass of port
1 large glass of white wine
1 tbsp redcurrant jelly
1½ qts chicken stock (a cube will do,
but the real thing would be better)
1 duck carcass, roughly chopped
3 pieces pithless orange zest
juice of 1 orange
3–4 tbsp heavy cream
squeeze of lemon juice
1 tbsp chopped mint

Serve with

croutons

Heat the duck fat in a roomy, solid-bottomed pan and in it fry the bacon until crisp. Add the onions, carrots, celery, mushrooms, garlic, and a little seasoning and continue frying all these until wilted and well colored. Stir in the tomato puree, mix it together with the vegetables, and cook the very devil out of it until it has lost all its vibrant red hue; rusty-colored is the look that is wanted here. Sprinkle over the flour and stir in. Complete this process by a further 5 minutes of gentle frying.

Add the port, wine, and red-currant jelly, stir in, and then incorporate the stock and the duck carcass. Stir everything together and bring to a gentle simmer. Scoop off the thick layer of scum that forms on the surface during this process and then leave to gently blip for about 40 minutes. Add the orange zest and juice, stir in, and continue simmering for a further 30 minutes. During the entire process, continue to try and control any further excess scum. Strain the soup into a colander suspended over a large, clean pan. Leave to drip for 10 minutes or so and then puree the result until very smooth. Now pass this through a fine sieve back into the (rinsed clean) original pan. Stir in the cream, lemon juice to taste, and mint. Adjust seasoning, reheat without boiling, and ladle into heated soup bowls. Offer a dish of crisp little croutons at table.

BRAISED DUCK WITH PEAS

This is the perfect simple duck supper for two. Scrupulously scraped new potatoes are the only necessary accompaniment here. The bacon I used was traditional Welsh and cut from a superb, fatty slab that I had bought from Carmarthen market. Try and find something similar; make sure it is taken from a whole piece.

Serves 2

a piece of fatty bacon (approx. 5 oz), cut into chunks
salt and pepper
1 small duck, if possible including giblets
1 onion, peeled and chopped
2 tender sticks celery, peeled and chopped
1 carrot, peeled and chopped
1 bay leaf
2 cloves garlic, peeled and crushed
1 glass of white wine
1 15-oz can of French petits pois *("à l'étuvée"* is
a good sign here)
several mint leaves, chopped

Preheat the oven to 300°F.

Take a large oval cast-iron pot that has a lid (Le Creuset is, of course, ideal here). Heat it and then gently fry the bacon chunks until the fat runs and begins to color. Lift them out of the pot and set aside on a plate. Season the duck liberally inside and out, introduce it to the hot bacon fat, and color on all surfaces until golden. Also lift out and put with the bacon. Fry the onion, celery, carrot, and bay leaf in the extensive amount of fat that has exuded from both bacon and duck, until lightly colored. Stir in the garlic at the last minute, give it a frazzle, and then pour in the wine. Enjoy its frothing for a moment or two and then tip in the can of peas, juice and all. Reintroduce the duck and bacon, bring up to a simmer, put on the lid, and cook in the oven for 1 hour.

Remove from the oven, lift the duck out onto a plate, and leave it until cool enough to handle. Meanwhile, allow the contents of the pot to settle and then remove the copious fat that has settled upon the surface with several sheets of paper towel. Neatly carve the duck from its carcass into two halves and reintroduce to the "pea stew." Reheat, stir in the mint, and correct the seasoning.

FENNEL

It took some time for me to be beguiled by fennel. Maybe this quirk developed simply because I had never really worked out what to do with – or to – it. In years gone by, if I ever found myself presented with fennel in circumstances beyond my control (e.g., *ordered* to cook it), my wayward interpretation would rarely receive rave reviews. After all, the law of good cookery demands that if one ever finds oneself cooking something one feels uncomfortable with, it is never going to be particularly special. Chestnuts cooked by me, for instance, will always be vile – but then surely a chestnut already knows that it was just one of those unfortunate mistakes in the first place. I do quite like the Mont Blanc at Angelina, Paris, however.

It is understood that an Italian knows more about cooking fennel than anyone else in the world. I am not quite sure why this should be so. Well, I sort of am, but not that interested in writing of such things. Moreover, you may have noticed that the chapter introductions in this book rarely delve into this type of research and information.

Although I find the provenance, history, and various whys and wherefores of each and every ingredient from all over the gastronomic globe extremely stimulating and informative when someone else has done all the work, I find it a tedious task to delve into for myself. Or for you. As far as I am concerned, this is the job of *Larousse gastronomique:* the serious cook's bible. I prefer to burble a bit. And if there is one thing above all that *Larousse* simply does not do, it is to burble. Furthermore, where do you think everyone else who writes about food provenance culls the info from? There is, of course, the wonderful new Alan Davidson masterwork *The Oxford Companion to Food* (Oxford University Press, 1999), which is, no doubt, an even more useful and up-to-date crib sheet.

So, naturally, it was the Italians (via Elizabeth David, Anna del Conte, Franco Taruschio, and Marcella Hazan) who taught me to understand the joy of fennel. The familiar fat green and white fennel in its bulb form, now so readily available in good corner groceries and most supermarkets, is known as Florence fennel. (Florence is a little-known city about a third of the way down Italy, with a big church thing in the town center.) Now, although I am sure that bulb fennel can also be grown in Emilia Romagna, Umbria, and Piedmont, it is understood that the finest is grown in land that surrounds the city of Florence.

The same, of course, is said of *les champignons de Paris,* traditionally grown in the Île de France, the region which encircles the capital. And then there are those early potatoes from the richly loamed, ozone-misted island of Jersey. Ah! Now then. Big rant. Slight diversion. Are not these fabled and fabulous tender tubers, the Jersey Royals, fast becoming a bit of a joke? As far as I am concerned, as each year's grossly extended crop continues to appear on the market they might just as well have been grown in a polluted allotment somewhere just within the M25 motorway, for all the taste and texture they exhibit.

As I write (early February 2000), I sadly expect to see a select few Royals for sale in my local greengrocers by the end of the month, clustered together in their typical wooden pannier, all immaculately sand-dusted and ranging in size from big marble to small Victoria plum. They don't fool me now, these sad impostors, unnaturally greenhouse- or poly-tunnel-forced upon the unsuspecting public for silly money. And money it surely is, at the tangled root of this problem.

Not having a potato chapter in this book forced me into that, I suppose, but it needed saying, don't you think? But finally, to conclude, the so-far unsullied fennel bulb is at its best either gently braised, baked with butter or oil, and finished with Parmesan (the Florentine cook's favorite way) or shaved raw into very thin slices and dressed with lemon juice and olive oil. Freshness, in all cases, being of the utmost importance. For the record, I should tell you that there is also wild fennel, fennel seed, and fennel herb – both the bronze- and green-fronded species – to further find out about. The city of Florence is further famous for spinach and tripe dishes and a grilled T-bone steak. And I've not so much as even glanced in *Larousse* for those little nuggets of info.

FENNEL À LA GRECQUE

This is particularly good as an accompaniment to grilled or cold poached fish such as (respectively) mullet or salmon but it is equally nice eaten all on its own, as a vegetable dish or first course. It is important that the fennel is extremely fresh, with the central parts good and white and its feathery fronds perky and bright green.

Serves 4

5–6 small, very fresh bulbs of fennel, trimmed and neatly quartered
20 pearl onions, topped, tailed, and peeled
salt and pepper
juice of 1 small lemon
1 tbsp Pernod or Ricard
¾ cup dry white wine
1 tsp fennel seeds, dry-roasted in a small
frying pan until fragrant
2 cloves garlic, peeled and sliced
2–3 sprigs of thyme
2 bay leaves
4–5 tbsp extra-virgin olive oil
1 tbsp chopped parsley, worked together with any fennel fronds too, if you like

Put the fennel and onions in a large pot so that they are almost in a single layer. Season and sprinkle over the lemon juice and Pernod or Ricard. Add the wine, fennel seeds, garlic, herbs, and oil and put on a low heat to cook. Stir together briefly, once it has come to a simmer, and cook very gently, covered, for about 45 minutes.

By this time the vegetables will be very soft and deeply flavored. Allow to cool to tepid or room temperature before tasting the juices to ascertain a correct seasoning. Spoon into a serving dish and sprinkle over the parsley, and fennel fronds if using.

FENNEL SOUP WITH PARMESAN CREAM

This is a model of a cream soup. A simple creamed vegetable soup is fast becoming a rarity in these days of incessant garnish. As far as I am concerned, the only "garnish" to such a bowlful is a sprinkle of very small, crisp croutons. Anything else simply gets in the way of the very idea; by which I mean, in this case, probably some diced fennel. I mean, why laboriously puree and sieve if you then put lumpy bits back in? Croutons, however, are different. Croutons do nice things to the inside of the mouth.

Having said all that, I have to confess to adding just a little extra something to this particular fennel soup; but lumpy it is not. It is a luxurious Parmesan cream that accompanied the finest potato gnocchi I have ever eaten, in Piedmont, a couple of years ago.

Serves 4

1 large onion, peeled and chopped
14 oz fennel bulb, trimmed and chopped
2 tbsp olive oil
2 tbsp butter
2 cloves garlic, peeled and chopped
2 tbsp Pernod (or Ricard, pastis, etc.)
½ cup white wine
2 cups plus 2 tbsp light chicken stock (a dissolved cube will just do)
salt and white pepper
⅔ cup whipping cream
about 2 tbsp freshly grated Parmesan

Serve with croutons

In a large pan, very gently stew the onion and fennel in the oil and butter until really soft, without coloring. *Note:* This should take *at least* 20 minutes, and is an essential step for any properly flavored, creamed vegetable soup. Add the garlic and stew for a further 5 minutes. Add the Pernod and light it with a match, shaking the pan a little until the flames subside. Pour in the wine and cook fast for a few minutes (simply to allow the harsher edges of the wine to dissipate quickly) then turn the heat down once more, add the stock with some seasoning, cover, and simmer quietly for 30 minutes. Puree in a blender for as long as you can bear it (a food processor is not as good here), before pushing the result through a fine sieve into a clean pan. Reheat but do not boil. Ladle into 4 heated deep soup bowls. Gently heat the cream in a small pan and whisk in the Parmesan until dissolved. Divide between the 4 soup bowls, spooning it over the surface of each serving. Hand a bowl of croutons at table.

BRAISED PORK BELLY WITH FENNEL

Do not be concerned that there is not enough liquid for this dish. Just wait until it is cooked, and you will see what I mean.

Serves 4

3 lb belly pork in the piece, nice and thick, bones intact and rind well scored
2–3 tbsp pork fat or dripping, or some very ordinary olive oil
salt and pepper

1 tbsp Pernod
½ cup white wine
2 large bulbs of fennel, quartered
about a dozen medium-sized fruity tomatoes, cut in half
16 cloves unpeeled garlic, bruised with the back of a knife
2–3 bay leaves
1–2 sprigs of thyme
a generous sprinkle of fennel seeds
3–4 pieces of lemon peel (no pith)
juice of 1 lemon

Serve with

boiled or creamed potatoes

Preheat the oven to 275°F.

Put a cast-iron or similar pot (one that has a tight-fitting lid) onto a moderate flame to become quite hot. Rub the pork all over with a little fat or oil, so that when seasoned the salt, pepper, herbs, or spices will stick easily; without this necessary embrocation, all will fall off. Incidentally, this simple procedure seems to me such an obvious, very important one when roasting or braising that I am constantly amazed as to how no one else ever mentions it. But, then, it is also quite astonishing how many recipes I read these days that omit any mention of salt and pepper at all during this preliminary stage. What is cooking coming to?

Anyway, add your chosen fat to that heated pot and then gingerly put in the salted and peppered pork loin; this, naturally, will splutter somewhat, so reduce the heat accordingly. Turn and burnish the meat over several minutes until the skin turns a uniform gold, with sporadic pustules appearing here and there. Lift out and put on a plate. Tip off and discard almost all the fat, then pour in the Pernod and wine. Allow these to bubble and seethe together, using a whisk to pick up any sticky brown bits that have collected in the bottom of the pot.

Return the pork to the pot (including any juices that have leached out of it), tuck in the fennel pieces, tomatoes, garlic, bay leaves, and thyme sprigs around it, then sprinkle with the fennel seeds. Put a few pieces of lemon peel amongst the vegetables too, and squeeze lemon juice over everything. Bring the pot up to a moderate simmer over a gentle flame, cover the meat with a sheet of wax paper cut to fit, put on the lid, and place in the oven. Cook for 1½–2 hours, turning the meat once during this time. Serve the pork carved into thick slices (bones and all) with all its messy vegetables spooned around it together with plenty of juices – and not without some plainly boiled or creamed potatoes too, I would think.

GNOCCHI

T he two motion pictures known as *The Godfather* and *The Godfather Part II,* realized by a genius of film directing, one Francis Ford Coppola, remain among a handful of movies that I will never, ever tire of watching. My friend Stephen Fry and I share this view, often boring the pants off chums around a dinner table by quoting lines from each of these two films: "Tom, can you get me off the hook – for old times' sake?" or "Don't forget the cannoli!" or "Fredo, you're my older brother and I love you," etc., etc. . . . And so it goes on and on. However, neither of us can quote one single line from *The Godfather Part III.* To those similarly afflicted by its two predecessors, this is not exactly surprising either.

Although it was not exactly a *great* film, we were both able to recall one particular, very good scene from this mildly disappointing movie. And it is the scene where Michael Corleone's nephew (played by Andy Garcia) demonstrates to his cousin (played by Sofia Coppola) how to fashion perfect gnocchi in the dimly lit kitchen of his neighborhood restaurant, after hours. This is a moment of such sensual filmmaking that I would go as far as to say that, along with the game of chess played by Steve McQueen and Faye Dunaway in the original version of *The Thomas Crown Affair* (I hesitate to even suggest that a remake actually exists), Coppola's gnocchi-making scene is cinematic sexual foreplay of a uniquely rare quality.

Incidentally, in that other fine film *Goodfellas,* the scene where Big Paulie slices cloves of garlic with a razor blade for the making of *tomatosauce* (all one word – and it was noted that the thinner the garlic was cut, the easier it melted into the sauce) while serving a prison sentence is also rated very highly as a quite gorgeous scene by me and

Fry. Slightly less arousing, maybe, but as a moment of supreme gastronomic integrity in the cinema it is unsurpassed.

Admittedly, languorously rolling small pieces of flour and potato paste along the inner tines of a table fork with your thumb before deftly flicking them onto a flour-dusted kitchen table may not necessarily be seen as everyone's idea of carnal stimulation, but it is a motion of enormous satisfaction to those who care to do things right, merely hungering for gastric fulfilment and a good result.

And doing good is something to be treasured in the dormant domestic kitchen *de nos jours* – particularly so, for heaven's sake, if it is Italian good. Surely, as only one small part of the current culinary darling within the modish British housewife's perceived repertoire, the fashioning of Italian gnocchi might be seen as something quite fun to do? Even without the possibility of humpy-bumpy later with Mr. Garcia (or, of course, with Ms. Coppola . . .).

I think the finest gnocchi I have ever eaten appeared as one course out of several within the limited-choice dinner at a strange hotel in northern Italy, near the town of Asti, Piedmont, in the spring of '99. Everything concerning the hotel and its services was quite appalling. Everything concerned with dinner and breakfast was beyond reproach. Infuriation experienced at its most complicated. Only in Italy. Ironically, in true Piedmontese fashion, where egg is here seen as an unnecessary binder, these gnocchi were not given the fork treatment. This traditional practice, however, may be realized in the double parsley recipe. Surely an offer you can't refuse.

PIEDMONTESE POTATO GNOCCHI WITH PARMESAN CREAM

The most trusted Anna del Conte (the gnocchi recipe is based on one of hers) confirms that the important difference between Piedmontese gnocchi and those of the Veneto is that the former should not contain any eggs. Only flour is used as a binder with the mashed potatoes, thereby rendering the mixture softer and less substantial in texture – rather like my mother's potato cakes, which were a treat of a late Sunday afternoon when I was a boy, gently fried in butter and anointed with more of it, then kept hot in front of the sitting-room fire in a Pyrex dish.

Note: It is imperative that the gnocchi are made quite soon after you have finished making the dough.

Serves 4

For the gnocchi

1½ lb potatoes, scrubbed clean
1 tsp salt
¾–1 cup all-purpose flour

For the Parmesan cream

1 cup whipping cream
about 3–4 tbsp freshly grated Parmesan
salt
a little strong chicken stock (optional)

If possible, steam the potatoes in their skins, until very tender (boiling them only adds to the invasion of treacherous water). Peel the skins off as soon as possible, using a dish towel to protect your hands, and cut them up into chunks. Pass through the finest blade of a vegetable mill (mouli-légumes) onto a dish towel or sheet of wax paper and allow to dry out. Put a large pan of salted water on to boil.

Once dry, place the potato on a work surface and sprinkle over the salt. Then, little by little, sift over the flour, working it into the potato with your fingers using a gentle kneading movement, until the mixture feels like biscuit dough—at least, until workable and with just the merest trace of stickiness. You will certainly need the full ¾ cup, and maybe a little more. Tear off large pieces and roll each into a long sausage shape, about the thickness of a chipolata. Cut into small, candy-sized slices with a sharp knife and put on a floured plate.

Drop the gnocchi into the pan of (gently) boiling water, a dozen or so at a time.

Once they float to the surface, which does not take long, allow them to poach for a further 30 seconds or so, lift out with a slotted spoon, drain well, and put on a plate. Keep warm while you cook the rest.

To make the sauce, simply heat the cream, whisk in the Parmesan, season, and simmer until slightly thickened; the stock is an aid to over-thickening and can also add body to the sauce. Divide the gnocchi between 4 hot plates and spoon over the sauce.

PUMPKIN GNOCCHI WITH BUTTER AND SAGE

I am not a huge fan of pumpkin per se, but when it is reduced to an intensity of flavor as in this gnocchi recipe and then pulverized together with the rather strange but traditional inclusion of crushed Amaretti biscuits, its elusive flavor comes through very nicely indeed.

Serves 4

1 2¼ lb wedge of seeded pumpkin, skin attached

12 oz peeled potatoes, cut into large chunks

2 whole Amaretti biscuits – that's 4 halves after unwrapping

4 tbsp freshly grated Parmesan, plus extra for the table

salt and pepper

¾–1 cup all-purpose flour

7 tbsp butter

2 large cloves garlic, crushed

12 or so sage leaves

Preheat the oven to 350°F.

Cut the pumpkin into large rough cubes (with the skin still on) and place in a baking pan. Cover with foil and bake for 1 hour. Switch off the oven, remove the foil, and leave in the oven for a further 40 minutes or so, to dry out. Meanwhile, steam the potatoes until very tender. Pass them through a vegetable mill (mouli-légumes) onto a dish towel or sheet of wax paper to dry out also.

Cut the skin off the pumpkin, pile the flesh into a dish towel, and squeeze out as much juice as possible. Place the flesh in a food processor with the Amaretti biscuits, Parmesan, and a little seasoning and puree until smooth. Tip out onto a floured surface and add to it the potato. Put a large pan of salted water on to boil.

Now, little by little, sift over the flour (you will certainly need the full ¾ cup, and maybe a little more), working it into the pumpkin and potato with your fingers using a gentle kneading movement, until the mixture feels like scone dough with a trace of stickiness and is a uniform pale orange color throughout. Tear off large pieces and roll each into a long sausage shape, about the thickness of a chipolata. Cut off small slices with a sharp knife and put aside.

Drop the gnocchi into the pan of gently boiling water, a dozen or so at a time. Once they float to the surface, allow them to poach for a further 30 seconds or so, lift out with a slotted spoon, drain well, and put on a plate. Keep warm while you cook the rest.

Gently heat the butter with the garlic until the garlic is tinged a light gold. Remove it and then add the sage leaves. Briefly fry until crisp and until the butter has also begun to take on a straw color. Divide the gnocchi between 4 hot plates and spoon over the butter and sage leaves. Hand freshly grated Parmesan separately.

PARSLEY GNOCCHI IN PARSLEY SOUP

There is something very comforting and almost − dare I say − sensuous about the combination of a voluptuous cream soup with these equally luxuriant little soft and savory dumplings. Sexy soup for cozy evenings.

Serves 4

For the soup

6 tbsp butter
2 large leeks, white parts only, sliced
2 small bunches flat-leaf parsley, stalks and leaves separated, stalks chopped
1 large potato, peeled and chopped
3 cups light chicken stock
salt and pepper
⅔ cup whipping cream

For the gnocchi

14 oz potatoes, scrubbed clean
1 small egg, beaten
1 oz flat-leaf parsley leaves, very finely
chopped indeed with ½ tsp salt and about ½ cup all-purpose flour

Serve with

a little freshly grated Parmesan

Melt the butter in a stainless-steel or enameled saucepan and sweat the leeks and the parsley stalks gently, uncovered, for 20 minutes. Add the potato, stock, salt, and pepper and simmer for a further 20 minutes. Coarsely chop the leaves of 1 bunch of parsley and add to the soup. Simmer for 5 minutes. Meanwhile, blanch the leaves of the other bunch of parsley in fiercely boiling water for 30 seconds. Drain and refresh immediately under cold running water, then gently squeeze dry in a dish towel.

Puree the soup in a blender with the blanched parsley until really smooth. Pass through a sieve into a clean pan, whisk in the cream, and adjust the seasoning. Keep warm.

To make the gnocchi, follow the method for making Piedmontese Potato Gnocchi with Parmesan Cream (page 97), but also work in the beaten egg and the parsley with the flour. Now, to form the classic ribbed gnocchi shape, take each slice and roll it along the inside of the tines of a fork using your thumb, flipping it off the end onto a dusting of flour. As you do this, your thumb will also form a little pocket on the underside. Cook as directed in the previous recipe. Reheat the soup without boiling and pour into heated deep soup bowls. Drop several gnocchi into each serving and sprinkle a little Parmesan over the surface.

Ices

As I write, buying good-quality ices in the British Isles has never been so easy. And, by the way, whilst in pedantic mode, I remain attached to this description "ices," knowing full well that it is archaic and rarely used, but if it's all the same with you, I'm sticking to it for now. I mean, I know that if I were to quietly saunter into the Leicester Square branch of Häagen-Dazs and request of the vendor, "Pray inform me as to the selection of delicious ices available to me this sunny day," I would be met with a blank stare. This is not to say that if, instead, I said, "Hey! Give us a large scoop of macadamia-nut brittle with double fudge sauce, chopped nuts, and make it quick," I might not be met with the very same blank stare. In fact, each of these vacant faces is actually saying, " 'Ere, no queue jumping, matey, get to the back like everyone else!"

I am most partial to a scoop of Häagen-Dazs; actually, slightly more than just the one, if the truth be known. In moments of the deepest and most tragic black holes it is possible to experience, it is almost always to the freezer for a large tub of Toffee Crème that I sidle. Well, I don't as much sidle as make a beeline, but it is the *idea* of sidling which suits the guilt to a T. Naturally, I always finish the entire tub: mostly because it is truly delicious but also because the act of total demolition is part of the therapy. Are there just a few more than several of you out there who are at all familiar with this scenario?

Thankfully, I haven't done the late-night sidle (it is usually late at night, isn't it?) for some time now. This doesn't mean I have grown tired of the flavor of Toffee Crème. Far from it. As far as I am concerned, this is H–D's greatest line to date, where a mild caramel ice is liberally swirled by beige veins of *dulce de leche*. This, the absurdly moreish South American spread made by slowly simmering gallons of milk and sugar until it turns to runny toffee, is also the basis of Nigel and Susan Mackenzie's original Banoffee Pie, invented in the kitchens of their restaurant, the Hungry Monk, Jevington, East Sussex.

Cleverly, the Mackenzies had managed to produce a version of *dulce de leche* simply by boiling cans of Nestlé's milk for hours, until the contents also eventually turned to a similar toffee goo. Some folk, eager to further follow their precise instructions and while temporarily forgetting about half a dozen cans of Nestlé's milk about to boil dry, are still to be seen scraping brown blobs from their kitchen ceilings: evidence of the explosion of many pressurized tin cans. My main reason for mentioning all of this is simply because Nigel and Susan Mackenzie have rarely been given full credit for the truly wonderful Banoffee Pie. And, I assure you, the Jevington original remains the best.

H-D apart, Hill Station, Rocombe Farm, and Green and Black's (their organic chocolate ice is very good indeed) are three further brands to look out for as makers of good ices in this country. Though Ben and Jerry may be really nice guys, with an excellent community spirit and a rare way with funky names for their particular ices, I have never really taken to them. For one thing I find their "bits" are too big and hard in the chunky ones and, for another, there are so many swirls and flavors going on that the very ice itself seems less than half the contents.

Most present-day quality ice-cream producers began by churning small amounts within a quiet domestic kitchen, simply to make their very first tub of perfect vanilla. So if you too want to create and eat the best ice of all, just go out and find yourself a good machine and get churning. You will never regret the purchase, the family will love you forever, and it is one of the surest ways of making an almost instant dessert: eggs, sugar, and milk heated together make custard. And frozen custard is possibly the most basic and delicious ice of all.

TANGERINE DREAM

The quite absurd title of this surprisingly delicious frivolity will, no doubt, be familiar to many middle-aged psychedelic hippie-rock cool cats — such as yours truly. However, in essence, this is nothing more than a deconstructed Mivvi. Do you remember those? Do you remember "Jubblees" too?

Serves 4

For the "tangerine" sorbet

2 cups plus 2 tbsp tangerine, satsuma, or
clementine juice, strained
6–8 tbsp sugar, depending upon
the sweetness of the fruit
juice of 1 small lemon, strained

For the "dream" custard

1¼ cups whole milk
4 egg yolks
2 tbsp sugar
2 tbsp Mandarine Napoléon liqueur

To make the sorbet, simply whisk the ingredients together in a bowl, chill, and then churn in an ice-cream machine until ready. Freeze as usual. *Note:* If you wish to make a proper sorbet you really must have a *sorbetière*.

For the custard, scald the milk in a heavy-bottomed saucepan. Briefly beat together the egg yolks and sugar and then strain the hot milk over them, whisking as you go. Return to the saucepan and cook over a very low heat (with a heat-diffuser pad if possible) until limpid and lightly thickened. Some say it should coat the back of a wooden spoon, but I don't go along with this theory; it should be taken further than this, almost until there is the odd simmering blip on the surface. When you think it is just about ready, give a final vigorous whisk, introducing the Mandarine Napoléon as you do so, and pour into a chilled bowl. Cover and place in the fridge until really, really cold. *Note:* If you are unlucky enough to split the custard, a brief whiz in a blender will usually rescue it.

To serve, arrange scoops of sorbet in chilled glasses and spoon some of the custard over each one.

LEMON ICE

It was my friend Hilary Rogers who first introduced me to this unique ice many years ago, in Pembrokeshire. I guess it is not really an ice at all in the conventional sense; more of a *semifreddo* – which, as Marcella Hazan correctly and simply insists, "means partly cold."

Note: This ice contains raw egg yolks.

Serves 4

8 large egg yolks
1 cup sugar
juice of 2 large lemons
1 cup plus 2 tbsp heavy cream

Beat together the egg yolks and sugar until very light, white, and fluffy. Gradually add the lemon juice, continuing to beat until the mass starts to rise up once more. Lightly whip the cream and carefully fold into the mixture until well amalgamated. Pour into a suitable container, put a lid on, and place in the freezer for at least 6 hours or overnight. The mixture, due to the high proportion of egg, remains naturally soft and creamy. There is no need to churn it; there is no need to remove it from the freezer and "give it a stir"; and there is no need – most definitely not – to scoop spoonfuls of it into a "tuile" or a "basket." Just chill a nice bowl, fill it with the ice, and place a teaspoon on the table.

WHITE COFFEE ICE

It is only when a good ice cream is flavored with coffee that I realize quite how extraordinary is its unique taste. It is not the creamy-capped *espresso,* nor the frothy filled thick cup of *cappuccino,* or even the lukewarm tall glass of a Venetian *latte.* (And why, pray tell, is a *latte* never, *ever,* hot in Venice?) For me, it is only once those magic roasted beans have infused a pan of warm milk, then been added to cream, eggs, and sugar and the whole lot churned to the palest, smoothest, frozen ivory cream, that I really get it.

Although I have not found an exact recipe for this, the inspiration comes from reading about an "exquisite white coffee ice-cream" from an "1837 edition of Guglielmo Jarrin's *Italian Confectioner*." I extracted this from deeply within Elizabeth David's very last work, *Harvest of the Cold Months* (Michael Joseph, 1994), which was, eventually, heroically compiled, completed, and edited by Jill Norman.

Complicatedly hidden amongst various references, it also seems that there was an extraordinarily fine ice-cream emporium known as Gunter's (originally of Berkeley Square, London, but then "removed to Curzon Street"), of which E.D.

had fond memories during the brief time she spent as an aspiring actress in her early twenties:

> Like everybody else who had been taken to tea at Gunter's or eaten their ices at a ball supper, I too remembered, in the immediate post-war years, those wonderful cream delicacies. There had been also a rare warm summer afternoon in 1934 or 1935 at the Open Air Theatre in Regent's Park, when one of the leading ladies, Miss Margaretta Scott, as I remember, treated the cast of *Midsummer Night's Dream* to ice-cream ordered from Gunter's and sent from Berkeley Square in huge pots which were circulated among the company in pails of ice.

Makes quite a lot

2⅓ cups milk
7 oz high-roast excellent-quality coffee beans
¾ cup plus 2 tbsp golden sugar
10 large egg yolks
1⅔ cups heavy cream

Put the milk onto a low heat and tip in the coffee beans and ½ cup of the sugar. Stir well, and bring up to a boil. Allow the milk to seethe up over the coffee beans once, remove from the heat, give it a brief whisk, and pour into a glass or stainless-steel bowl. Cover the bowl with a lid and suspend over a pan containing hot water for 1 hour; which is not to say boiling, but the idea is to keep the milk hot, and therefore continue to extract flavor from the coffee beans by sustained heat. What I tend to do is decant tepid water and then top up with water boiled up in a kettle – and do this about every quarter of an hour (well worth it if you enjoy cooking, pointless if you can't be bothered).

Strain the coffee-flavored milk through a fine sieve into a clean bowl and set aside. Discard the coffee beans. Beat together the egg yolks and remaining sugar until thick and pale yellow, then add the coffee-flavored milk to them. Gently whisk together and pour back into the (wiped clean) milk pan. Make a thin-textured custard with this mixture, being careful not to allow it to boil, but making sure that it does thicken lightly. Pour into a chilled bowl and whisk in the cream. Leave to cool completely and remove any visible surface froth with a spoon. Churn in an ice-cream machine in the usual way.

JELLY

As a child, what exactly was it about a package of Chivers Jelly that begged one to rip off a corner piece and secretly stuff it in one's mouth? In our house jelly was usually strawberry or lime – to be honest, it was either the red one or the green one, flavor was immaterial (also, it seemed to me, something quite irrelevant to Chivers at the time too), for that bouncy little cube was simply seen as a free sweet which lasted a nice long time in the mouth and was packed full of sugar. And yes, you know, they truly did bounce, those cubes, albeit in a random fashion. A red one once landed in Bodger's basket. Although a red cube of jelly covered in corgi hairs was not part of the plan, it represented only a minor setback. A brief rinse under a warm tap soon put paid to any unwanted garnish.

Mum used to make a delicious instant pudding by combining a melted packet of strawberry jelly, a can of strawberries, and a large can of condensed milk. I used to adore this – and also, as it transpires, did grown-up chums of mine I have mentioned it to, whose mothers frequently used to whip up a similar pale-pink treat. Perhaps the recipe was printed on all packets of Chivers Strawberry Jelly throughout the late 1950s and '60s.

For some strange reason, I named the finished dish Strawberry Flush. The mixed-up vocabulary of an eight-year-old can do anything it likes: with that certain deadly accuracy, fluff and mush surely makes flush, does it not? Or, overcome with a fascination for those popping pretty blue bubbles formed by a pull of the downstairs lavatory chain, could it instead have been *that* particular "flush" which prompted my accurate description?

I do, most certainly, vividly recall being endlessly intrigued by the workings of the flush lavatory around that time. In fact, so spellbound was I by one very exciting example at the rear of a Dutch cafe on our first Continental holiday (it was "push-button"!) that I was moved to flush it incessantly, resulting in a flood of biblical proportions, along with me in an equally terrifying flood of tears. Clearly a prototype requiring modification.

Anyway, the manufacture of a fine homemade jelly is one of the great culinary peaks. Whether savory or sweet, it takes time and trouble to perfect the art of jelly-making. Before the advent of such things as sheets of leaf gelatine or small packets of measured granules, jelly would usually be made using cow-heel or a calf's foot. Whether it is only these two extremities that are the constituents of manufactured "gelatin" is a matter for conjecture; my packet of Supercook brand will only admit to the following four words: "Gelatine origin: Several countries." Using one less word I guess it could also simply read "glue for cooking."

I have never actually made a sweet jelly using the old way of simmering a chopped-up calf's foot, as this truly seems just that little bit too much kerfuffle. And anyway, however much one attempts to refine the resultant liquid after long and slow simmering, won't there still be a faint lingering smack of extracted gristle, cartilage, and skin from a ruminant's foot? This matters not one jot when it comes to assembling the ingredients for a properly made beef consommé, but it might be more difficult to conceal in a spoonful of the following fragrant recipe for an orange jelly.

JELLIED CHICKEN CONSOMMÉ WITH TARRAGON CREAM

If you have already read the Vinegar chapter (page 269) you will know about the useful little condiment there that is the base of a good Béarnaise sauce. Well, here is a magical moment in which to employ it very successfully as a complementary embellishment to this sparkling bowl of chilled consommé. Read on.

Serves 6

For the chicken broth

2¼ lb chicken wings (or failing that, drumsticks – still relatively cheap), roughly chopped
1 pig's foot, split
3 sticks celery, chopped
3 leeks, trimmed, chopped, and washed
1 medium carrot, peeled and chopped
2 small onions, peeled and chopped
3 cloves garlic, bashed
4 ripe tomatoes, peeled and chopped
1 chicken bouillon cube
3 sprigs of fresh thyme
2 bay leaves
8 black peppercorns
6 sprigs of parsley
3 quarts water
1 cup white wine

For the clarification

9 oz ground turkey or chicken
4 egg whites, loosely beaten until frothy
1 tsp salt

For the tarragon cream

2 tbsp mayonnaise
4–5 tsp tarragon vinegar reduction (for Béarnaise sauce – page 272)
1 tbsp chopped tarragon
⅔ cup whipping cream
salt and pepper

Put all the ingredients for the broth into a large pan, bring up to a simmer, skim off any resultant scum, and cook at the merest blip for 2 hours. Pour through a colander into a clean pan and leave to drain and drip for 15 minutes. Remove any fat from the surface with several sheets of paper towel. Check for seasoning, taking into consideration that there is salt in the clarification mixture. Leave to cool.

Mix together the turkey or chicken, egg whites, and salt until all is a sloppy mass. Whisk into the cool broth over a medium heat for a few minutes, distributing the solids through the liquid thoroughly. Bring up to a simmer, checking from time to time that none of the ground meat has sunk to the bottom of the pan where it may be in danger of sticking and, therefore, scorching. Once a dirty sort of raft has formed on the surface, and the liquid is seething up from underneath it as occasional pustules and mini-blowholes, lower the heat source to its minimum and allow to burble quietly for 40–45 minutes.

As the stock gently blips through the crust it should be showing crystal-clear and be the color of tea. Now make a large hole in the crust with a spoon and lift some of it away. Using a ladle, transfer the clear liquid that lies beneath, through a damp muslin-lined sieve (or an old thin dish towel), into a clean pan. Collect all you can. Discard the crust, it has done its work.

Pour into a clean bowl and leave to cool before carefully placing in the fridge, covered, until set.

To make the tarragon cream, simply mix the mayonnaise, the reduction, and the tarragon together with a whisk and then slowly incorporate the cream, continuing to whip until lightly thickened – do not over-beat. Season to taste.

To serve, take roughly portion-sized amounts of jelly from the bowl and, using another bowl, gently break each serving down into small jellied lumps with the aid of a fork, taking great care not to work them too violently; otherwise they will cloud and turn opaque, which, with the best will in the world, is not the general idea here. Ladle into deep, chilled soup bowls or plates and judiciously spoon some of the tarragon cream over each one – or, if you prefer, pass the cream at table.

JAMBON PERSILLÉ

Possibly one of my top ten favorite things to eat, period. Endlessly satisfying from the first bite to the last, a thick slice or wedge of *jambon persillé* is the jewel of the *charcutier's* art: pink nuggets of ham, rivulets of green-flecked jelly, and a few cornichons on the side for essential pucker and crunch. Add a crisp length of good baguette and some very cold, very white unsalted butter and you have a feast fit for a king. Sadly, you will now find several bewildered young chefs who think it both witty and inspired to include bits of foie gras amongst the unsuspecting ham. Not surprisingly, I find this practice both insulting and misguided in the extreme.

**Feeds about 10 – it is irritating,
difficult, and frankly, pointless to make this for fewer**

For the initial cooking of the ham

3 lb (approx.) piece of ham
(although ham is usually leg meat, I have always found
shoulder ham to be best – and it is cheaper)
1 pig's foot, split
several sprigs of tarragon,
10–12 sprigs of flat-leaf parsley
and 2–3 sprigs of fresh thyme, all tied together as a bouquet garni
12 black peppercorns
6 juniper berries
1 750 ml bottle dry white wine

for the jelly

8 sheets leaf gelatin
2 tbsp tarragon vinegar
1 small bunch flat-leaf parsley, stalks removed (these can be included in
the bouquet garni too) and leaves chopped
freshly grated nutmeg
plenty of black pepper

Serve with

Sauce Gribiche (below)

Cut the ham, all fat and rind included, into (approx.) 3 in chunks. Put into a large room
pan together with the pig's foot, cover with water, and bring to a boil. Simmer for 10
minutes and then lift out with a slotted spoon and briefly rinse off under a running tap
any scum that clings to the meat and pig's foot. Discard the blanching water. Put into
another pan in which the pieces of ham and foot will fit snugly. Tuck in the bouquet
garni, add the peppercorns and juniper berries, and pour over the wine. If the meat is
not covered, top up with a little water. Bring up to a simmer, skim off any more scum
that may be generated, and turn down to the merest blip. Do not cover. Cook like this
for about 1½–2 hours, or until all meats are very tender when pierced with a skewer.

Now carefully lift out the pieces of ham onto a plate or dish. Strain the liqui
through a damp, double-thickness dish towel into a clean bowl. (If the liquid has bee

carefully simmered with the ham the resultant stock should be pretty clear, but if it should happen to be cloudy, allow it to cool and whisk in 2 lightly beaten egg whites. Put on a low heat, bring to a boil, and let the liquid seethe up 3 times through the egg whites. Switch off and leave to settle for 5 minutes, and then proceed with straining through the double-thickness dish towel.) This should measure to just under 2½ cups. If it is more than this, reduce the liquid a little until the approximate quantity is achieved.

Put the gelatin in a bowl of cold water and leave to soften; this takes about 3 minutes or so. Stir in the tarragon vinegar, squeeze the softened gelatin leaves in your hand to rid them of excess water, and add to the hot ham stock. Gently stir them in with a spoon until they are thoroughly dissolved.

Allow the stock to become cold in a cool place – not the fridge. When it has become lightly jellied, stir in the parsley, nutmeg, and pepper. Take the pieces of ham and, using a small sharp knife, cut the meat and any adherent fat (important for moistness and flavor) into approx. ½ in bits. Using a large metal spoon, stir the meat into the parsley jelly.

Rinse out a suitable 1 quart container (I use an oval white porcelain dish) with cold water, shake out, and then carefully fill the dish with the mixture and smooth the surface flat with a spatula. Try and push any bits of ham under the surface of the jelly so they are not exposed to the air to become discolored. Put in the fridge to set, and only then cover the surface with plastic wrap. Leave there for a further 12 hours before consuming.

When ready to serve, take a very sharp knife, dip it into hot water, and cut the *jambon persillé* into thick slices. If you wish to turn it out to do this, then dip the dish into hot water for a few seconds, loosen with a knife, and turn out onto a suitable wooden board or attractive serving dish. If you should choose this method, then decorate it with bunches of watercress. Serve with *Sauce Gribiche*.

SAUCE GRIBICHE

1 tbsp smooth Dijon mustard
2 tbsp tarragon vinegar
salt and pepper
about 1 cup peanut or other
flavorless oil – most definitely *not* olive oil
a little lukewarm water
1½ tbsp capers, drained, squeezed dry, and coarsely chopped
5 sprigs of tarragon, leaves only, finely chopped
5 hardboiled eggs, yolks only, sieved

Blend the mustard, vinegar, and seasoning for 30 seconds in a blender. With the motor still running, start pouring in the oil in a thin stream. When you have used about three-quarters of the oil, switch off and have a taste for acidity and seasoning. The mixture should have started to thicken somewhat and may need thinning down with some of the water; the desired thickness of the finished sauce should be similar to bottled salad dressing. Continue adding more oil if necessary and also some water perhaps.

When this basic dressing is complete, stir in the capers, tarragon, and egg yolks. Pour into a suitable bowl or sauceboat and hand separately around the table. Don't forget the cornichons and crusty baguette.

RED GRAPEFRUIT AND BLOOD-ORANGE JELLY
WITH CHAMPAGNE

As far away from a packet of Chivers as it is possible to imagine. This fresh and fragrant jelly is a joy and ever so simple to make. Shocking as it may sound to you, however, if I *were,* perchance, to be offered a small, punctured can of Carnation to pour over it I am not so sure that I would find it that easy to resist just a little splash or two . . .

Serves 6

4 red grapefruit
5 blood oranges
5 leaves gelatin
1 cup freshly squeezed orange juice
(strained through a fine sieve)
1 cup champagne

Cut the skin from both the grapefruits and oranges right down through past the pith, using a sharp serrated knife. The best way to do this – after cutting off a slice from the top and bottom – is to stand the fruits on their ends, cutting downwards in a curved motion, following the line of the cut fruit once it has been exposed by the knife. Continue in this fashion, rotating the fruit, until all the skin has been removed. Put the leaves of gelatin into a bowl of cold water to soak until spongy.

Now, taking the fruit in one hand, slice between and against the membranes to allow a segment to fall out, discarding seeds as you go along. Collect both grapefruit and orange segments in a bowl, juice and all. Once finished, strain off the juice into a small pan and put in the gelatin leaves. Warm over a low heat to melt the gelatin and strain once more into a measuring cup. Top up with the plain orange juice to reach 1 cup, and then slowly add the champagne to reach the 2 cup mark. Stir well, but carefully, as the champagne will froth.

Line a terrine mold with plastic wrap and pile in the fruit segments. Pour over the champagne and orange juice and gently move the fruit around with a fork to aid even distribution of solids and liquid. Put in the fridge to set for 1 hour and then cover the surface with a sheet of plastic wrap, not allowing it to make contact with the surface of the jelly. Leave in the fridge for at least another 4 hours, or, preferably, overnight. To serve, dip the mold into a bath of hot water for a few seconds and then carefully invert onto a chilled serving dish. Slice carefully, using a serrated knife that has been dipped into hot water.

LEMONS

I have always considered lemons to be one of the cook's great seasoners, whether to add zest and zing to a roast chicken, enliven a simple salad, curiously sweeten the bitterness of a dish of braised endives, or correct the balance of the emulsion of egg and oil in a mayonnaise. Of course, salt is the essential taste and flavor enhancer in all of these preparations but it is often that elusive sharpening of lemon juice which can joyously bring everything together.

One of my earliest memories of the magical taste of lemon came from a spoonful of my mum's homemade lemon curd (or cheese, as it is known in the north of England). As it sat heavily upon my tongue I vividly recall not wishing to swallow the luscious, deeply yellow ointment (egg yolks were always very yellow then), so smooth and sexy was its texture; well, perhaps not sexy to me *then,* I guess, but most certainly orally welcome to this imaginative infant at the time. But once the blob inexorably trickled over the palate and settled upon my impatiently awaiting taste buds, it was as if a thousand lemons had burst inside my mouth. You may well be muttering, "Hmmm . . . talk about pretentious . . ." – mutter away all you like, I don't give a damn. After all, it was me licking the teaspoon clean, not you.

Syllabub was the next lemon treat and that was made by me, all by myself. (This was several years later, at the age when the description "sexy" had begun to have some sort of meaning.) I had read that the (sixteenth-century?) recipe for this frothy mass originated from many squirts of the richest new milk from a cow's udder (no doubt from beneath the prettiest Jersey) directly into a pail of sweet wine—or mead, maybe?

And, so the story goes, the curdling of these two opposing liquids turned out to be something so ambrosial that it was abundantly clear to all that an exciting new pudding had unwittingly been created. Perhaps it was the dairy maid who discovered this exciting coagulation while canoodling with a randy stable lad who had a half-drunk bottle of mead stuffed down his trousers. Who knows? What I do know, however, is although those curds and wine may well have tasted "goode and pewer"– maybe even fit for the "master's table" – a sorry and separated mess they would have looked as a workable recipe of today.

Being a stickler for authenticity at all times and coupled with a healthy regard for not tampering with a perfectly sound recipe, even I can see that this sixteenth-century "receipt" required, how shall we say, a little work? Even so, to spend four-hundred-odd years perfecting a recipe seems a heck of a long time in anyone's book. I blame the stable lad. No giddy ideas of aiming for three Michelin stars for that boy then.

LEMON MOUSSE CAKE

This absurdly simple dessert is based upon the one called *Macaronade au Citron* from a cookbook written by the French chef Jacques Maximan, published in the mid-1980s. It became a favorite of mine while working in the kitchens of the Hilaire Restaurant around that time, in London's Old Brompton Road. The lemon mousse that makes up part of the cake could also be served in its own right as just that, so delicious it is.

Serves 4

For the macaronade

2 egg whites
1 cup confectioners' sugar
¼ cup ground almonds
the grated zest of 1 lemon

For the mousse

2½ leaves of gelatin, pre-soaked in cold water until softened
¾ cup lemon juice
1 cup heavy cream
⅓ cup sugar
a little extra sifted confectioners' sugar

Serve with

fresh raspberries

Preheat the oven to 400°F.

Beat the egg whites to the soft-peak stage. Sift the confectioners' sugar and almonds together and, very gently, beat them in slowly, together with the lemon zest. Place a sheet of cooking parchment on a flat baking sheet and spread the mixture into 2 circles of about 4–5 in diameter using a palette knife. Bake in the oven for about 10 minutes, or until pale golden and with lightly crusted surfaces. Remove, leave to cool for several minutes, and then carefully lift off the paper and put to dry on a cooling rack, top surfaces down.

Melt the gelatin over a low heat with a couple of tablespoons of the lemon juice. Add the rest of the juice to it and set it upon a bowl of ice to chill, stirring occasionally until just beginning to gel. Whip the cream with the sugar until loosely thick and then slowly incorporate the lemon juice/gelatin mixture while continuing to beat until the mixture is thick and voluptuous.

To assemble, place one of the macaronades on a serving plate, smooth side up, and carefully spread with the mousse right up to the edges, smoothing around the edges with a palette knife dipped in hot water. Gently press the second macaronade on top and tidy up any stray bulges of mousse. Sift the extra confectioners' sugar over the surface and put to chill for no longer than 2 hours before serving. Fresh raspberries as an accompaniment are particularly fitting here.

LEMON AND GINGER SYLLABUB

Syllabub is one of the very nicest of traditional English desserts. It should be light and almost frothy, insubstantial and tart, with the merest hint of spirit and wine in the background. The addition of stem ginger here seems to me a most natural one, being yet another particularly traditional English ingredient and also very good when partnered by plenty of cream. (Do you remember when you could find Stem Ginger and Cream on many, many restaurant and hotel dining room dessert menus in Britain in the 1960s and '70s? *Awfully* good, wasn't it?)

Serves 4

½ a 750 ml bottle fragrant, medium-sweet white wine
⅓ cup ginger syrup (taken from the jar of stem ginger)
2 tbsp cognac
2 tbsp Ginger Wine
the thinly pared rind of 2 small lemons (absolutely no pith;
use a potato peeler), and their juice
1¼ cups heavy cream
3 globes stem ginger, finely diced
1 globe stem ginger, thinly sliced

Put the wine and ginger syrup into a stainless-steel pan and reduce by half. Cool, and add the cognac, Ginger Wine, lemon rind, and juice. Cover with a lid or plastic wrap and leave overnight to infuse.

The following day, strain the liquid through a fine sieve into a pitcher. Put the cream into the bowl of an electric mixer and slowly start to beat it. (For an even better texture, hand-beat using a traditional wire balloon whisk.) Add the wine infusion a little at a time, beating gently, until all the liquid has been absorbed. *Do not over-beat.* Gently fold the diced stem ginger into the mixture, pile into chilled glass dishes, and chill for 1–2 hours. Just before serving, drizzle a little extra ginger syrup over each portion and decorate with a thin sliver of stem ginger.

LEMON CHICKEN SOUP WITH PARSLEY AND CREAM

Now then, how often do you see a decent, properly made cream of chicken soup on a menu these days? Never, is the simple answer. Although this one is made from scratch, a most passable one may also be fashioned from a leftover roast or from the remains of a boiled chicken dinner – if anyone does such a thing anymore. Mind you, trying to find a boiling fowl in the first place these days is almost impossible.

Serves 4

12 chicken wings
1 chicken bouillon cube (optional, but don't
be too prudish over this)
2 carrots, peeled and chopped
3 sticks celery, chopped
1 leek, trimmed, thickly sliced on the diagonal, and washed
1 medium onion, peeled and stuck with
three cloves, one of these securing a bay leaf
a few sprigs of thyme
1 small bunch flat-leaf parsley (leaves removed and reserved, stalks
roughly chopped to add to the stock)
1 glass of white wine
2 small lemons
salt and white pepper
2 tbsp basmati rice
⅔ cup heavy cream

Put the chicken wings into a deep pot. Just cover with cold water and plop in the bouillon cube. Slowly bring to a boil while keeping a beady eye on the scum that will surely rise to the surface as a nasty gray blanket. Reduce the heat to a simmer and carefully lift off the scum with a large spoon until the surface is quite clean.

Tip in the vegetables, thyme, and parsley stalks, and add the wine. Once more bring up to a gentle simmer, skimming off any further scum that emanates from the vegetables. Once this is done, adjust the heat to its very lowest: it should merely shudder and blip, and for about 45 minutes.

Strain the broth through a colander suspended over a clean pan and leave to settle for 10 minutes. Pick out, say, 6–7 wings, remove and discard their skin, and lift the flesh from the bones. Chop this and put into a small bowl. Discard the remaining wings and vegetables. (You could, of course, use the remaining wing meat in sandwiches.) Lift all surface fat from the strained broth with a few sheets of paper towel and return to the stove. Remove 4–5 strips of zest from the lemons (absolutely no pith whatsoever) and add to the broth with a little salt, if necessary, some pepper, and the rice. Bring to a boil (more scum will form, be assured) and further simmer for 10 minutes. Meanwhile, squeeze the juice from the lemons.

Puree the soup with about a third of the reserved parsley leaves and about two-thirds of the lemon juice in a blender until very smooth indeed. Strain through a fine sieve and reheat with the cream and the rest of the parsley, finely chopped. Taste for seasoning and add more lemon juice if you think it needs it.

LETTUCE

I will always remember shopping with my friend Fay Maschler in a supermarket (Waitrose?) in the Finchley Road, for a dinner I was helping to cook that evening at her home, then in leafy Belsize Park.

She is a decidedly forthright and opinionated woman, and I soon found myself swiftly returning a collection of "interesting leaves" (it *must* have been Waitrose) to the chilled salad cabinets. Fay had said to me, a touch witheringly, "Oh, come on, dearie" – her favorite term of endearment – "let's just have some nice, ordinary lettuce. I'm sick and tired of constantly having to mess with all those silly leaves, particularly that awful lollo rosso which tastes of quite nothing at all. Don't you think lettuce is nice anymore, Simon? Imagine all those nice and slippery pale yellow inner leaves, simply dressed with an ace vinaigrette?"

In the swiftest of turnarounds, I bleated, "Why, yes, of course, Fay. Couldn't agree more!" Fay began to rummage furiously. "I reckon on one lettuce per person. What do you think?" Quickly counting them as I wheeled the cart towards the checkout, I replied, "I guess so." Then, with a twinkling smile, she insisted, "Come along, it's you who are supposed to be doing the shopping." Quite so.

It turned out to be a ripping dinner and the lettuce salad was duly applauded. "You see," concluded Fay, "everyone would actually prefer a nice lettuce salad in a restaurant, but apart from being too timid to request one, they just aren't offered it anymore even if there is the remotest chance of lettuce being available." She was right, of course, then – and remains so to this day. It is worth noting that this dinner took place at least ten years ago, yet nothing has changed as far as a lettuce salad is concerned. Surely it is not only the supermarket shopper who buys lettuce?

Ironically, the common or garden round lettuce is now rarely offered in the more discerning, independent grocery store. Tiny leaves of peppery arugula, yes; carton upon plastic carton of pre-washed and trimmed clumps of mâche (lamb's lettuce), sure; mizuna, landcress, oak leaf, batavia, curly endive, pale yellow torpedoes of chicory, and the inevitable lollo bloody rosso. It would not surprise me to be offered the freshest clippings, harvested from a superior, organic wheatgrass field somewhere in West Sussex, one day soon – and at £10 the kilo, no doubt. But you won't find a really fresh lettuce anywhere.

So, then, is it only the everyday indiscriminate supermarket habitués who now idly pick up the familiar round lettuce simply because they always have done? In my local Tesco in west London, at *all* times of the day and *all* year round, that lettuce is never, ever out of stock. Perhaps they chuck out loads of them at the close of business every day. Who knows? Maybe there remains a resolute clique of British housewives who are eternally resigned to churning out that dreadful high-tea salad of old, complete with weeping bottled beets, gray eggs, cress, cucumber, and salad cream, but still utilizing only the very outside leaves of the lettuce? But somehow, I think not. That particular high tea has long been replaced by the microwaved pizza.

I will always be indebted to Fay for reintroducing me to the purity of the simple lettuce, as I had long discarded it in favor of more enticing Continental foliage suddenly available to me from burgeoning supplies spilling willy-nilly into the London markets during those heady years of the 1980s. So I was pleased to be saved all those years ago in the Finchley Road, once more embracing a handful of lettuces.

Lettuce is also very nice cooked in soups and vegetable dishes and also braised alongside a roast pigeon, say. And it is still very good along with beets, egg, cress, cucumber, and homemade salad dressing for that high tea, just so long as you adhere to the following recipe explicitly.

AN ENGLISH LETTUCE SALAD

Quite superb when done with care. Quite abominable when carelessly thrown together by a Llandudno landlady – that is for instance, not pointedly. I mean, it could be a Chelsea or even a Mayfair landlady and one who won't give you dessert unless you eat it all up. That's if you actually want dessert.

Serves 4

6 hard-boiled eggs, separated: the yolks sieved
into a bowl, the whites coarsely chopped for adding to the salad

For the salad dressing

2 tsp sugar
salt and cayenne pepper
2 tsp dry English mustard
1½ tbsp tarragon vinegar
1¼ cups heavy cream
1 tbsp coarsely chopped fresh tarragon

For the salad

6 hearts of some very fresh Boston lettuces,
separated into leaves, washed and dried
12 thin spanking-fresh spring onions,
trimmed and sliced into 1 in lengths
12 radishes, washed, halved, and put into ice-cold water
for 30 minutes, to crisp up
½ a cucumber, peeled and not too thinly sliced
a few leaves of mint, torn to shreds

To make the dressing, whisk together the egg yolks, sugar, seasoning, mustard, and vinegar. Add the cream and tarragon and mix thoroughly. Arrange the ingredients for the salad in a large shallow dish, employing good taste the while, so achieving as natural a look as possible. Sprinkle over the chopped egg whites and then spoon over the cream dressing in dribbles and swirls. Serve right away.

BRAISED BIBB LETTUCES WITH BUTTER
AND SPRING ONIONS

Although it may not exactly come as a great surprise to you, not very many people cook lettuce. Well, you should learn to, as quickly as possible. And right now seems as good a time as any. I feel sure you will be both thankful and surprised in equal measure once you have tasted the result.

Serves 4

6 tbsp butter
8 Bibb lettuces, trimmed of a few
of their outside leaves, well washed and dried
salt and white pepper
a bunch of spring onions, trimmed and sliced into ¾ in lengths
1 tbsp white wine
chopped chives

Using a deep, lidded pot melt the butter and put in the lettuces. Season and then add everything else but the chives. Bring up to a simmer, turn the lettuces over, mingling the onions amongst them, and put on the lid. Turn the heat down to its very lowest and cook the lettuces for about half an hour, turning them over again, until extremely tender and floppy. Lift off the lid, turn up the heat, drive off most of the excess liquid, and, once more, turn the lettuces over. You may notice during this process that the edges of the lettuces have become lightly scorched in places. This is as it should be. Very good with the gentler-flavored game birds, such as partridge or pheasant.

ROMAINE LETTUCE HEARTS, COLD CURRIED
SHRIMP, AND EGGS

In essence, Coronation Chicken made with shrimp, but every bit as good, if not more so. As delicious a first course for a summer weekend lunch eaten in the garden as I can think of. It also has a particularly English ring about it too, don't you think? And what could be more spiffing than that?

Serves 4

For the curry essence

¼ cup chopped onion
1 tbsp sunflower oil

1 demitasse spoon Madras curry powder
1 tsp tomato puree
⅔ cup red wine
⅓ cup water
2 tbsp smooth mango chutney
1 bay leaf
salt
sugar
a touch of pepper
a slice or two of lemon plus a good squeeze of juice, possibly more

For the curried prawns

5–6 tbsp mayonnaise
1 lb whole cooked shrimp in the shell (these have usually been
frozen, but are of quite good quality and much better than peeled shrimp), peeled
8–12 inner leaves from a crisp
romaine lettuce, washed and dried
3 hard-boiled eggs, shelled and cut into quarters
cayenne pepper (optional)

To make the "essence," gently stew the onion in the oil until transparent. Add the curry powder and cook for a few minutes longer. Add tomato puree, wine, water, chutney, and bay leaf. Bring to a simmer and add salt, a little sugar, pepper, and the lemon slices and juice. Simmer for a further 5–10 minutes. Strain through a fine sieve, pushing down on the solids with a small ladle, and cool. Add by degrees to the mayonnaise until you are happy with the taste. Mix with the shrimp just to bind, spoon into the lettuce leaves, and arrange the quarters of egg amongst them. Lightly dust with cayenne pepper if the mood takes you. (I'm forever in just this sort of mood.) Excellent eaten with lots of brown bread and butter.

Note: You will find that you have more "essence" than you actually need, but once sieved and cooled it can be decanted into screw-top jars and kept in the fridge for a few weeks.

LINGUINE

Not only do I find the word linguine most attractive to pronounce: *lingweeeeee-neh* – I also reckon its shape is one of the most appealing of all pastas when wrapped around the tongue. Curiously, linguine is a rare pasta within the indexes of most of the reputable Italian cookbooks I have, but when I finally found a brief description, the gist of it seemed to suggest flattened spaghetti. And, in fact, that is exactly what it is: not as wide as fettuccine or tagliatelle, but a bit thicker than trenette. And trenette is often understood to be the most favored pasta for dressing with pesto.

It was *The Times* restaurant critic Jonathan Meades, I recall, who first alerted me to the traditional Genoese inclusion of potatoes within a dish of pasta dressed with pesto. Initially, this rocks the boat of all reason: starch and yet more starch, all within the same plate of food, can hardly be seen as a thoughtful notion. As you might have already guessed, it is a quirky marriage that is most sublime.

This muted mingle of manufactured bland strands of paste with nuggets of earthy tuber suddenly makes me realize quite why we like a chip butty so much, or a forkful of roast potato, Yorkshire pudding, and gravy. And there is yet another version in this vein where *borlotti* – or other *fagioli* – take the place of the potato amongst the tangle of pasta which sounds equally delicious to me, I must say.

I remain convinced that one deeply sad day very soon we will come across this assembly stacked, as a teetering tower: the potato slices, swirls of ribbon pasta sandwiching them together, a smear of pesto sauce as adhesive and with this absurdly composed nonsense finally topped off with a whimsical lid that is the "Parmesan crisp," neatly trimmed to fit. Remember, you first read about it here.

Furthermore, I am absolutely sick and tired of this incessant desire to continually "garnish" each and every dish with this cretinous coil of twiddled pasta turrets. My, how I loathe them. And then there is this other growing fashion: that witty little raviolo pillow, all plumped up with some nonsense – often wildly inappropriate – and slithering around a huge white soup plate like some demented dodgem car.

The very latest impertinence, however, and, be assured, soon to overtake the previous two, is the use of a spoonful of risotto to titivate an assembly. Most often, it is seen as a soggy disc lurking underneath a mountain of other ingredients, the rice overcooked to pudding consistency so that it "molds" to shape. None of these traditional Italian staples deserve such ignorant treatment, for it is in their very nature to be presented as stars in their own right, which makes them shine so brightly. So, for heaven's sake, just leave them be!

LINGUINE WITH PESTO AND NEW POTATOES

As I find it quite impossible not to include a few sprigs of mint when boiling new potatoes, you will simply have to excuse me this particularly English habit on this occasion or, of course, choose to leave it out. However, I do find that basil and mint have a true affinity with each other; so much so, that I would seldom consider making the Italian lotion known as salsa verde without including both basil and mint – as well as, of course, copious amounts of parsley too. Hey, it's entirely up to you. After all, it is only a hint of mint we are talking about here.

Serves 2

For the pesto

the leaves from a small bunch of basil
1 clove garlic, peeled and crushed
1 tbsp pine kernels, lightly toasted in a dry frying pan
salt and pepper
2½–5 tbsp olive oil
½ tbsp freshly grated pecorino or
Parmesan cheese

For the linguine

3½ oz small new potatoes, scrupulously scraped clean
2 3 sprigs of fresh mint
5 oz good-quality dried linguine
extra grated Parmesan

First make the pesto. Using a mortar or food processor, pound or process to a paste the basil, garlic, and pine kernels, together with a little salt and pepper. Then add enough of the olive oil in a thin stream to produce a loose-textured puree. Finally, quickly mix in the cheese. Set aside.

Cook the new potatoes with the mint in a small pan of boiling salted water until tender and leave them in their water. Cook the linguine in another pan of boiling salted water until tender. Suspend a colander over a large serving bowl and drain the linguine. Lift out the colander and allow the pasta to drain. Tip the draining water out of the bowl and wipe dry. (This draining process allows the serving bowl to be heated through for serving.)

Add 4–5 tbsp of the potato-cooking water to the pesto to loosen it, drain off the rest of it, and slice the potatoes in half lengthways. Toss all three ingredients together in the warmed bowl and hand extra Parmesan at table.

LINGUINE WITH SHRIMP AND DILL

A luscious combination this, and a fragrant one too, with its tones of aniseed, lemon, and pulverized shrimp shells; more Scandinavian than anything to do with Italy, one might almost say. But it is a thoughtful assembly nonetheless and just the sort of thing to serve up for an early supper eaten out of doors on a balmy summer's evening – be it in Stockholm, Siena, or Swindon. Well . . . perhaps not Swindon.

Serves 2

1 lb shell-on shrimp, fresh or frozen
2 shallots, peeled and finely chopped
1 clove garlic, peeled and chopped
4 tbsp butter
1 tbsp Pernod
1 demitasse spoon white wine vinegar
1 small glass of white wine
2 ripe tomatoes, chopped
⅔ cup whipping cream
salt and pepper
grated rind and juice of ½ a small lemon
5 oz dried linguine
1 demitasse spoon freshly chopped dill leaves

Remove the heads from the shrimp and peel their tails. Place the peeled shrimp tails in a bowl and keep cool in the fridge. Put all the shell debris to one side.

Gently fry the shallots and garlic in the butter until softened. Add the shrimp-shell debris and turn around in the pan over a high heat for a couple of minutes. Add the Pernod and allow to sizzle for a moment, then introduce the vinegar and wine. Add the tomatoes and then simmer this mush together for 20 minutes. Tip into a blender or food processor and puree to a pink slurry. Tip into a sieve and, using the back of a ladle, force every last scrap of juice from this slurry into a saucepan. Bring the resultant juice to a simmer. As it approaches this moment, skim off the copious scum that settles upon the surface. Reduce by half and then stir in the cream. Bring back to a boil and simmer until unctuous and the consistency of thin custard. Check the seasoning and add the lemon rind and juice. Keep warm.

Cook the linguine in a large pan of boiling salted water until tender. Drain, return to the pan, and add the sauce and peeled shrimp tails. Sprinkle over the dill and gently heat everything together while also turning all the ingredients over and into each other so as to cohere both pasta and shrimp with sauce and dill. Once you are sure that all is good and hot, serve without delay.

BAKED LINGUINE WITH HAM AND CHEESE

Now I have never actually eaten this gorgeous-looking dish, all bubbling and variously pustulated as it is deftly spooned out of its well-burnished oval dish, day in day out, in Signor Cipriani's Venetian *istituzione,* Harry's Bar. The next time I go there – and I promise myself this each and every time – I will only have the *gratinati.* But, of course, I don't. I have watched others eat it, oh yes. And stared, transfixed, as it is decanted from its deceptively diminutive dish: the creamed béchamel, the ham, the cheese, all dripping lazily from the strands of pale pasta as it curls up on the plate like a large family of sleepy worms. This is super slop, the best there is, famously fluid the world over. You simply have to forgo anything else to eat, that's all. And, as I always want my custard pancakes for afters, I regretfully veer away and, as if on automatic pilot, once again request the *fegato.* I know my place.

The following recipe is based upon the *Tagliolini Gratinati al Prosciutto* recipe from *The Harry's Bar Cookbook,* by Arrigo Cipriani, and is how I prepared it at home.

Serves 4

1 tbsp butter
2 oz sliced prosciutto, cut into julienne strips
12 oz dried linguine
5 tbsp freshly grated Parmesan
½ cup béchamel sauce (use a recipe for this that you are familiar and happy with,
but do not make it too thick)

Preheat the broiler.

Bring to a boil plenty of salted water. Melt one-third of the butter in a large frying pan and add the prosciutto. Cook gently for a minute or two, stirring constantly. Cook the linguine in the boiling water for a couple of minutes, until *al dente.* Drain well in a colander, add to the ham, and toss together briskly with a further third of the butter and half the Parmesan.

Spread the pasta evenly in a shallow oval ovenproof dish. Spoon the sauce over the surface and sprinkle with the remaining Parmesan. Cut the remaining butter into bits and scatter over the top. Place under the broiler for a couple of minutes or so, until golden and bubbling. Serve at once, with more of the Parmesan passed separately.

LOBSTER

A few years ago I had one of the most frustrating conversations I can recall ever (it eventually turned into a full-blown argument), with a highly respected American food writer and journalist. I met him in New York, where he lives. We had enjoyed a jolly dinner at a new restaurant (a freebie, I think, which sort of says it all) and, towards the end, touched upon the subject of lobster. This shift in the conversation turned out to be a very big mistake.

This man just knew it all. Naturally, the American lobster was the finest in the world, the *Homarus americanus,* to which he incessantly referred and loftily lionized. He was convinced that this type of lobster could not be found in the UK . . . (I thought at the time, slightly bewildered, that here we have a right one.) And, furthermore, however much I tried to convince him that it surely could, and was every bit as fine a specimen (I tactfully chose not to say it was better), with its beautiful brittle blue/black carapace, as opposed to the almost "plastic"-shelled, dull brown U.S. cousin, I could see I was fighting a losing battle. I also tentatively suggested that I found the flesh of our native *Homarus* a little sweeter with a more dense, almost fudgy texture to it. This was all complete nonsense, as far as he was concerned.

But it did not stop there. Oh no. Apparently, we had never known the existence of freshwater crayfish in any of the rivers and lakes of Britain. Granted, there are not many of our indigenous species left now, as they have all been gobbled up by some (other) ignoramus who decided, some years ago, to introduce the American species into our waters: the voracious and vicious "signal" crayfish which has since all but destroyed our native creature. For I remember well, in my early teens, catching sight of my very first British crayfish as it idled awhile beneath the crystal-clear waters of the infamous Strid, in Bolton Abbey, Yorkshire, where many foolhardy young lads over the years have come to a watery death, bravely attempting to leap across this ferociously fast stretch of turbulent flume. But there it was, the British crayfish in all its glory.

And then we touched upon the question of scampi. These are not langoustines, Dublin Bay prawns, or anything to do with them, my smirking host insisted. No, not at all. They were another thing altogether and only lived in the deepest waters of the Veneto lagoon. They were very large, apparently, these scampi, and were not to be found anywhere else at all. Interesting that, for soon after I arrived back home, our Crustacea van at Bibendum just happened to be selling some magnificent creatures that weighed in at just over half a kilo each.

I smiled, but at the same time also felt very sad for this preposterous person who, having over one short evening almost reduced me to tears with his pomposity and ignorance, would never be able to sit down to a plate of one of our very own hot-buttered lobsters or freshly boiled langoustines. Surely, he wouldn't even be able to look them in the eye, would he?

HOMARD CHAUD CHAMPEAU

As an assistant chef at La Normandie Restaurant et Bar, Birtle, near Bury in Lancashire, it was up to me, come the English summer months (no constant invasion of year-round imported *Homarus americanus* in those bygone days, thank heavens), to dispatch live lobsters for chef during the hectic evening dinner service. And it was a full-time job. So many customers came specifically to eat M. Champeau's astonishingly fine lobster that he would even take the trouble to telephone them personally, alerting them to the debut of the season. It was only when I eventually tasted the finished dish that I understood why there was always this mini-stampede up that winding lane to Birtle.

You will need one very large frying pan, or two smaller ones.

Serves 2

two 1–1¼ lb live lobsters, preferably female
3 tbsp olive oil
4 tbsp butter
salt and cayenne pepper
1 tbsp finely chopped shallot
1 tbsp finely chopped garlic
2 tbsp Pernod
2 tbsp cognac
1 tbsp chopped parsley

Kill each lobster by inserting a large, very sharp, strong knife directly through the head at the point where you can quite clearly see a small cross-section of detail in the shell structure. Make it a swift stab directly downwards and then bring the knife sharply through the head section. Quickly turn the creature through 180° and finish the job by hewing the remaining section in two with one blow, which will allow the two halves to fall apart. Remove the crumbly little stomach sac from the head of each half and also any thin, dark digestive tract running through the tail flesh. Break off the claws from the body and crack them with the side of the knife for ease of eating later, once cooked.

Preheat the broiler.

Put the frying pan on the stove and in it heat together the olive oil and butter. Once foaming slightly, add the lobster halves and claws. Season the exposed flesh with salt and cayenne pepper and allow to sizzle gently for several minutes. If you have a lid that will fit the pan, cover and stew quietly for 10 minutes or so; otherwise secure with a sheet of foil. Then remove the lid or foil, increase the heat a little, and baste the lobsters liberally with the buttery juices for a good 2 minutes. Lift out the lobsters to a heatproof dish and put under the broiler 4–5 inches from the heat to complete the cooking. *Note:* The shells should by now be a bright red color and the flesh slightly raised from the confines of the carapace.

Tip the shallots and garlic into the pan juices and fry until soft and slightly golden. Turn up the heat and add the Pernod and cognac. You may flame the alcohols, but this is not entirely necessary; whatever happens, they will certainly seethe and bubble in the pan. Once the fats and alcohols have nicely mingled together, return the lobsters to the pan and, once more, baste with the resultant sauce, adding the parsley as you so do. I think you will believe me when I say that this is one of the finest cooking smells I have ever come across in my life. Any accompaniment to this dish simply gets in the way, but you may like a squeeze of lemon juice.

A SUPERIOR LOBSTER COCKTAIL

However much you think I may have lost my marbles over this recipe, I assure you that the end result is a refreshingly light and fragrant take on the original – whatever that might be. The curious combination of melon and cucumber (although they are, after all, related) is actually very fine, and with the further addition of tomato – that all-in-one fruit and veg – the garnishing trio is now all set to provide backing to the solo lobster.

It was the remarkable and most individual Jimmy Last, now long-departed cook and proprietor of the Howard Arms, Ilmington (a country inn a few miles south of Stratford-upon-Avon), who was instrumental in alerting me to this inspired combination of sweet fruit, grassy cucumber, piquant cream dressing, and shellfish. He also used to roast the finest ducks in the land, which he reared in his back garden, having fed them on bits of bread which had previously been soaked in milk and cognac. The like of such individualists, alas, we shall surely never see again.

Serves 2

the meat from 1 small cooked lobster
(approx. 1 lb whole cooked weight)
1 small and ripe Charentais melon, halved horizontally, seeds removed
¼ of a large cucumber, peeled and deseeded
1 ripe tomato, peeled, quartered, and deseeded
2–3 tbsp mayonnaise (not made with olive oil)
2 tbsp sour cream
1 tsp tomato ketchup
3–4 drops Tabasco
2–3 drops Angostura bitters (optional)
a squeeze of lemon juice
the crisp heart of a Bibb lettuce, shredded
1 tsp snipped chives
cayenne pepper

Cut the lobster meat into small chunks and place in a roomy bowl. Remove the flesh from the melon halves, reserving the skins, and dice into similar-sized pieces, but only add about two-thirds of it to the lobster as otherwise its flavor will dominate. (It goes without saying that it would be sensible to utilize the most dice-friendly scoops of melon flesh for the cocktail and eat the untidy remainder.) Place the 2 emptied melon skins in the fridge. Dice the cucumber and tomato flesh a little smaller and put with the lobster and melon. Put to chill.

Using a small bowl, mix together the mayonnaise, sour cream, ketchup, Tabasco, bitters (if using), and lemon juice. Combine two-thirds of this sauce with the fruit and fish medley and carefully fold together. Sparsely fill the base of each melon shell with a little of the shredded lettuce. Now pile the cocktail mixture on top of the lettuce and then tidily coat each portion with the remaining sauce. Sprinkle with chives and ever so lightly dust with cayenne pepper – an affectation we just cannot resist, and so love to do.

LOBSTER WITH FENNEL PUREE AND LOBSTER OIL

In the village of Maussane-les-Alpilles, Provence, there is a producer of olive oil the like of which I have never encountered anywhere else in Europe. I do not usually get my knickers in a twist over olive oil, being quite happy to use what comes my way. (The very idea of attending an "olive oil tasting" is enough to make me sick – which it probably would, come to think of it.) Yes of course I am choosy, but I am not daft.

As far as I am concerned, that Maussane oil is more about the taste of the olive, whereas oils of similarly good standing from Italy primarily concern themselves with purity and finesse; a case, perhaps, of the French farmer versus the aristocratic Italian estate. This lobster and fennel thing requires, most definitely, the substantial stamp of a muddy boot rather than the caress of soft calf leather.

Serves 2, as a first course

For the lobster and its oil

a 1¼ lb cooked lobster
¾ cup of olive oil
½ a small onion, chopped
1 stick of celery, chopped
1 clove garlic, bruised
¼ tsp fennel seeds
1 bay leaf

For the fennel puree

1 large fennel bulb, cut into sixths
salt and freshly ground white pepper
2 tsp Pernod
1 tbsp olive oil
2 tbsp crème fraîche

Preheat the oven to 325°F.

For the lobster and its oil, first remove the lobster from the shell, extracting all its meat. Wrap the meat in plastic wrap and reserve in the fridge until ready for use. Using a heavy knife or large pestle and mortar, reduce all the shell of the lobster to debris, by chopping or pounding, respectively; it is important that this procedure is most thorough. Place the debris in a pan and stir in the rest of the ingredients. Place over a low flame, heat until a continuous series of bubbles rises through the solids for 2–3 minutes, and then switch off the heat, remove the pan, and cover it. Leave to infuse, somewhere close to the stove and where there is residual heat, for at least 1 hour.

Meanwhile, make the fennel puree. Put the fennel in a small lidded oven dish with the seasoning, Pernod, and olive oil. Warm through on top of the stove until just beginning to simmer, then put on a lid and cook in the oven for around about 1 hour, or until the fennel is very tender indeed. Remove from the oven, tip into a blender (a food processor is OK, but it will not result in so smooth a texture), and reduce to a fine puree. Pass through a fine sieve into a small bowl. Whisk in the crème fraîche. Keep hot over a pan of barely simmering water.

Tip the lobster-shell-and-oil infusion into a sieve suspended over a bowl. Allow to drip while you warm through the pieces of lobster meat, which is best achieved by arranging them upon a sheet of foil and then gently steaming for a couple of minutes or so.

To serve, attractively display the lobster meat on two warmed plates, dish up some of the fennel puree alongside, and, finally – and without drowning it – spoon a little of the lobster oil over the lobster. Offer lemon quarters also, in case anyone finds the assembly too rich.

Note: It is not really possible to make just the correct amount of lobster oil for 2 servings, so freeze the remainder. If you haven't the faintest idea what else to do with it, then perhaps this sort of recipe was never your sort of thing in the first place. Try the Superior Lobster Cocktail instead (see page 133).

MILK

Lovely, lactic, luscious, limpid milk. Such an easy alliteration and so effortlessly descriptive for one little word. I fondly remember a friend in my kindergarten class who had a bit of a speech problem, even over the simplest of words. Even those four little letters would struggle to erupt from his trembling lips, eventually emerging as a most difficult "miiiiiik."

Michael and I always looked forward to our tiny bottles of fresh milk each and every breaktime, all cold, fresh, untreated, deeply flavored, third-of-a-pints. The great trick – assuming, that is, you are old enough to know what the dickens I am talking about – was to be able to puncture the foil cap with the straw without it buckling, so sinking it directly into two inches of top-of-the-milk cream – almost as a sharpened twig through the ice on a frozen pond. As I recall it was here that Michael's particular precision skills came to the fore.

As you read this, the nearest carton available to you which has anywhere near the taste of that little bottle is something now called "breakfast milk." This package is whimsically decorated – there are blue skies dotted with clouds, verdant green fields, caramel-colored Jersey cows with big eyes – and, to remind you quite how "special" this milk is, it is fitted with an absurdly complicated individual pouring spout.

I mean, Tetrapak cartons are not exactly the easiest things to open at the best of times but do they *truly* imagine that to offer this unusual facility in the side of the pack convinces average shoppers that they have purchased something special? The option of an elite pouring action, perhaps? Whatever. It used to be known as "gold top" and is just the right stuff for pouring over a morning bowl of Frosties, with the milk really, really cold for best results.

Many young chefs these days who may like to think they are *au fait* (or whatever the Italian translation is for this) with all aspects of Italian cookery have probably never cooked a true *salsa balsamella* (béchamel sauce), so obsessed they are now with which particular olive oil to use, how to include balsamico in almost anything at all, making sure their potato peeler is to hand at all times for endless shavings of Parmesan, and whether or not their *cavolo nero* is quite ready for the *ribollita*.

Il salsa balsamella is such a staple "ingredient" in northern Italy (where fatty butter and milk contrast nicely with the olive-oil-rich south) that many of the region's most delicious indigenous dishes would not exist without its luxurious lactic balm. But then this sauce is made with flour, isn't it? As far as the modish sauce chef today is concerned, a bag of flour has 666 written all over it.

MACARONI PUDDING

Originally known to me as macaroni pudding, this milk pudding was a favorite of mine as a child. The ingredients are the same as for rice pudding, with the rice being replaced by the pasta. Penne, apart from being easier to get hold of than macaroni these days, seems to be a better vehicle here as all the milky sauce that is produced during the cooking flows deep inside the quill-like tubes, making the finished result all the more soft and slippery.

Serves 4

1 quart whole milk
1 vanilla bean, split lengthways
⅓ cup sugar
5 oz penne
⅔ cup light cream
freshly grated nutmeg

Preheat the oven to 300°F.

Put the milk, vanilla bean, and sugar into a shallow ovenproof dish that will also sit happily over a naked flame. Bring to a simmer and then stir around with a whisk, pushing around the vanilla bean, which will help to disperse its little black seeds into the milk. Tip in the penne and add the cream, stir around, and bring back to a gentle simmer. Grate plenty of nutmeg over the surface, to give an even dusting, and then place in the oven and cook for approximately 1 hour and 15 minutes. Have a look from time to time, as the surface should remain pale golden throughout; turn the temperature down a touch if it seems to be getting too dark. Remove from the oven and leave to cool for 10–15 minutes before eating, as this sort of pudding is infinitely better eaten warm rather than piping hot.

Note: The pudding should be very slightly runny when it emerges from the oven. The starch in the pasta thickens the hot milk, which it continues to do as the pudding cools slightly. Clearly, for once, considering the cooking time here, the phrase *al dente* is redundant; but then I don't believe this recipe has anything at all to do with Italian cooking. Nevertheless, it is a truly delicious milk pudding.

SMOKED HADDOCK CHOWDER

The name chowder originates from the French *chaudière,* which refers to a type of cauldron. To me, it will forever be associated with a milky fish soup with bacon and potatoes in it. For those who daily sit at the counter of the Oyster Bar in Grand Central Station, New York City, slurping down huge bowls of Manhattan clam chowder, this would doubtless be seen as nothing less than the thought of a demented heretic. I actually don't get the point of Manhattan chowder, as all too often it seems to me little more than a rather insipid tomato soup with some clams floating in it – and with not a drop of milk in sight. But, then again, they have every right to say that the following recipe of mine is "Hey! Way outta line there, goddamit!"

Serves 4

4 thick slices bacon, diced
2 small leeks, white part only, split lengthways, thinly sliced, washed, and drained
6 tbsp butter
12 small waxy potatoes, peeled and thinly sliced
salt and pepper
2 cups light chicken stock
1 fresh corn cob
1 cup whole milk
1 lb smoked haddock, skin and bones removed
2 coarsely chopped hard-boiled eggs
2 tbsp chopped parsley
1 tbsp chopped chives
a squeeze of lemon juice
a few drops of Tabasco (optional)

Sweat the bacon and leeks in the butter until both have melted and softened nicely. Add the potatoes and some seasoning. Stew together gently for a further 10 minutes. Add the stock, bring up to a simmer, and, as it does so, deftly remove any resultant scum that appears on the surface with a ladle. Now remove the corn from the cob by placing it on its end and running a knife down the sides, slicing off the kernels with determined strokes until fully denuded. Add these to the chowder and simmer for 15–20 minutes, or until the potatoes and corn are tender. Pour in the milk and add the smoked haddock in one piece. Once more, bring up to a simmer and, almost immediately, lift out the haddock with a spatula and put on a plate. Once it has cooled a little break the fish into flakes with your fingers. Now stir in the eggs, parsley, and chives and sharpen with lemon juice, and Tabasco if using. Reintroduce the smoked haddock, reheat, and adjust the seasoning.

JUNKET WITH VANILLA AND NUTMEG

Junket is one of the most underrated desserts. Particularly English and good for you too. Considering that every single pastry chef in the land seems to have gone panna cotta potty recently (do they all sleep with each other or what?), this will, no doubt, be the next wobbly wonder on the dessert menu. Very lactic. Very milky milk.

Serves 4

1⅔ cups cream-top milk (if available) or whole milk
⅔ cup whipping cream
½ a vanilla bean, split lengthways
2–3 pieces of lemon peel (absolutely devoid of pith)
1 tbsp sugar
1 tsp rennet
freshly grated nutmeg – pre-ground will *not* do

Pour the milk and cream into a very clean pan, add the vanilla bean, lemon peel, and sugar, stir together, and, very gently, warm to blood heat (98.4°F – use a thermometer if you are not sure). Lift out the vanilla bean and lemon peel and stir in the rennet. Pour into a shallow china dish, immediately grate some nutmeg over the surface, and leave on the kitchen table to set. Do not put it in the fridge. It should set in about 20–30 minutes. If you like to eat it cold, which I very much do, then place it in the fridge after it has set. It is delicious with loosely beaten and lightly sweetened cream, and a dribble of honey, if you like, which I very much don't. In Cornwall they traditionally like to serve it with their local clotted cream. Much as I also adore this dense and heavy ointmentlike cream, I find that it interferes with the very gentle set of a true junket.

MINCE
(GROUND MEAT)

Now then, listen here. Although a celebrated chef may be able to turn his hand to the finest Hollandaise emulsion, a perfect provençale daube, or – if he is particularly gifted – maybe even a pressed leek terrine with lobster, foie gras, truffles, caviar, beets, lovage leaves, and a soft-boiled egg, all wrapped up in swathes of blanched Savoy cabbage leaves, it takes a thoughtful, most particular, almost fastidious cook to turn out a decent panful of savory mince.

As you might have guessed, all that nonsense with the pressed leeks was simply the private thought of a fictitious (though clearly ambitious) chef with delusions of greatness, purely invented by me at my most cynical. Though – heaven forbid! – the prospect that such an abomination might ever become reality is, worryingly, not entirely outside the realm of possibility. It remains abundantly clear, however, that whether he or she be fact or fantasy, neither of them would consider a simple plate of mince to be in any way connected with gastronomy or "Modern British" cooking.

As an example, my friend Sally Herdman-Newton is one who is extremely knowledgeable about the precision required to turn out fine mince. Being Scottish (with a sprinkling of Russian) may help to explain her expertise, but the real reason why Sally makes such very *good* mince is because she also happens to be a learned, highly intelligent, and genuinely natural cook. She is not alien to vivid seasoning, nor averse to a sprinkling of dried mixed herbs if they happen to be to hand, and also understands the importance of piquancy in her mince, a dash of ketchup (Heinz, naturally), Lea & Perrins, and Burgess anchovy essence being other essential seasonings.

It goes without saying that while an overture of chopped onions and carrots fried in dripping provides necessary aromatic strength, they could never, in a thousand years, be called a *mirepoix* – celebrated chef-speak for chopped veg. When I phoned Sally *re* mince she also shrieked, "And don't forget, my boy, it *must* be dry! There's nothing worse than slippy-sloppy mince. Ask my darling ma. She knows. Learnt it all from her, bless her heart."

It's also a funny old thing that when one talks to the average fortysomething (my generation) about memories of mince, all most of them do is go dewy-eyed over Bolognese sauce. This makes me feel mildly disappointed that they have never been given properly cooked mince at home, all dark brown and rich, bejeweled by tiny chunks of carrot and traces of slippery, gently gilded onion. A *ragù alla Bolognese* is all well and good in *trattoria* and *ristorante,* but it isn't mince as we know it. I mean, there are chopped chicken livers in it for one thing.

My mum's mince was always bolstered by mashed potatoes. Sally's ma probably also serves bashed neeps (mashed swede to Sassenachs and mashed turnips to Yanks) as well. I suppose that if savory mince were ever to be elevated to Michelin three-star status, each of these vegetable accompaniments would be either piped, quenelled (in the shape of a molded ovoid achieved by playing about with two wet tablespoons), or maybe even "pillowed." Could this be the moment when a pile of steaming mince on a large white plate will properly be referred to as "a duvet of lightly herbed and spiced savory chopped steak"? I just can't wait.

VEAL RAGÙ

I remain convinced that the majority of those who still like to cook a Friday night spag-bol (spaghetti Bolognese) regard it as nothing more than an easy filling meal, dismissing in the shake of a colander its integrity and fine tradition. The two main points that are of the greatest importance to the success of this ubiquitous dish are that the meat *ragù* (the "bol") is cooked very, very slowly over a long time, so creating an essential fondancy and richness, and, when combined with pasta, the *ragù* should merely dress rather than swamp it, as countless British food pictures of the past – and still lurking about in the present – have led us to believe it should have: the cow-pie look.

Serves 4

2 medium onions, peeled and finely chopped
6 tbsp butter
1 large carrot, peeled and finely diced
3 celery stalks, peeled and finely chopped
2 cloves garlic, peeled and chopped
11 oz coarsely ground veal
3½ oz chopped chicken livers
¾ cup dry white wine
freshly grated nutmeg
salt and pepper
¾ cup passata (unseasoned tomato sauce)
¾–1¼ cup milk
½ cup whipping cream
2 tbsp freshly chopped flat-leaf parsley

In a heavy-bottomed, cast-iron cooking pot, fry the onions in the butter until soft. Add the carrot, celery, and garlic and fry for a few minutes further until all are pale golden. Add the veal in small amounts, turning up the heat a little and frying carefully, breaking up the meat with a wooden spoon as you go. Tip in the livers, stir around for a moment, and introduce the wine a little at a time with the heat turned up full. Allow the wine to bubble away to almost nothing, so becoming absorbed, before adding more.

Once all the wine has been used up, season with nutmeg and salt and pepper and pour in the passata. Stirring constantly, bring the *ragù* to a simmer, reduce the heat, and leave to cook gently for 30 minutes. Now stir in ¾ cup of the milk and continue to cook at the lowest possible temperature. (Use one of those heat-diffuser pads if you have one or cover the pot and cook in a very low oven.) Allow the *ragù* to merely "blip" for about 1–1½ hours, stirring from time to time and adding more milk when necessary. Add the cream, stir in, and continue to simmer for a further 30 minutes. Check the seasoning and stir in the parsley. Ready to use.

THAI PORK RISSOLES WITH SWEET AND SOUR DIPPING SAUCE

This heavenly aromatic mixture is hot and spicy and with all the flavors that one associates with Thai cooking. The rissoles can be eaten as a cocktail snack or a first course, according to size.

Serves 4 as a first course, or up to 10 as cocktail snacks

9 oz lean pork
9 oz fatty pork belly, including skin
2 stalks of lemon grass, tender bulbous part only
6 lime leaves
¾-in piece galanga ginger (or ordinary fresh ginger), peeled
3 cloves garlic, peeled
2 large shallots, peeled
1 tsp shrimp paste
2 large red chillies, seeded
1 demitasse spoon green peppercorns
5 leafy sprigs of fresh cilantro, roots included if possible
10 mint leaves
a little salt
1 tsp ground turmeric
2 tbsp Thai fish sauce *(nam pla)*
3 tbsp fresh bread crumbs
vegetable oil for frying

Serve with

sliced cucumber
cilantro sprigs
lime wedges
Sweet and Sour Dipping Sauce (see below)

Put the first 12 ingredients through the coarse blade of the meat grinder, twice. Place in a mixing bowl and add the salt, turmeric, fish sauce, and bread crumbs. Blend thoroughly with your hands, squeezing the mixture in a clutching manner, until all i well amalgamated. Cover with plastic wrap and put in a cool place for at least 2 hours so that the flavors blend and ripen.

Form into small walnut-sized balls if you wish to serve them as cocktail snacks, o larger, slightly flattened cakes for a first course. The smaller size is best cooked i deepish hot fat, in a frying pan for about 5 minutes. The larger version should be frie gently, still in a frying pan, but using only a couple of tablespoons of oil, for 5 minutes on each side. Both will turn out well crusted and a deep brown color, with the insides moist and golden from being stained with turmeric and chillies. Serve hot with sliced cucumber, cilantro sprigs, lime wedges, and the following sauce.

SWEET AND SOUR DIPPING SAUCE

½ cup rice vinegar
⅓ cup palm (or golden granulated) sugar
1 tbsp Thai fish sauce (*nam pla*)
1 tbsp soy sauce
1 small red and 1 small green chilli, seeded and finely chopped
(leave the seeds intact if you wish for a more fiery taste)

Boil together the vinegar and sugar until syrupy. Stir in the fish sauce and soy. Allow to cool and add the chillies. There may be too much sauce here, but it keeps for ages in a screw-top jar in the fridge.

SAVORY MINCE (GROUND BEEF)

I could eat a nice bowl of savory mince once a week, if the truth be known. It is surely one of the most gratifying of all comfort foods. But it must be carefully made. Then, in my book, *everything* I cook I try to do as carefully as possible; it is a habit born of some quirky desire to sit down and eat something of excellence rather than something second-rate. Am I old-fashioned? I think I might be (with apologies, but with respect, to Dame Edna Everage).

Some might suggest that there are a few too many spurious additions to the following recipe that do not quite follow the tradition of British – or Scottish – savory mince. Whatever, it remains quite a few steps up from a can of Dinty Moore.

Serves 4

7 oz onions, peeled and chopped
6 tbsp butter
7 oz carrots, peeled and diced
7 oz flat dark-gilled mushrooms, diced
1 tbsp peanut oil
1 lb chuck steak, coarsely ground
7 oz bacon, coarsely chopped (leave the rind on, as it will add richness and flavor)
1 tsp mixed herbs
½ tbsp tomato puree

a 14 oz can chopped tomatoes
¾ cup beef stock (or canned consommé)
1 tbsp tomato ketchup
½ tbsp Worcestershire sauce
salt and plenty of white pepper

Serve with

creamed potatoes

Start by frying the onions in the butter until well colored, in a large heavy-bottomed pan. Add the carrots and mushrooms and continue cooking gently for a further 10 minutes or so. Tip out the vegetables onto a plate and reserve. Briefly wipe the pan clean, pour in the oil, and heat until smoking. Put in the ground beef and bacon and briskly fry until golden brown. Add the mixed herbs and tomato puree and cook for 5 minutes over a fairly high heat until the puree loses its very red color. Add back the vegetables, together with the canned tomatoes, stock or consommé, ketchup, and Worcestershire sauce, season, and simmer very gently, uncovered (preferably on a heat-diffuser pad), or in a low oven with the lid on, for about 1 hour, stirring from time to time. The final consistency should be thick and rich and not at all too liquid. Eat with creamed potatoes.

MINT

As far as culinary smells are concerned, mint, for me, epitomizes an English kitchen in summertime. As you might guess, my association with such things originates from the very happy kitchen in which I grew up. Of course, I didn't actually "grow up" in a kitchen, you understand, as I had my own bedroom too and was allowed to wander in and out of any other room in the house without so much as a by-your-leave.

It is just that in that particular kitchen, where I would have a daily chat with Mum (after having walked home from school all alone aged five from the bus stop a mile away, and in the dark, in winter) while she did the ironing, the conversation would often turn to what we were going to eat for tea. And – particularly in that hysterically delicious and nirvana-like time that was the waning weeks of the spring term – Mum would invariably say, once having neatly folded the last cream Clydella shirt: "Could you just nip out to the garden and pick some mint for the new potatoes, darling?"

I was out there in a flash, most often clambering over the wall into the adjacent field where a new, flourishing crop of furry-leaved apple mint had recently thrived even more successfully than in our own garden. I would pick only the tippy-top stems of those early shoots, thinking they were the prettiest and also the most suitable for our pan of simmering tender yellow marbles, as once they were drained through the green-and-cream-enameled colander they would be that much easier to pick out and throw in the trash. I know this all sounds a bit H. E. Bates, but I remember it as if it were yesterday. And I enjoyed every single moment of it very much indeed.

Quite why the French have always turned their culinary noses up at us over our love of mint sauce with roast lamb I do not know. I suppose that, along with *le rosbif et le pouding Yorkaise et les "feesh and cheeps,"* our mint sauce is one of the only original tracklements (no translation for *that,* in French—it means savory sauces or relishes) that doesn't exist, in any form whatsoever, within *la cuisine française.* Well, all the better for that, say I. (The very finest and deep traditions of French cookery, however, continue to remain unsurpassed; at least for me they do.)

So *pourquoi* has it been, pray, that over the last fifteen years or so those same diminutive sprigs of fresh mint that I used to pick for Mum from over the wall have come to decorate every single French dessert from Biarritz to Boulogne? They're plonked on everything: *le gratin des framboises; la tarte aux pommes caramélisée à la minute; les trois boules de glace vanille "bourbon."* What are they for? From where did they suddenly appear? And what caused the rush to return so quickly, and with so much force, to the very shores from whence they came?

Quicker than you could say "dust my bottom with icing sugar and flood my belly button with raspberry *coulis,*" little green sprigs began to decorate desserts from Penzance to Pitlochry. And still adorn such confections to this day. Now look here, don't be ashamed, just chop 'em all up with sugar and add a splash of vinegar, then at least the poor herb is actually used rather than daintily picked off, discarded to the side of the plate, and then thrown away.

MINT AND ELDERFLOWER GRANITA

Even though I feel absolutely sure that someone else in the world has also introduced mint and elderflower within chilly circumstances, I did think of this splendidly refreshing combination all on my ownio. It is a perfect partnering if I might say so and all the better for being a rough granita rather than a smoothy old sorbet.

Serves 4–6

2 cups plus 2 tbsp elderflower cordial
2 cups plus 2 tbsp water
juice of 1 lemon
juice of 1 lime
a large handful of mint leaves, finely chopped

Chill a shallow metal pan in the freezer in advance.

Mix all the ingredients together in a bowl. Place in the pan and put in the freezer for about an hour before having a look. What you are looking for is ice crystals forming around the edge of the pan (completely opposite to ice cream or sorbets, as here the ice crystals are the essential charm of the thing). Once the crystals have reached about 2–3 inches towards the middle of the pan, gently lift them with a fork into the not-so-frozen mixture. Return to the freezer. Have another look in about half an hour and repeat the forking. Continue this procedure until all the mixture has formed crystals. Now tip into a suitable lidded plastic container and store in the freezer until ready to use; it will keep its granular texture for a few days, but after that the granita starts to firm up into a block.

FRESH COCONUT AND MINT CHUTNEY

One of the easiest and simplest recipes in the entire book and astonishingly good to eat with char-grilled lamb cutlets or a fillet of fried fish. Nothing more to be said here, really.

Enough to fill a standard-sized storage jar (about 1½ cups [12 oz])

3½ oz mint leaves
6 garlic cloves, peeled and crushed
2 tsp dry-roasted and freshly ground cumin seeds
2–3 tsp sugar
1–2 tbsp Asian fish sauce
5–7 tbsp lime juice
5–6 small green chillies (seeds removed or not, it's up to you)

½ cup thick coconut milk (cream of coconut)
3½ oz creamed coconut (this comes in a block), grated
salt, if necessary

Puree all the ingredients except the salt together in a food processor or blender until completely smooth, test for salt, pour into a storage jar, and chill. Eat with all sorts of cold and hot dishes whenever the mood takes you, which will be frequently. Keeps fresh-tasting for about 3 days, but will last, at a push, for 1 week.

FRESH MINT ICE CREAM WITH CHOCOLATE AND BOURBON SAUCE

The very idea of wishing to put Kentucky Bourbon anywhere near food is anathema to most of you, I guess. Well, it almost is for me too. Apart, that is, from this once-in-a-blue-moon exception. One Sonia Blech, erstwhile chef of Mijanou restaurant in London's Ebury Street, used to put a lot of bourbon in her dishes. And a lot of nuts too. Other dishes which did not include either of these ingredients (of which there seemed to be precious few) were very nice indeed and the wine list was an absolute joy.

I assure you that this ice-cream frivolity is an absolute joy too. Mint and chocolate are well-known associates of old. But it is the affinity that mint and bourbon have with each other, as exemplified by that wonderful Kentucky drink called the Mint Julep, which initially inspired the following recipe.

Serves 5–6

1 quart whole milk
8 egg yolks
1 cup sugar
1 small bunch fresh mint, leaves only
1 cup plus 4 tbsp heavy cream (as cold as possible without freezing it; this simply helps to arrest the cooked custard from *over*cooking)
2 tbsp crème de menthe (optional, but it remains elusive and is a quite delicious addition – and also lends an almost imperceptible pale-green tinge to the ice cream)

For the chocolate sauce

5 oz best bittersweet chocolate
2 tbsp cold water
2 tbsp sugar
4 tbsp slightly salted butter
2 tbsp Kentucky Bourbon (or another brand if this proves difficult to find)

Scald the milk. Whisk together the egg yolks and sugar until light and fluffy. Slowly pour in the milk while continuing to whisk. Pour the mixture into a heavy-bottomed saucepan and cook over a very gentle heat, constantly stirring with a wooden spoon. As the mixture perceptibly begins to thicken – do not let it boil – also stir in the mint. Once fully thickened immediately pour it into a metal bowl, or another cold pan (hot liquids cool quickest in metal) and stir in the very cold cream. Leave as it is for 5 minutes and then strain through a fine sieve into a bowl. Add the crème de menthe if using. Once completely cold, pour into an ice-cream machine and churn and freeze according to the manufacturer's instructions.

To make the chocolate sauce, first place the chocolate, water, and sugar in a small, thick pan. Stir together over a lowish heat until smoothly blended. Beat in the butter – added in small flakes – then incorporate the bourbon. Serve the sauce hot or cold.

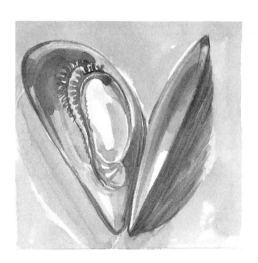

MUSSELS

As far as ready-to-go products are concerned, mussels are surely one of the very finest examples. During my apprenticeship in a French restaurant in the early 1970s, however, it was a different story entirely. I used to dread the weekly winter arrival of a truly huge sack of Morecambe Bay mussels, which was so weighty it needed me and another lad to carry it from the delivery van. But I particularly recall that it was the real work of cleaning the little blighters before they could get anywhere near the heat of the stove that filled me with dread.

And they were absolutely filthy. In fact, so deeply caked with the detritus of a million rock pools were these molluscs that one felt maybe, just the week before, Poseidon himself had expressly ordered all the barnacles in the world to swiftly attach themselves to my particular sack of mussels in readiness for the immense task that lay ahead. And there was much weed. And sand. And there were dead mussels too, of which the very deadest ones of all smelled so bad they would cause me to retch uncontrollably.

Today's mussels are now so squeaky-clean and washed one wonders whether they have ever actually grown anywhere near the sea at all. This, of course, is not the case, rather it is just me having a boisterous little rant with myself as to why the hell this was not the case when I was a toiling assistant, left out in the chilled Lancastrian air scraping and washing the entire mussel harvest of the entire northwest English coast – at least, it seemed at the time – when instead I could have been filleting sole, chopping parsley, hiding in the staff lav or even being mildly taunted by Chef for a good ten minutes. It was just so damned *cold* out there with the mussels, all on my own, cursing and shivering.

So to reiterate my initial observation that mussels may now be seen as one of the finest ready-to-go products available to all both pleases and annoys me at one and the same time. For each and every time I visit my fishmonger, idly pick up a plastic bag of mussels, and toss it about between my hands, all I am concerned with – albeit only for a minute or two – is the plight of the poor wretches who have had to clean them all for me. But maybe they are now all washed and scraped by some magical machine, which is progress most rare. Thankfully, it is also rare to find even a half-dead mussel lurking among a bagful today.

Much improvement, therefore, on the production side of things. Any sign of an increase in domestic sales? Oh, come on! I mean, just why is it that whereas the market stalls and blue-tiled fish shops or the simplest of seaside restaurants along the coast of Brittany and Normandy offer, respectively, mountains of fresh mussels to buy to take home and many steaming cauldrons of *moules marinières,* the possibility of purchasing one single flimsy pale-blue plastic bagful on the seafront in Brighton, Newhaven, or Hastings on even a Friday afternoon or spooning up a single hot bowlful of the same is practically zilch. Truly, a very sad state of affairs.

MUSSEL RISOTTO

Shellfish risottos are the exception to the rule, where it seems that olive oil, rather than butter, is the correct fat to use. Maybe I am talking a lot of nonsense by saying this but, somehow, it feels absolutely bang on for this savory slop of rice, mussels, and tomato. A touch of dairy right at the end, nevertheless, simply to slick it all together remains the right thing to do.

Serves 2

2 onions, peeled and chopped
4 tbsp olive oil
¾ cup dry white wine
2¼ lb mussels, cleaned and debearded
⅔ cup light chicken stock
2 very ripe, large fresh tomatoes, peeled, cored, seeded, and chopped
½ cup Carnaroli rice (my particular
choice, but any other suitable rice for risotto [see page 215] will be just fine)
1 clove of garlic, peeled and very finely chopped
1 tbsp chopped parsley
a tiny pinch of dried chilli flakes
a little salt, if necessary
1 tbsp softened butter

Before you do anything at all, have ready a large colander suspended over a pan and in the sink. Soften half the onion with half the olive oil in a large pan that will accommodate the mussels. Turn up the heat, pour in the wine, add the mussels, shake the pan about a bit, and put on the lid, still over a high heat. After about 2 minutes, remove the lid and shake and toss the mussels so that those initially underneath now appear on top; you will notice, from this action, that the mussels from beneath have already started to open. Replace the lid; cook for a further 2–3 minutes and then repeat the shaking and tossing motion. Depending upon strength of heat, you may have to do this once more, but if it looks as if most of the mussels are now open, tip the whole panful into the colander in the sink. Leave to drain for at least 5 minutes, giving the colander an occasional shake to ensure that all remaining juices drip through.

Once the mussels are cool enough to handle, extract all the meat from their shells and collect it in a bowl. Cover and set aside. Take the mussel-cooking liquor that has now collected beneath the colander and strain it through a very fine sieve into the stock. Pour this mixture into a pan and place over very low heat to keep hot, but not to boil. (You may not necessarily use all of this; any leftover can, of course, be frozen for a subsequent occasion.)

In an entirely new solid-bottomed pot, heat the remaining olive oil. Soften the remaining onion in this and then add the tomatoes. Briskly cook together for a few minutes until reduced to a sloppy paste. Add the rice and stir around in the tomato mess until thoroughly coated with it. Introduce the first ladle of the hot stock and vigorously stir in. Only consider incorporating a second ladle once this has been fully absorbed. And so on, until the rice is nearly cooked; taste a grain: it should still possess "bite."

Now add the shelled mussels and stir in, together with what should, hopefully, be the final ladleful of stock. Sprinkle in the garlic, parsley, and chilli flakes and carefully fold everything together, while also making sure that you do not pulverize the naked mussels, which are now fragile, having been robbed of their protective shells. Taste for salt – probably not necessary – and finally stir in the spoonful of softened butter. Cover the pot with a lid and leave to settle for 5 minutes. Serve from the pot at table, directly onto hot plates.

SPAGHETTI WITH MUSSELS AND PESTO

This gloriously simple dish of mussels with pasta might possibly be one of the finest plates of food I have ever eaten at Riva, the eponymous Italian restaurant in Church Road, Barnes, a brisk fifteen-minute walk from the south side of Hammersmith Bridge. Its proprietor, Andrea Riva, his loyal chef, Francesco Zanchetta, and each and every charming member of the staff who look after the dining room are, without doubt, a rare and shining example of everything that is right and proper about honest restauration.

Serves 2, as a light supper

For the pesto

the leaves from a small bunch of basil
1 clove garlic, peeled and crushed
1 tbsp pine kernels, lightly toasted in a dry frying pan
salt and pepper
3–5 tbsp olive oil
½ tbsp freshly grated pecorino or Parmesan cheese

For the mussels

1 tbsp olive oil
1 lb cleaned mussels
a generous splash of white wine
5 oz good-quality dried spaghetti

155

Have ready, in the sink, a colander suspended over a large pan. Also, have another pan full of salted, simmering water on the stove.

Using a mortar or food processor, pound or process to a paste the basil, garlic, and pine kernels, together with a little salt and pepper. Then add enough of the olive oil in a thin stream to produce a loose-textured puree. Finally, quickly mix in the cheese. Set aside.

In a large pot, heat the olive oil and then tip in the mussels. Once they are starting to sizzle add the wine. Put on the lid and allow to cook for 2–3 minutes. Remove the lid and shake around the mussels so that those on top (slightly open) are replaced by those on the bottom (fully open). Replace the lid and cook for 2–3 minutes more. Once you are happy that all the mussels have fully opened, drain into the prepared colander.

While the mussels are draining, bring the pan of salted water to a full rolling boil and cook the spaghetti in it until *only just* tender. As it cooks (for about 5 minutes) lift the mussels from the colander, and drain their collected juices from beneath through a fine sieve into a small bowl. Suspend the colander once more over the pan and drain the spaghetti into it. Immediately return the spaghetti to its (now empty) cooking pot and tip in the mussels. Now dilute the pesto with a little of the mussel-cooking liquor, but only so much as to turn it into a loose slurry. Stir this into the mussels and spaghetti with great care while also reheating the whole assembly. Once each and every strand of pasta is coated green and all is hot, serve it up.

MOUCLADE

Although one might haughtily suggest that the French have never quite understood the correct use of Asian seasoning – *"un point de couteau de poudre de curry,"* par example – it nevertheless remains that there are few more successful and hugely enjoyable dishes than this one. Moreover, if the dish is made using some carefully roasted and ground spices of one's own invention rather than a commercial brand (a good-quality one, of course), somehow the final result just does not taste quite the same. Ditto Coronation Chicken.

Serves 2

4 tbsp butter
3 shallots, peeled and sliced
1 large clove of garlic, peeled and sliced
1 demitasse spoon Madras curry powder
1 small glass of dry sherry
3 lb cleaned mussels
2 tbsp softened butter
1 tbsp flour

a generous pinch of saffron stamens
½ cup milk
⅔ cup whipping cream
a squeeze of lemon juice
salt, if necessary

Before you do anything at all, have ready a large colander suspended over a pan and put it in the sink. Now melt the butter in a very large pot (which should possess a lid) and in it fry the shallots and garlic until soft, but uncolored. Add the curry powder, stir in, and cook over a gentle heat for a few minutes. Pour in the sherry and briefly allow to bubble vigorously over a high heat. Tip in the mussels, shake the pan about a bit, and put on the lid, still over a high heat. After about 2 minutes, remove the lid and shake and toss the mussels so that those initially underneath now appear on top; you will notice, from this action, that the mussels from beneath have already started to open. Replace the lid, cook for a further 2–3 minutes, and then repeat the shaking and tossing motion. Depending upon strength of heat, you may have to do this once more, but if it looks as if most of the mussels are now open, tip the whole panful into the colander in the sink. Leave to drain for at least 5 minutes, giving the colander an occasional shake to ensure that all remaining juices drip through.

Strain the collected juices through a fine sieve into a clean pan. Now start the moderately tedious job of detaching the empty shell of each mussel from its full partner, depositing the useful half into a bowl and discarding its divorcée – along with any stubborn ones that have failed to open. Reheat the strained mussel broth (removing any resultant scum in the process) and allow to simmer gently. Mix the butter and flour together in a small bowl until smooth. Now, using a whisk, gradually incorporate the butter and flour mixture (known as a *beurre manié* in classical French cooking) into the simmering broth until very smooth and slightly thickened. Add the saffron, milk, and cream and stir in. Bring back to a simmer and cook for a further 5 minutes. Add lemon juice to taste and a little salt, if necessary. Reintroduce the mussels, heat through for a few moments, and divide between two large preheated shallow soup plates.

ORANGES

I truly abhor peeling oranges with my bare hands. Moreover, even to observe someone else doing it almost makes me wince. Even if my fingernails were as sharp and strong as those belonging to an orang-utan I would still shy away from this messy, difficult, and ultimately disappointing procedure. Generously taloned friends over the years have kindly offered to peel oranges just for me but still I find it difficult to enjoy the result of their sterling efforts.

I mean, does not *everyone* know full well that it is quite impossible to manually peel an orange without leaving almost all of its inner, bitter white pith behind? Although I may be possessed of the eternally pedantic palate, do you not all agree with me that this unwanted downy bloom quite ruins the taste of every single segment? And then there are all those tiny bits of rind that get caught underneath the nails followed by squirts of sticky juice all over your hands . . . For me, this only confirms that this entire rigmarole is a non-starter in the first place. And, wouldn't you know, whenever this messy undertaking is forced upon one it only ever takes place as far as it is possible to be from a source of running water.

Let us be sensible here: the only way to enjoy the delights of a clean, neat orange segment is by accurate and precise carving, using a long, sharp stainless-steel knife. It does not require a great deal of skill, this carving thing, as more than anything else the action is neatly guided by the contours of the fruit itself.

Once you have cut a neat disc from each end of the orange – which so clearly reveals the clenched extremities of its segments all at once – it should then be steadied on a chopping board. Using the same sharp knife, neatly cut an initial carving of peel from the edge of the exposed flesh while following the curvature of the orange itself.

from top to bottom. This tentative maneuver once completed, simply trace the continuing exposure of flesh-to-peel with the knife blade, making a similar curved motion around the entirety of its circumference.

You should now have close to an immaculate, naked orange orb. Holding this in one hand – and over a bowl from which you intend to eat the orange (exactly the same procedure applies to grapefruit) – neatly slice each segment from between its clearly marked protective membranes while removing perfect wedges each and every time. Once this final operation is complete, squeeze the exhausted framework over the fallen segments by hand, extracting all remaining juices.

Now *that* is what I call a peeled orange and, truly, this is no big deal. When you especially wish to do something properly – and all good cooking is, without question, a proper procedure – it all just depends on how deep is the desire for propriety in the first place.

So, there is the orange at its most pure and chaste. Within the realms of ambitious cooking, however, it is also the oils and aromas of the orange that play a distinctive part in all manner of sweet and savory dishes. That is not to say its juices play no part at all, but when called upon for inclusion in, say, a dessert sauce or a game or duck gravy, these lotions invariably need a boost of thinly pared, pithless zest to accentuate that distinctive orange tang.

Atypically, when it comes to marmalade, it is both the aromatic zest *and* its bitter pith which impart our most traditional preserve of all with all its contradictory, bittersweet flavors – which, I guess, knocks my pith theory (difficult to say, that) neatly on the head.

The massive amount of sugar used in the making of marmalade helps just a little bit here, or (I remain convinced) it would never have caught on. Not in a month of Sundays. I also always need a convenient source of warm running water even after spreading marmalade on buttered toast; which is precisely why I choose to eat breakfast sitting at the kitchen table rather than in my car, for example.

STEAMED MARMALADE SOUFFLÉ

Now then, this is not a soufflé in the traditional sense of the word, as it is only made from egg whites. (The yolks are used in the custard that accompanies it.) In fact, it is more like one large floating island instead of several small ones – like those that you would normally see served in a restaurant. This recipe originates from the kitchen of the late Mary Shaw (MBE), much loved and highly respected cook of Inverlochy Castle, Fort William, Scotland.

You will need a double boiler with a capacity of at least 2 quarts, preferably more. If not, then use a bowl of similar capacity that will sit suspended over a pan.

Serves 2 – with enough for seconds

For the custard

1 cup whole milk
½ a vanilla bean, split lengthways
3 egg yolks
2–2½ tbsp sugar
1 tbsp Cointreau or Grand Marnier

For the soufflé

3 eggs, separated
5 tbsp sugar
3 tbsp coarse-cut marmalade, melted
grated rind of 1 small orange
juice of ½ a small lemon
a little softened butter

To make the custard, simmer the milk with the vanilla bean and leave to infuse for 10 minutes. Beat the egg yolks and sugar together and then strain over the flavored milk and whisk to blend. Cook over a moderate heat, stirring all the time with a wooden spoon, until lightly thickened. If you mess it up and it looks as if the custard has split, whiz in a blender, which always works a treat. Add your chosen liqueur and stir in. Leave to become very, very cold in the fridge, as the contrast between the hot soufflé and ice-cold sauce is very agreeable.

Meanwhile, beat the egg whites in a large bowl until fairly stiff (as you might when making meringues) and then start to beat in the sugar, little by little, until all is glossy

160

and thick. Carefully fold in the marmalade, orange rind, and lemon juice until well amalgamated. Butter either the top half of the double boiler or a bowl, and spoon in the mixture, leveling off the top. Do make sure there is enough room for the soufflé to rise by at least one-third further. Cover with a piece of buttered foil, allowing room for any extra rising. Steam over gently simmering water for around about 45–60 minutes. The soufflé is cooked when it feels firm to the touch.

Once the soufflé is cooked, carefully turn out onto a deep cold dish and flood the custard around it.

JOUE DE BŒUF À L'ORANGE

This is the very first recipe I cooked from Michel Guérard's book *Cuisine Gourmande,* possibly the book that has influenced me more in my life with cooking than any other. Naturally, at the time— more than twenty years ago now— it was a little difficult to readily purchase ox cheeks from my local butcher. Come to think about it, I never actually asked for them, simply requesting several large lumps of top rump without a second's thought, assuming no such thing actually existed outside of France.

Perhaps those deeply flavorsome cheeks were always lurking there under the counter in a similar way that spooky Mr. Briss, the butcher of Royston Vasey, occasionally keeps "something special." Something special is certainly an accurate description of this superb dish of braised beef, that's for sure. The following version is based upon the original with a few tweaks here and there by me, but with every possible respect.

Serves 4

2 oranges
1 lemon

For the marinade

3 oz flat mushrooms, diced
4 oz carrots, peeled and diced
5 oz onion, peeled and diced
2 large sticks celery, peeled and diced
2 cups plus 2 tbsp dry white wine
a few sprigs of thyme
2 bay leaves
2 tbsp olive oil
1 whole ox cheek (approx. 1¾ lb), lightly trimmed

4–5 tbsp olive oil
salt and pepper
3 cups light veal or beef stock or strong chicken stock
3–4 tbsp crème de cassis
2–3 tbsp heavy cream

Remove the zest from 1 of the oranges and the lemon using a potato peeler, making sure that they contain no pith whatsoever. Juice all 3 fruits and add to the marinade ingredients. Cut the zest into thin strips (julienne) and blanch in a small pan of boiling water. Drain in a sieve and then refresh under cold running water. Set aside.

Mix all the marinade ingredients together in a large bowl. Cut the cheek into 4 equal pieces and bury it in the marinade. Cover, and place in the fridge overnight.

Preheat the oven to 275°F.

Lift out the pieces of cheek from the marinade and flick off all bits of chopped vegetable that cling to them. Lay on folded pieces of paper towel and dry thoroughly. Also pick out the sprigs of thyme and bay leaves and put aside. Drain the marinade into a sieve suspended over another bowl, and keep the juices for later.

Take a roomy casserole dish and in it heat the olive oil. Season the cheeks and gently fry in the oil until crusted and brown on all surfaces. Lift out and put on a plate. Now introduce the drained vegetables to the oil and cook, stirring occasionally, until lightly colored. Off the heat, push them to one side of the pot with a wooden spoon and tilt the pan. Using crumpled sheets of paper towels, soak up the excess oil from the pan and discard. Return the cheeks to the pan together with the drained juices from the marinade, the stock, cassis, and about three-quarters of the reserved orange and lemon zests. Gently mingle everything together, bring up to a simmer, cover with a sheet of wax paper (cut into a circle, to fit) pressed down onto the meat, put on the lid, and braise in the oven for 1½–2 hours, or until very tender indeed when pierced with a skewer. Place back upon a gentle heat, remove any excess grease from the surface with paper towel, and stir in the cream. Check for seasoning, allow to bubble for a few more moments, and strew the surface with the remaining orange and lemon strips.

ST. CLEMENT'S CREAM

One of cooking's magic tricks, this one. How very helpful indeed it is that by simply boiling cream and sugar together, stirring in orange and lemon juices, and leaving the mixture to cool, everything just sets like a dream. All on its own. This is exactly the sort of recipe that should be taught in schools up and down the country, but isn't. *And* it has a song to go with it.

Enough to fill 6 large ramekins

For the cream

juice of 2 large oranges
2 cups plus 2 tbsp heavy cream
⅓ cup sugar
grated rind of 2 lemons
grated rind of 1 large orange
juice of 2 lemons

For the orange jelly

1 leaf gelatin
⅔ cup freshly squeezed orange juice
juice of ½ a lemon
1 tbsp Grand Marnier (optional, but it does give the orange jelly a bit of a boost)

Put the orange juice into a small pan and, over a low heat, reduce until syrupy – by about three-quarters, I guess. Put to one side. Bring the cream, sugar, and rinds of the fruits to a boil in a large pan. (The size of the pan is important here, to allow for the expansion of the cream as it boils.) Boil all together for exactly 2 minutes. Take off the heat and whisk in the lemon juice and reduced orange juice. Leave to infuse for 15 minutes. Now strain everything through a fine sieve into a bowl and then ladle into the ramekins. Chill for at least 4 hours.

To make the jelly, first soften the gelatin in cold water until soft and spongy. Bring the orange and lemon juice *just* to a boil, noted particularly by the moment when a scum forms on the surface. Immediately strain through a piece of muslin into a clean pan and stir in the softened gelatin whilst the juice is still hot. Add the Grand Marnier if using. Leave to cool to room temperature and then carefully spoon about 1 tbsp over the surface of each "cream." Return to the fridge to chill for a further hour before serving.

OYSTERS

On the first two occasions that I consumed a quantity of oysters I was violently ill. Before this I had eaten the odd one or two without any ill effects whatsoever, and, furthermore, had absolutely loved the taste. So it turned out that not until I had decided to go the whole way, and downed a grown-up dozen or so (I was the *tiniest* bit apprehensive but six just seemed such a cop-out), did things begin to go seriously wrong. But, as you will soon discover, I was most determined not to be beaten by these bivalves.

My initial dozen were the plumpest and juiciest collection. They were from the Helford estuary in Cornwall and eaten in the dining room of La Normandie Restaurant in Birtle, near Bury in Lancashire, my first place of toil and to where I had now returned, several years later (1977), as a paying guest. It was a truly wonderful dinner. Memorable. Doubly memorable, as it happened, as I experienced it all over again at six o'clock the following morning . . . except this time it was all the wrong way round. Bugger, I thought, I can't stomach the damn things. And for something so very delicious, this was an enormous blow to me.

Forward one year, almost exactly, to Pembrokeshire. Boxing Day lunch 1978 in the city of St. David's. There was much talk in the area at the time about how some enterprising folk were cultivating native oysters in an estuary close to the county town of Pembroke. I knew well the owners of the hotel in which we were to enjoy lunch, and had always looked upon them as being equally enterprising chaps. So it came as no surprise to find that they were indeed offering these local oysters amongst the choice of first courses that very day.

Did I dare? Did I wish to spoil the remaining few days of what had turned out, so far, to be a very happy Christmas break? Should I have the safe option of the *potag bonne femme*? Almost as if spoken by someone else altogether, the words "A dozen of your finest oysters, please, David!" had, seemingly, escaped my lips before I'd so much as taken a sip from my glass of festive fizz.

It was to be 6 P.M. this time. And much, much worse. I was laid up for two days. Thank heavens I was staying with my parents for the duration. While Mum fussed, cooed, and tucked in damp sheets, Dad administered kaolin and morphine and made occasional cups of weak, sweet tea. Meanwhile, all I could think was that the *potage bonne femme* would, most likely, have been really, really horrid. All warm and watery, stringy and thick. In fact, just like . . . oh, dearie, dearie me.

Early December 1979. Isle of Wight. Researching for the *Egon Ronay Guides*. Sitting at the bar of a really nice pub a few miles outside the town of Yarmouth, enjoying a glass of draft Guinness. Good mood. It was Friday. Last lunch of the week. My ninth. I glanced at the blackboard: "Local native oysters, £5 the dozen" – or some such silly price of twenty-odd years ago. Third time lucky? Delicious with the stout, no question. I wondered what the johns would be like on the ferry . . . Oh, sod it.

"A dozen of your finest oysters, my good man!" I said. I didn't actually say it like that at all, of course, but however I demanded of him I recall that it sort of came out as a timid squeak. "With the utmost pleasure, young man! I shall sally forth and shuck them personally," he retorted. He didn't say it like that either, but what he surely *did* go on to say was that he had just the sixteen oysters left and would I like to eat the lot for the price of twelve? (Oh no, noooo . . .) "Yes! Whyever not! How very kind!" I squeaked again. "Well . . . better have another Guinness then, hadn't I?" . . . (help!)

No doubt the johns on the ferry were a vision of loveliness: frothy blue-flush, a bar of brand-new Camay, linen hand towels, and pointy toilet paper. I'll never know. Sometimes you just can't win.

OYSTER VELOUTÉ

Because there is not going to be anywhere near enough juice to collect from the oysters for this "soup" it is necessary to obtain it from elsewhere, hence the inclusion of mussels. Apart from anything else, I have always considered mussel stock as being one of the very finest fish broths one can use, both for soups and sauces. As far as the mussels are concerned, once they're cooked and shelled, simply pop them in a small plastic bag, pour over just a little of their cooking liquor – a couple of tablespoonfuls or so, just to keep them moist – and put them in the freezer for another use: in risotto, with pasta, or added to a paella, for example.

Serves 4

2 lb cleaned mussels
¾ cup dry white wine
¾ cup light chicken or fish stock
2 tbsp basmati rice
2 leeks, white part only, sliced
1 small fennel bulb, chopped
6 tbsp butter
18 large oysters, shucked, kept in
their shells with all their juices
⅔ cup whipping cream
freshly ground white pepper
a squeeze of lemon juice
1 tbsp snipped chives

Wash the mussels well in plenty of cold water, picking through them to remove any stray beards or barnacles. Put into a roomy pan and pour over the wine. Put a lid on and bring to a boil, shaking and stirring the mussels as you go. When you see that they have opened (the cooking process should not take much longer than about 5 minutes), drain into a colander suspended over another pan or bowl. Shake the colander to draw out any remaining liquor and then shell the mussels, putting the meat into a small bowl.

Decant the mussel liquor through a double sheet of muslin into another pan together with the chicken or fish stock. Slowly bring to a boil and, as it does so, whip off the gray blanket of scum that appears on the surface. Add the rice and simmer until the rice is fully overcooked; this is intentional. Put this stock and the rice to one side. Using a smaller saucepan, quietly sweat the leeks and fennel in the butter until softened. Incorporate into the mussel and rice stock and stir in. Simmer all the components together for a further 20 minutes.

Lift each shucked oyster out of its juices, briefly dip into a bowl of cold water, and deposit in another clean bowl; this removes any clinging particles of shell and grime that may have attached themselves. Once you have done this, strain the juice through a fine sieve back over them. Put only 6 of them, together with some of their juice, into the canister of a blender. Blend with half of the mussel and rice broth until really smooth and pass through a fine sieve into a clean pan. Blend the remainder of the broth and repeat.

Stir in the cream, bring to just below a simmer, and check the seasoning; you should need no salt at all, but certainly some pepper. (I sometimes like to use Tabasco here instead.) Now add the remaining 12 oysters and all the juice. Warm through until the oysters have plumped up slightly, but beware of overcooking them. Squeeze in a little lemon juice to taste and stir in the chives.

OYSTERS KIRKPATRICK

An Australian, Mr. Anders Ousback – gourmet, restaurateur, gifted ceramicist, wit, and raconteur (all-round clever dick, one might say) – informs me that this is the original and, therefore, correct name for what has long been known in Australian culinary circles as oysters *Kil*patrick.

Apparently the dish is named after the mayor of San Francisco who officiated in that fair city around the turn of the century. (A. O. says it was 1908, but let's not quibble here.) Originally, it was understood to be simply oysters grilled with bacon and Worcestershire sauce. I'm not so sure about the sauce, but bacon has long been a favorite of mine with hot oysters; angels on horseback to name but . . . well, just the one example, I guess. Anyway, here is the second one, without the L&P sauce but with élan.

Note: Place the shells as nearly horizontally as possible; this can be achieved by strewing the container you are using with rock salt.

Serves 2

12 large oysters, shucked,
their juices strained into a small stainless-steel pan,
and their muscles loosened from the base shell
2 tbsp crème fraîche
3–4 thin slices of bacon
(pancetta, for preference), cut into 12 small squares

serve with

lemon
Tabasco

Preheat the broiler.

Mix together the oyster juice and crème fraîche and bring to a simmer, whisking. Allow to thicken slightly. Now place a square of bacon on top of each oyster and spoon a little of the oyster cream over, just to mask the bacon. Pop under the broiler for 4–5 minutes or until the bacon is curling at the edges and the oysters have noticeably stiffened from the heat. Serve directly. Add a squeeze of lemon and a healthy dash of Tabasco.

HOT OYSTERS WITH LEEKS AND CURRY SPICES

Another hot oyster dish, and a surprisingly good one it is too, considering that curry flavors with oysters sounds a touch on the wacky side. I can only say that it excited me very much the first time that I tried it. You only have to cook them to find out for yourselves.

Note: Place the shells as nearly horizontally as possible; this can be achieved by strewing the container you are using with rock salt, as in the previous recipe.

Serves 2

12 large oysters
1 large leek, white part only, sliced thinly, washed, drained, and dried
4 tbsp unsalted butter
1 tsp curry powder
very little salt
1 tbsp dry sherry
⅔ cup heavy cream
½ a small egg yolk
a squeeze of lemon juice

Shuck the oysters or have them shucked. Whoever does the job, any juices must be saved as they are opened, so this should be done over a small bowl. Extract each oyster from its bottom shell with a small, sharp knife and allow to slide into the bowl, juices and all. Once this is done, scrub the oyster shells well with a brush and warm water all over, then dry under a hot broiler – and leave this on, as you will need it later. Also, heat the oven to its lowest temperature. Now lift each oyster from its juices, dip each one quickly in a bowl of water (this is simply to make sure there are no clinging particles of shell still attached), and put it in a small pan. Strain the juices over them using a fine sieve. Put to one side.

In another pan, stew the leek in the butter until very soft. Add the curry powder and the merest sprinkling of salt. Allow to stew for a minute or two and then add the sherry. Turn the heat up and cook for about 1 minute, bubbling. Suspend another sieve over the oyster pan and drain the leeks into this, pressing down lightly with the back of a spoon so that their buttery juices drip out. Arrange the oyster shells in an ovenproof serving dish which has been thickly spread with rock salt, and deposit a teaspoon or so of the leeks into the bottom of each shell.

Heat the oysters ever so gently over a low flame until they have stiffened slightly – about 2 minutes. Lift them out with a slotted spoon and lay each one atop one shell of the leeks. Keep warm in the oven covered with foil and with the door wide open. Now bring the juices to a boil and rapidly reduce by two-thirds. Add the cream and bring back to a simmer, whisking the while. As the sauce begins to thicken, remove from the heat and immediately whisk in the egg yolk until the sauce is somewhat frothy and noticeably further enriched. Add a squeeze of lemon juice. Whip the oysters out from the oven and spoon the sauce carefully over each one; it matters not a jot if some of the sauce dribbles over their edges. Place under the hot broiler for about 1 minute, or until the surfaces are lightly burnished and a little puffed around the edges. Serve at once, directly from the dish.

PANCAKES

Pancakes are the great instant dessert – or maybe a sweet or little treat, call them what you will. A pancake is there for the making, just whenever you wish to eat one. For as you know, or at least you ought to, eggs, flour, and milk can be thrown together in minutes to make a simple batter. In fact, it takes less time to soften a tub of stiff Häagen-Dazs ice cream in the fridge until *just* the right texture than it does to whisk together a pancake batter; mind you, the thought of a scoop of Häagen-Dazs's Toffee Crème wrapped inside a freshly made warm pancake . . .

Well, anyway. Mum was always most adamant that we should not reserve the cooking and eating of pancakes just for Shrove Tuesday. And, being the thrifty cook she certainly was, it seemed glaringly clear to her that flour, eggs, milk, sugar, and a squeeze of lemon were also a pretty cheap set of ingredients. Furthermore, for an easy dessert so clearly enjoyed by all, to not think of making it only because it was not the right day would have been – to quote Dad – "just playing silly beggars."

But this insane British tradition lives on, as thousands of Stepford Wife–like mothers in early spring feel that they should fling pancakes around the kitchen simply to amuse the children. Then, once the embarrassed laughter has died down and the kids have been released back to the telly, the efficient modern mum quietly opens the lid of the freezer and deftly slides a packet of ready-made supermarket pancakes into the microwave. And with a triumphal smooth of her immaculate apron opts to drizzle them with forty-year-old balsamic vinegar and fresh ewe's milk ricotta. "Now then, you two, how about trying this new recipe I saw on *Ready, Steady, Cook!*" "Um . . . yeah, Mum, sure . . . er . . . is there any ice cream?" Damn right, sonny.

English pancakes, as soon as they are ready, simply need a light sugaring, drenching of lemon juice, and a loose fold-up. That's it. Plain and simple. And, let me tell you now, Mum's pancakes were not even tricky and thin French *crêpes*. Oh no. They were simply English pancakes. Not even thick Scotch pancakes. Or American pancakes with bacon and maple syrup and buttermilk and blueberries and fried eggs and yet another pancake on top. Never. Our pancakes, in essence, were nothing more than very thin and flat Yorkshire puddings cooked in butter. Batter is just batter – and all the better for being nothing more than just that. Naturally, the desire to learn how to cook pancakes in the first place helps enormously here.

Once you have made this batter (a basic recipe follows) and are ready to make pancakes, first and foremost make sure you have a nice and sturdy pan for the task at hand. One that measures approx. 8 inches in diameter is about right here, with slanted sides and – perhaps most important of all – a perfectly flat bottom; an uneven pan will cook an uneven pancake, however much an expert you might imagine yourself to be.

First of all have the pan good and hot. Now add a generous amount of vegetable oil (or other flavorless oil) to the pan and heat until it begins to smoke slightly. Pour this away into a bowl (discarding it once cold) and return the pan to a more moderate heat. Add a ladle of batter to the pan (my ladle measures ⅓ cup and is about right), swiftly swirling it around so that it covers the whole surface as quickly as possible. As soon as the underneath of the pancake has started to set – clearly indicated by a golden crusting around its edges – flip it over with a spatula, cook for a few more seconds on the other side, and then chuck it in the trash.

Do not be disillusioned by this. One of the most effective ways to "season" a pancake pan so that all the following pancakes will perform obediently is to ruthlessly sacrifice the first one. It has both absorbed that first film of oil and, as it were, also primed the surface. You may now continue to make pancakes in the same way as described for the first one. No further lubrication of the pan will be needed as the batter recipe already includes melted butter. Once each pancake has been cooked on both sides, simply tip it out onto an awaiting plate. Stop making pancakes when the batter runs out and the plate is piled high.

Finally, there is no need whatsoever to interleave small sheets of wax paper between pancakes to, supposedly, prevent them sticking together; one simply peels one away from the other to separate them. Those who wish to make pancakes simply to freeze them for another day, so saving them the trouble of making them on *another* day (the terminally bewildered, in other words) often suggest this packaging aid just in case. The "just in case" cook, I guess, is the one that packaged frozen pancakes were solely intended for.

CHICKEN AND SPINACH PANCAKES

I think I am right in saying that this particular recipe originated – well, at least it did to me – at the Box Tree Restaurant in Ilkley, Yorkshire. Its supremely gifted amateur chef–proprietors, Malcolm Reid and Colin Long, were pioneers of innovative cooking in this country way before the likes of . . . well, just about anyone in the last ten years, to be brutally frank.

I firmly believe that the secret of their success lay in the simple fact that they truly adored eating superb food and, with this in mind, they decided that they would also like to learn to cook it, serve it, and then charge unsuspecting Yorkshire folk a great deal of money to come and eat it.

So they simply opened a restaurant. In Ilkley. In 1962. I mean, for two gentlemen from Leeds who, until then, had been salesmen in the rag trade this must surely have been looked upon as a venture into lunacy, to say the very least. Yet their only training as potential professional restaurateurs had simply come from observing their betters: all their spare time and money were spent on eating in the finest restaurants in France. Marco Pierre White spent time at the Box Tree as an apprentice yet has always (allegedly) professed that he has never set foot in that country. He didn't copy that idea, then.

Serves 6

For the pancake batter

¾ cup all–purpose flour
a pinch of salt
1egg
1 egg yolk
1 cup milk
4 tbsp butter, melted

For the pancake filling

4 tbsp butter
1 large onion, peeled and chopped
2 cloves garlic, peeled and chopped
9 oz skinless chicken breast, cut into large chunks
9 oz spinach, trimmed of stalks, washed, and thoroughly dried
2 tbsp cream cheese
salt and pepper
¼ tsp freshly grated nutmeg

For the béchamel sauce

¾ cup milk
2 cloves
1 small onion, peeled and finely chopped
1 bay leaf
salt and pepper
3 tbsp butter
2 tbsp all-purpose flour
5 tbsp heavy cream
3 tbsp freshly grated Parmesan

First make the pancake batter. Simply put all the ingredients in a blender and blend well. Pour through a sieve into a pitcher and allow to stand for at least half an hour. Take a 6-in. frying pan, add a smear of butter, and allow to become hot. Pour in just enough batter to cover the base of the pan. Once it is pale brown on the edges, flip over with a palette knife and cook for a few more seconds. Tip out onto a sheet of wax paper or a dish towel. *Note:* The first pancake is often a bit of a mess; if so chuck it out and then start afresh.

You should not need to use too much extra butter in the pan as you cook the pancakes, just a trace now and again as the pan becomes dry. (The melted butter in the mix usually adds sufficient lubrication.) The yield should give you slightly more than 12 pancakes, to allow for a few messy ones. Keep on one side while you make the pancake filling.

Melt the butter in a deep, large frying pan and fry the onion and garlic together until softened and just starting to turn pale golden. Add the chicken and turn around in the pan until just starting to stiffen. Add the spinach and allow to wilt down, stirring all the time. Turn up the heat to drive off some of the moisture, but not all; it should remain a bit wet.

Tip this mixture into the bowl of a food processor, add the cream cheese, salt, pepper, and nutmeg, and process briefly until homogenized, but do not make it too smooth; otherwise it will become pasty. Tip out onto a plate to cool.

Preheat the oven to 350°F.

To make the sauce, heat together the milk, cloves, onion, bay leaf, and seasoning. Remove from the heat, cover, and leave to infuse for 15 minutes or longer. Now melt the butter in a heavy-based saucepan, and stir in the flour to make a roux. Strain the milk into the roux and whisk thoroughly. Bring to a simmer, gently, over a low heat for a good 10 minutes. Strain again and adjust the seasoning, stir in the cream and 1 tbsp of the Parmesan, and keep warm.

Lightly butter an oval baking dish that will accommodate 12 small rolled-up pancakes. Fill each pancake with a generous tablespoon of the mixture and roll up.

Place in the dish and spoon the sauce carefully over the pancakes. Sprinkle over the remaining Parmesan and bake in the oven for 30 minutes, or until the surface is gilded and burnished in parts.

HARRY'S BAR'S CUSTARD PANCAKES

As one among many moments of uncontrollable greed that have punctuated my life with food, a mid-afternoon snack of these superb pancakes (having already enjoyed a long lunch at Da Fiore and looking forward to dinner at Harry's Dolce) was, to put it mildly, a little excessive even for me. Apart from anything else, I had already enjoyed a serving of them the previous evening. But then, ah, but then, to those who understand quite how seductive is the taste of great food it matters not one jot that a gradual buildup of evening hunger is so jeopardized by teatime pancakes. And there is always the option of the early evening Fernet Branca if problems arise.

Serves 4

For the batter

¾ cup all-purpose flour
a pinch of salt
1 egg
1 egg yolk
finely grated rind of ½ an orange
1 cup milk
4 tbsp butter, melted

For the custard cream

1⅔ cups milk
⅓ cup sugar
2 pieces of pithless lemon zest
3 large egg yolks
2 tbsp all-purpose flour
1 tsp pure vanilla extract

For the pancakes

a little extra sugar
½ cup Cointreau

First make the pancake batter. Simply put all the ingredients in a blender and blend well. Pour through a sieve into a pitcher and allow to stand for at least half an hour. Take a 6-in. frying pan, melt a small amount of butter in the pan, and allow to become hot and sizzling. Pour in enough batter to just cover the base of the pan. The first pancake is often a bit of a mess; if so chuck it out and then start afresh. This is good for "seasoning" the pan anyway.

You should not need to use too much extra butter in the pan as you cook the pancakes, just a trace now and again as the pan becomes dry. (The melted butter in the mix usually adds sufficient lubrication.) Try and make the pancakes as thin as you dare, flipping them over in the usual way with a spatula, and then lay out on a dry dish towel as each one is cooked. The yield should be about 12 pancakes. Wrap in foil while you make the custard cream.

Put the milk, 2 tbsp of the sugar, and the lemon zest into a heavy-bottomed saucepan and bring to a boil. Remove from the heat and leave to infuse for several minutes. Discard the lemon zest. In a bowl, whisk the egg yolks with the remaining sugar. Whisk in the flour a little at a time until the mixture is smooth. Continuing to whisk, incorporate the milk in a steady stream until well blended. Pour back into the pan and cook very gently, stirring constantly with a wooden spoon, over a low heat, until the mixture is very thick and there is the occasional boiling blip. Allow to "cook out" for a few more minutes, still stirring and, if possible, using one of those heat-diffuser pads. Stir in the vanilla. Allow to cool before filling the pancakes.

Preheat the oven to 450°F.

A rounded tablespoon of the custard is spooned onto the middle of the open pancake (have the better-looking side of the pancake underneath, so that it shows at its best when arranged in the baking dish); the pancake is folded over in half and then, with more care, folded over once more into the shape of an open fan, or, prosaically, a quarter circle. These are then laid in the lightly buttered oval dish, delicately sprinkled with sugar, and popped into the oven for about 5–10 minutes. The sugar becomes crunchy on the surface, the custard warms through, and the very thinnest edge of the pancake burns a little. This is how they arrive at table in Harry's. But then the finishing touch that makes them really come alive is the dousing in Cointreau. Do this whilst the dish is still hot from the oven and then light with a match. Tilt and swirl the dish so that the alcohol mingles with the butter and sugar and forms a sauce of sorts. The flames will eventually subside. In my opinion, nothing else is necessary to the dish but, unusually for such a perfectly restrained restaurant as this one surely is, the mode at Harry's is to serve the dish with a scoop of – delicious in itself – homemade vanilla ice cream.

YORKSHIRE PUDDING WITH SWEET WHITE SAUCE AND GOLDEN SYRUP

Bizarre as this recipe may sound, if you like very sweet and intense desserts then this is exactly the one for you. As a child I adored it and could never eat it too often. And, you know, think of the French *clafoutis* (oh, so fashionable just now, so much so that I recently witnessed an English chef in his own restaurant in Cannes misguidedly attach this label to a crème brûlée with rhubarb: why do people diminish tradition these days without so much as a second thought?); it is actually no more than a sweet Yorkshire pudding. A batter pudding, in fact – and I cannot think of a more mundane and economical recipe which, once cooked and assembled, offers such paradoxical pleasures.

Serves 6

For the batter

2 eggs

1 cup all-purpose flour

¾ cup milk

5 tbsp cold water (I sometimes use fizzy mineral water, thinking that it may
add more air to the puddings, but I may be talking absolute rubbish here.)

a pinch of salt

For the sweet white sauce

2½ cups whole milk

4 tbsp butter

⅓ cup all-purpose flour

⅔ cup whipping cream

¼ cup sugar

a tiny pinch of salt

For the puddings

a little plain oil or dripping

Serve with

2–3 tbsp warmed Golden Syrup

First make the batter. If you have a method for making Yorkshire puddings that you are already happy with, then use that. Otherwise, I find the easiest way is to put everything into the bowl of a food processor or a blender and switch on. Blend until very smooth and then pass through a sieve into a suitable container. Leave to rest for at least half an hour.

Preheat the oven to 425°F.

Meanwhile, make the sauce. First scald the milk. Melt the butter in another pan and stir in the flour. Allow to cook together, without coloring, for about 2–3 minutes, stirring constantly. Slowly add the milk, whisking or stirring in, until smooth and glossy. Stir in the cream, sugar, and salt. Leave to simmer and blip, controlling the heat with a heat-diffuser pad if you have one, for 7–10 minutes, so that the sauce mellows and the flour cooks through. Keep warm, covered, until the puddings are cooked.

Take your favorite 6 large pudding dishes or a pan with 12 smaller molds in it (cupcake pan), and add 1 tsp of oil or the equivalent amount of dripping to each one. Place on the top shelf of the oven to heat until smoking. Remove, and then pour in the batter to fill to about three-quarters up the dishes or molds. Immediately put back onto the top shelf of the oven and bake for 25 minutes, or until golden brown and well puffed up. Serve without delay, swamped with sauce and trickled with a little syrup – not too much, or the thing becomes intolerably sweet.

PEARS

One of the most astute observations on the contrary pear was noted exactly by the great Eddie Izzard during one of his wonderful shows. Izzard's gripe and frustration are well grounded. You buy a couple of pounds of slightly under-ripe, clean, and unblemished pears, with the innocent intention of allowing them to ripen up over a few days at home. "Hmmm, yes, I will arrange them in *that* bowl I think, put them on the sideboard, and enjoy them with some Roquefort on Friday when Michael and Gloria are coming for supper." Then, as if by magic, that very afternoon they will suddenly decide to blotch and bloat, their insides turning to a fluffy mass of woolly flesh, bereft of both taste and texture.

In fact, so frustrating is the fresh pear that when wishing to use some to fashion a hot pear dessert, such as the one that follows, I will often find myself reaching for a can of Del Monte. ("This cook he need a perfect pudding? He say yeah!") But then – and I know I am not alone here – I have always enjoyed a can of fruit, so long as it has been stored in the fridge for a few hours to become really cold. Similarly, it perfect partner, a welter of Carnation Milk, should also be well chilled for maximum enjoyment.

If you want to cook pears from raw, then buy them rock-hard – which, I am convinced, is what the canny canners do anyway. An impenetrable pear will *always* perform, just so long as it is cooked in a balm of sweet and fragrant syrup, preferably perfumed with a nice black bean of vanilla, a bay leaf perhaps, and – though certainly not for me – a curly brown scroll of cinnamon bark.

The first person to cook me some pears in this fashion was Mr. J. Gordon Macintyre, who owns a most individual hotel in Nairn, in the Scottish Highlands. H has been proprietor, chef, actor/manager of his own in-house theatrical productions, and general all-round *bon viveur* for well over thirty years now, continuing in a tradition inherited from his father before him. I remember these delicious pears arriving at the table in a deep earthenware pot, still lightly steaming from their poach and with the scent of sweet vanilla pervading the dining room along with a final heady boost of a slug of *eau de vie de poires Williams* that had been poured in at the last minute.

POACHED PEARS WITH VANILLA AND EAU DE VIE

You may, if you wish, choose to serve these whole. However, I prefer to do away with the aesthetics of the thing and cut them in half, making quite sure that no trace of pips or fibers remains. The best and neatest way to core pears is to use a small melon-baller. Serve the pears warm, rather than hot or cold.

You will need a large bowl (preferably metal) that has been put in the freezer for 30 minutes.

Serves 4

6 firm William pears
pared rind and juice of 1 small lemon
5 tbsp golden granulated sugar
1 vanilla pod, split lengthways
1 large glass of sweet white wine (a Muscat would be good)
1¼ cups water
4–5 tbsp *eau de vie de poires Williams*

For the crème Chantilly

⅔ cup whipping cream, very well chilled
⅔ cup double cream, very well chilled
3 tbsp confectioners' sugar
vanilla seeds scraped from a split ¼ of a fresh vanilla pod

Peel the pears and cut them in half lengthways. Place in a bowl and sprinkle over the lemon juice, turning them over and around with your hands. Scoop the core out with the melon-baller, forming a neat hemisphere. Remove any fibers with a small knife. In a roomy stainless-steel or enameled pan mix together the lemon rind, sugar, vanilla pod, wine, and water. Bring to a simmer and cook gently for 5 minutes. Slip in the pears and poach for around 15–20 minutes or until *just* tender when pierced with a knife; they should also look a little transparent. Add the *eau de vie*. Put a lid on and leave to cool to lukewarm, by which time the pears will be fully cooked.

Meanwhile, make the crème Chantilly. It is important that all is cold for this most lovely of whipped creams; this allows for any chance of the cream separating whilst being beaten. Put everything in the bowl and hand-whisk the cream using fluid motions until loosely thick, but on no account very thick. This does not take as long as you think it might. And it is a special further pleasure to see the difference between hand-whisked and electrically aided beaten cream.

PEAR AND GINGER CAKE

I have slightly adapted this recipe from Jane Grigson's Springfield Pear Cake in her wonderful *Fruit Book* (first published by Michael Joseph, 1982). It is yummo-scrummo beyond belief. I have made it a touch more gingery by adding some powdered ginger to the mix and also think that the ginger-wine flavored cream works very well here too.

Serves 4–5

For the top

6 tbsp slightly salted butter

5 tbsp granulated sugar

2 tbsp syrup from a jar of preserved ginger

3 or 4 large firm pears

juice of 1 lemon

For the cake

½ cup plus 1 tbsp softened butter

5 tbsp sugar

¾ cup self-rising flour

1 tsp baking powder

1 tsp ground ginger

2 tbsp ground almonds

2 large eggs

3–4 tbsp syrup, once more, from the preserved ginger jar

4 knobs preserved ginger, coarsely chopped

Serve with

heavy cream

sugar

Ginger Wine

Take a nonstick cake pan (9–10 in x 1¾ in), set it over a low heat, and put in the butter. Once it starts to melt, start to move it around the pan, brushing some of it up the sides. Add sugar and the ginger syrup and heat until amalgamated, toffeelike and bubbling slightly. Remove from the heat. Peel, core, and thinly slice the pears, turning them in the lemon juice so they do not discolor. Arrange them in a sunflower effect on the toffee base. Preheat the oven to 375°F.

Tip all the cake ingredients – except for the chopped ginger – into a food processor and whizz to smoothness. Tip into a bowl and now stir in the chopped ginger. Pour it over the pears and smooth over the surface. Bake in the oven for 45 minutes, then turn the heat down to 350°F. Keep a watch on the surface, as it can start to brown quickly towards the end of the cooking time; if so, cover with a sheet of foil. The cake is cooked when the edges have started to shrink away from the sides of the pan. Test with a skewer, which should come out clean.

Remove from the oven and leave to cool in the pan for about 10 minutes. Run a knife around the edge of the cake, place a large plate on top, and – watching out for hot juices – invert the cake. Serve warm, in thick wedges, with lightly sweetened heavy cream that has had a little Ginger Wine beaten into it.

PICKLED PEARS

We prepare endives in this fashion at Bibendum. Their first outing accompanied slices of cold salt duck (the idea and full recipe originally given to me by Gay Bilson, one of Australia's most original and important restaurateurs; truly a gifted and inspired woman, though now retired from the culinary scene), but the preparation also works well with pears. They are excellent served alongside cold cuts, particularly with cured bits of pig in all its myriad forms.

To fill a 1 quart Ball jar

4 large, under-ripe pears
juice of ½ a lemon
1 cup tarragon vinegar
½ cup sugar
1 star anise
1 small knob of fresh ginger (unpeeled),
thinly sliced
4 cloves

Peel and halve the pears lengthways, then core and thickly slice them and put into a bowl. Squeeze over the lemon juice and mix together with your hands. Reserve.

In a stainless-steel or enameled pan, mix together all the other ingredients. Bring to a boil, reduce the heat, cover, and simmer gently for 30 minutes. Allow to cool for 10 minutes and then pour it over the pears, including all bits and pieces. Stir together with a spoon and leave to cool. Carefully spoon everything into a Ball jar or similar, seal, and leave to macerate for 1 week before using. Best kept in a cool place or, to be safe, in the fridge, where the pears will survive for at least a month.

PEAS

My friend Lindsey Bareham likes frozen peas so much that she finds it difficult not to recommend them in the recipes she writes in her popular London *Evening Standard* cooking column, five days a week. I tease her mercilessly over this, but at the same time I fully understand her devotion to them. I love frozen peas too, and if the truth be told, doesn't everyone? I am also rather partial to canned peas, but somehow these only ever taste quite right when French-canned.

I have a particularly vivid memory of eating several slices of stuffed goose neck with peas in a restaurant somewhere in the Dordogne. Having argued with my parents over cheese as to whether my peas had been *"en boîte"* or *"frais"* (it was *boîte* all the way, as far as I was concerned), it was down to Dad to ask the waiter as to their provenance. It only took one discreet, sage nod from the waiter to know that I had been proved correct. Pubescently precocious, you might think, but at least I was keen to know. And if you want the best canned peas, look for those that have not only been canned in France, but are also labeled *"petits pois à l'étuvée."* These are the very best.

When you come to think about it – and most people rarely do – a more perfectly frozen vegetable than the pea you could never wish for. Of course, there are some bewildered folk who also buy frozen sprouts, carrots, and even cauliflower – and possibly a packet of six frozen ready-risen "Aunt Bessie's Yorkshire Puddings" too, to cap it all.

Well, I also ponder that these are the very same people who will similarly roast a leg of defrosted New Zealand lamb in early June, at precisely the moment when a joint of home-grown lamb is at its very finest. Yet, curiously, both the frozen pea and the canned pea somehow manage to dodge each and every prejudice, judgment, or ridicule thrown at them. It may be very small, very green, and rather sweet, but the power of the pea should not be taken with a pinch of salt. Well . . . maybe just a little.

Unless you grow peas in your very own garden and pick, pod, and cook them for supper within minutes, you will rarely enjoy the treat that is supposed to be the fresh pea. Although seduced on many occasions by early arrivals of fresh peas into my local grocery store, my initial elation has often been very short-lived: once they are cooked, my seemingly lovely panful of peas is now only fit for pureeing into soup. For it is no myth that when a pea is picked its inherent sugar begins to convert to starch right away.

But what is it that makes the frozen pea so impressively sweet? I mean, is this how a homegrown garden pea would *really* taste if we were able to emulate the dawn-treading harvest of the leviathan that is the Birds Eye pea harvester? Whatever the reasoning behind the gigantic success of frozen peas and why they possibly remain the most popular vegetable in the land, it is as a couple of buttered spoonfuls alongside a serving of roast duck, lamb cutlets, or even a Fray Bentos steak and kidney pie that their intense sweetness is most appreciated. Now if you think I'm about to instruct you how to heat up a Fray Bentos pie, you need your bumps feeling.

ALMOST INSTANT "PEA AND HAM" SOUP

Although it may, on the surface, seem that there is no particular skill required in its making, this soup remains one of the nicest I have made and, further, eaten. Is that *just* about enough to assuage the guilt of reaching for the can opener?

Serves 4

1 large onion, peeled and chopped
6 tbsp butter
2 Bibb lettuces, shredded
2 cans of top-quality French peas
(look for the legend "*à l'étuvée*" on the label), average size 10–12 oz
3 cups chicken or ham stock
salt and pepper
several mint and tarragon leaves
⅔ cup whipping cream
5–6 very thin strips bacon, gently cooked until crisp and brittle

Gently stew the onion in the butter until softened. Add the lettuce and stir in. Tip in the peas, juice and all, and then add the stock. Bring up to a boil and skim off any resultant surface scum with a ladle. Season lightly and simmer for 20 minutes. Puree with the mint and tarragon in a blender until very smooth indeed (a food processor is an alternative option, but the consistency will not be quite so velvety) and then pass through a sieve. Reheat and then stir in the cream. Finally, adjust the seasoning, pour into heated soup bowls, and break up bits of bacon over the surface of each serving.

CHILLED PEA, PEAR, AND CUCUMBER SOUP

An unusual combination but one that works beautifully; once you have tasted the first cool, smooth spoonful you will see what I mean. The idea was originally inspired by a soup that John Tovey used to make, with watercress in place of the cucumber. Equally nice, but I feel the cucumber helps to further transform it into a chilled soup that has summer sprinkled all over it. The addition of mint also adds to the effect.

Serves 4

4 tbsp butter
2 medium white onions, peeled and chopped
1 small cucumber, peeled and chopped
7 oz frozen peas

3 cups light chicken stock
(if you want a totally vegetarian version, use
vegetable bouillon)
salt and pepper
2 ripe pears, peeled, cored, and diced
⅔ cup whipping cream
1 tbsp chopped mint (apple mint is particularly good here)

Serve with

pears, peeled, cored, and diced (optional)

Melt the butter in a roomy pan and add the onion. Allow to stew quietly for 5 minutes or so and then add the cucumber. Stir in and cook both until limp and tender. Tip in the peas and stock and bring to a boil. Skim off any resultant scum that forms on the surface, season, and simmer for 20 minutes.

Puree with the pears in a blender and then pass through a sieve into a bowl. Allow to cool to room temperature and then stir in the cream. Adjust the seasoning once more if necessary and place in the fridge, covered, until really cold; there is nothing worse than a tepid cold soup. Ladle into chilled soup bowls and sprinkle with mint. *Note:* You may further wish to garnish the soup with a small dice of fresh, ripe pear, simply for a contrast of textures.

SPICED LAMB MEATBALLS WITH PEAS

I have always enjoyed eating the keema curry (chopped lamb) that they serve at the Standard Indian restaurant in Westbourne Grove in Bayswater, west London. They also do it with peas. For me, this almost makes it a keema deluxe, if you know what I mean and with tongue very firmly in cheek. I have always loved the Standard and have been eating there on and off for more than twenty years. Nothing much has changed there in all that time, which is, as far as I am concerned, as veritable as boons can possibly get. In this recipe the ground lamb has been compressed into koftas: Indian for meatballs. Very deluxe indeed.

Serves 4

4 small onions, peeled and finely chopped
4 cloves garlic, peeled and finely chopped
4 tbsp vegetable oil
1⅔ lb ground lamb shoulder

2 tbsp coriander seeds
and 1 tbsp cumin seeds, dry roasted together in a frying pan
until fragrant, then ground with a pestle and mortar or coffee grinder
2 tsp ground turmeric
1 tbsp garam masala
½ tsp chilli powder
1 tsp freshly ground black pepper
1 tsp salt
1 tbsp chopped fresh mint
1 egg, beaten
flour
4 tbsp butter
½ stick cinnamon
4 cloves
4 ripe tomatoes, peeled and chopped
12 oz frozen peas
⅔ cup plain yogurt
juice of 1 lemon or lime
a dozen or so mint leaves, coarsely chopped

Serve with

plain boiled rice or boiled potatoes

Fry the onions and garlic in the oil until golden brown. Cool on a plate. Mix into the ground lamb together with the spices, salt, mint, and egg. Form into balls the size of a walnut, roll in flour, and fry in the butter in a roomy, shallow pan until golden brown all over. Put in the cinnamon and cloves and fry for a minute or so together with the meatballs. Now tip in the tomatoes and peas, allow them to collapse somewhat and exude their juices, and stir in the yogurt. Cook the meatballs for a further 20 minutes. Finally, add the lemon or lime juice, mint, and a little more salt if necessary. Serve right away with some plain boiled rice, boiled potatoes, or if you prefer, nothing at all.

PEPPER

I first learned about the magical properties of pepper when I was first taught to make the classic (French, that is) *steak au poivre*. I guess I must have been all of sixteen and a half years old at the time and was working during the school holidays in my very first professional post as assistant chef to the Champeau family at their restaurant La Normandie, a few miles from my hometown of Bury.

I remain convinced to this day that my time there – which, once I had finally left school, constituted my first year's full-time employment – was the most important grounding a keen young cook could then have wished for, and, thinking back for a moment, maybe not that much different to the discipline instilled in me while away at school. But then, for me, making mayonnaise was a damn sight more fulfilling than that tedious round of rugger, chemistry, history, and hazing; well, the latter was occasionally quite interesting . . .

The smells that constituted the preparation of the Normandie kitchen's *steak au poivre* will forever be impregnated within my sensory memories. It started, naturally, with the grinding of the pepper itself. This was usually assigned to me. Now, although this might have seemed a tedious and boring task to many of the more experienced chaps in the kitchen, it was a revelation to me; indeed, everything was revelatory to me then. Even the way in which the washing-up was done was fascinating.

But firstly, I was told, it was essential that the peppercorns should be an equal quantity of both black and white: "Aroma from the white with the fire of the black is what gives the steak a perfect heat," confided Chef Jean-Pierre. I measure this *petit truc* of early learning as one of the most significant lessons in the art of seasoning food. Almost more important still, however, was the sieving of the pepper once coarsely ground.

We used a funny old wooden coffee grinder to do the job, hand-cranked and with a little drawer underneath to collect the grains. The grinder needed to be set to its coarsest aperture so that the corns would emerge in minuscule chunks, but there was always plenty of dusty excess that accompanied these. To have included this fine powder on the surface of the steak would have been the ruin of it and, consequently, M. Champeau's reputation. Which is why his particular *steak au poivre* remains quite perfect and proper, rendering all other sad renditions, even to this very day, as poor imitations.

So, one must always be quite careful with pepper. Along with everyone else I often find myself drifting when I include seasoning in a recipe; you know, "salt and pepper," as if pepper is just something that accompanies salt. I recall the crazy Ainsley Harriott barbecuing something on the TV a couple of years ago that included a seasoning of chilli, cumin, lime juice, fish sauce, coriander, and olive oil (actually, pretty well every single dish in that barbecue series used these ingredients); but even then, there was the inevitable "salt and pepper" added from a great height, sprinkled and ground into the simmering brew below. My point is that having the (salty) fish sauce, the (hot) chilli, and the (aromatic) cumin in there, surely the inevitable salt and pepper becomes a touch redundant?

Sadly "S & P" has simply become a habit rather than a thoughtful addition, and added only because . . . well, because one always does.

HAKE CUTLET AU POIVRE

Make sure to check the freshness of the hake before you even consider doing this dish. Although its flesh is naturally softer than most, it should still have a definite resilience when prodded. The skin should also shine, and its body look sleek and smell fresh and sea-sweet. Hake somewhat resembles cod. Choose 4 cutlets from a large fish for the best results here and make sure that you request of your fish store that they scale and trim the fish before cutting the cutlets. In fact, it might be well worth buying the whole fish and keeping the tail portion for another dish and have it filleted there and then. Assuming the fish is as fresh as can be, these fillets will keep in the fridge, well wrapped up, for 2–3 days.

Serves 4

2 tbsp coarsely crushed black and white peppercorns, sieved to remove excess powder

4 large hake cutlets

salt

a little flour

2 tbsp light olive oil

4 tbsp butter

2 tbsp cognac

4 tbsp strong chicken or veal stock

1 tbsp parsley

Serve with

wedges of lemon

watercress

plainly boiled new potatoes

Get a heavy-bottomed frying pan good and hot. Sprinkle the pepper over 1 surface only of the cutlets and press in well. Season with salt and dip carefully into the flour on both sides. Add the oil to the pan and allow to become hazy. Gently lower each cutlet into the oil, pepper-side down, and leave to become crusty – about 4–5 minutes; you may need to turn the heat down slightly during this time, but do not move the fish too early as it may stick.

Now turn the fish over with a spatula or tongs and cook for a further 5–7 minutes. Once turned, add the butter and allow to froth. Turn the heat down and baste the fish with this buttery lotion as it finishes cooking. Check to see if the cutlets are cooked through by wiggling the central bone with your finger: it should start to come away from the flesh quite easily. Remove the hake and put on a warmed serving dish.

Turn the heat up once more under the pan and, when frothing, pour in the cogna and set alight with a match. Once the flames have subsided, add the stock and stir together. Bring up to a boil and reduce slightly, whisking together until syrupy; you may need to add a further sliver of butter here. Add the chopped parsley, swirl in, and pour over the hake. Serve with the lemon wedges and sprightly clumps of watercress. Good with plainly boiled new potatoes.

SALSA PEVERADA

I first came upon this unique sauce while cooking in the kitchens of Bibendum. Looking to do something a little different than the usual red-currant–sweet game gravy touched by a little orange, which is my favorite with a roast mallard, I came across this unusual Italian number in the pages of one of Marcella Hazan's cookbooks. (I *think* it was the *Second Classic Italian* one.) This is my adaptation (Hazan encourages one to so do with this recipe) from *The Essentials of Classic Italian Cookery* (Macmillan, 1992).

With great respect, we may not quite see this as a "sauce" in the terms that we are familiar with; frankly, it seems almost more akin to a *ragù*, so chunky it is with chopped sausage and chicken livers. Be that as it may, it is nonetheless a splendid and most delicious recipe to know. Also, apparently, the recipe is deeply steeped in Italian cooking history, dating back to medieval times. And, while speaking of *ragù*, I have, most successfully, used it in that very way with some freshly made pappardelle.

Makes enough to accompany 4 main courses

4¼ oz English pork sausages – the very best you can buy: Duchy Originals (the finest), Musks, or your favorite from your local butcher (Hazan insists that "so-called Italian sausages that contain fennel seeds" are too strong here.)

4¼ oz chicken livers, trimmed and roughly chopped

4–5 gherkins, chopped

1 demitasse spoon capers

1 small onion, very finely chopped

5–6 tbsp olive oil

salt

plenty of freshly ground white *and* black pepper

grated rind of 1 lemon

⅔ cup dry white wine

1 demitasse spoon sherry vinegar (wildly non-Italian, I know, but it really works very well here!)

1 tbsp chopped parsley

½ tbsp chopped mint

Skin the sausages and put them in a food processor with the livers, gherkins, and capers. Grind to a smooth and creamy consistency. Fry the onion in the olive oil until golden.

Add the sausage mixture and stir it around well until it has freely broken up into the tiniest browned nuggets. Add salt, plentiful and equal amounts of both peppers, and the lemon rind and stir in. Add the wine, briefly mix in, and set it over the merest thread of heat to quietly stew for a good hour, adding occasional splashes of water if it starts to become too dry. Finally, incorporate the vinegar and herbs.

Spoon over roasted and jointed game birds or, as I suggested, use as a judicious dressing for fresh (or dried) pasta. If choosing the latter route, I feel, for once, the traditional accompaniment of grated Parmesan would be gilding the lily.

QUATRE ÉPICES ("FOUR-SPICE")

It was to Michel Guérard's masterwork *Cuisine Gourmande* (first published in Great Britain by Macmillan, in 1977) that I turned when wishing to attempt to make my very first terrine of fresh foie gras — as, of course, did many of my contemporaries at the time. Ever since then, if I taste a terrine of foie gras made by someone else (other than M. Guérard himself, naturally) that does not contain a pinch of this extremely useful collection of spices, I, firstly, always know that it is not there and, secondly, do not particularly care for it. Also useful in countless other pâtés, terrines, stuffings, and — dare I say it? — the very English pork pie.

Enough for a small potful

3 oz white peppercorns
3 oz black peppercorns
4 tsp freshly ground cloves
1 oz ground ginger
1¼ oz whole nutmeg, broken into pieces
with the back of a heavy knife before grinding

Mill together in an electric coffee grinder until a fine powder. Sieve into a bowl and spoon into a small screw-top jar.

PLAICE

Why is it that a nice fillet of plaice (a European flounder) seldom makes it onto restaurant menus these days? Cod has recently enjoyed a renaissance – and not before time – but the simple, unassuming, well-behaved, and delicious plaice seems to be forever submerged in the deep-frier. "And nowt wrong wi' that," I jocularly admit, having eaten my fair share of battered fillets of plaice in Lancashire during the first twenty-odd years of my life. And the finest plaice and chips I ate were always fried in beef dripping – and I trust that it remains as always.

I have never quite understood why some folk continue to turn their noses up at this perfectly reasonable means by which to fry fish. Surely it is not unusual to add deep flavor to the batter surrounding a piece of fish with something such as melted beef suet? I mean, many southerners who regularly frequent Chinese restaurants in the capital and surrounding commuter-belt towns must be well aware that meat flavors and fish have always been eminently compatible. For example, a hot pot of crisp belly pork (yet another famous Lancastrian tradition – with tongue very much in cheek . . .) cooked together with either oysters or eel at Poon's Restaurant just off London's Leicester Square neatly trashes this prejudice against juxtaposition. Health reasons are hardly a serious issue here, especially as everyone seems to be obsessed with cooking all sorts of things in endless quantities of duck and goose fat just now; even a neatly trimmed fillet of salmon *en confit,* having been gently "seized" in a trembling bath of duck or goose fat, is all the rage. (Succulent as some may find this method of preparation, I find the process and result over-rich in the extreme. Give me the batter-encrusted bit of cod in beef fat anytime.)

Anyway, to return to the fish itself. I hazard a guess that most of you are really only familiar with portion-size fillets of plaice, all neatly tucked together and displayed upon the fish store's slab or chilled supermarket facility. Yet, at the height of the British flounder season — which seems to be around midsummer — a whole, super-fresh plaice can regularly tip the scales at around about the 4½ lb mark; a weightier flat fish with real flavor at an affordable price I cannot think of.

When you feel, fondle, and squeeze a fish this good, it surely beckons to be bought forthwith — even though your initial intended purchase might well have been three mackerel, a pint of frozen shrimp, or a couple of tired tuna steaks. Once trimmed of fin, beheaded, and cleaned, a whole plaice such as this can be baked with ease and also with much success.

Buttered liberally, moistened with a little lemon juice (the addition of white wine or vermouth that is the usual enhancer of, say, turbot and brill I find is lost on the singularly odoriferous plaice), boldly seasoned, and finally secured by foil, it is simply the heat of a hot oven that is necessary to cook a whole plaice to perfection. By virtue of its naturally intrinsic moisture (plaice is the "wettest" fish of all), plaice can literally stew in its own juice.

It goes without saying that a firm or magisterial turbot affords one the occasional — albeit pricey — treat, but our fine spanking-fresh plaice should not be looked upon as a common companion to its aristocratic cousins. And although this orange-spotted fellow may often be looked upon as ranking lower in the piscatorial roll of honor than is necessarily good for it, those who are able to recognize a good fish without it slapping them in the face can feel fully confident that "Somewhere . . . there's a plaice, for us . . ."

FILLET OF PLAICE WITH HERB CRUST

I first cooked fillets of fish baked with a herb crust in Pembrokeshire, in the summer of 1974. The fish I used at the time was sea bass, scaled and filleted about a half hour after it had arrived in the kitchens of Druidstone Hotel, where I was then working as a young chef. The filleting bit always had to wait awhile, it being difficult to fillet a sea bass that is still moving about.

The dish resurfaced many years later on the menu of the Hilaire Restaurant, in London's South Kensington, where I also resurfaced in 1983. I now think that fat fillets of plaice are an even better vehicle than those lively sea bass. The particular "wetness" (see page 194) that is so characteristic of plaice carries and complements this crust in possibly the most successful fashion of all.

Serves 4

For the herb crust

2 cups fresh bread crumbs
2 tbsp chopped flat-leaf parsley
½ tbsp chopped tarragon leaves
½ tbsp chopped chives
½ tbsp chopped dill
grated rind of 1 small lemon
salt and pepper

For the plaice

7 tbsp butter
1 large clove garlic, bruised
1 tbsp Pernod
(optional, but Pernod adds a warmth of aniseed
flavor to the fish, making it taste ever so nice)
4 fillets of plaice, skinned and trimmed
salt and pepper
flour
beaten egg

Serve with

lemon juice
mashed potatoes

First make the herb crust. Put the bread crumbs in a food processor, then add all the herbs, lemon rind, and a little seasoning. Process cautiously, as the moisture in the herbs has a tendency to suddenly turn the fresh bread crumbs pasty. Once the crumbs have become lightly tinged with green, tip out onto a tray to dry out a little. *Note:* You will not use all the mixture. Secure the remainder tightly in a plastic bag and freeze for another occasion, as it is impractical to make a smaller amount.

Preheat the oven to 425°F.

Melt the butter in a small pan, and add the garlic, and Pernod if using. Allow to bubble together for a couple of minutes, remove, and discard the garlic and set the butter aside. Season one surface of each of the plaice fillets, dip them in the flour, the egg, and finally into the bread crumbs, making sure that the crust is evenly dispersed. Lay out in a lightly buttered oven dish, and spoon over the flavored butter. Bake for 20–25 minutes, or until the crust is spotted with brown bits. Eat with a squeeze of lemon and some mashed potatoes.

GOUJONS OF PLAICE WITH CILANTRO DIPPING SAUCE

And here, if you don't mind, is yet another crumbed dish. Have you ever come across those wonderful Japanese dry bread crumbs in gaily colored cellophane packets? Fry Star I think they are called, and an absolutely first-class ingredient to aid the success of a fine and crisp crumb coating to anything you might wish to deep-fry. They are also known as "panko."

Although clearly a great deal more costly than grinding up bits of leftover bread in the usual manner, the reward fully outweighs the added expense. I think the secret lies in the simple fact that the "crumbs" are manufactured from raw dough into the minutest extrusions and then baked into trillions of tiny shards. Search them out in your nearest Oriental supermarket. (*Note:* These crumbs are not suitable for use in the previous recipe.)

Serves 2, as a first course

For the dipping sauce

the leaves from a small bunch of cilantro and, if possible, its roots
12–15 mint leaves
2 cloves garlic, peeled and crushed
3 small green chillies, seeded and chopped
2 tsp sugar
juice of 3 limes
5 tbsp Thai fish sauce *(nam pla)*
5 tbsp water

For the plaice

2 large fillets of plaice, skinned and trimmed
salt and pepper
flour
beaten egg
panko or homemade bread crumbs
lemon

To make the dipping sauce, work all the ingredients together in a food processor until well mixed but not a puree.

Season the strips of plaice, dip in flour, then in the egg, and finally evenly coat with bread crumbs. Deep-fry in hot oil (350–375°F.) for 3–4 minutes, drain on paper towel, and lightly salt once more. Serve on individual plates laid with a paper napkin and decant the sauce into small dishes, for dipping.

BAKED WHOLE PLAICE WITH LEMON BUTTER SAUCE

Having any fish cooked on the bone is always preferable to having it off. I'm sorry, I'll write that again: fish is always best cooked on the bone.

Serves 2

2 large whole plaice, trimmed of head, tail, and frilly edges
oil
salt and pepper

For the lemon butter

juice from 1 large lemon
2 tbsp water
½ cup plus 1 tsp butter, cut into small chunks

Preheat the oven to 450°F.

Oil both sides of the fish and liberally season the orange-blotched dark side. Place in a buttered oven pan and bake on the top shelf for 10–15 minutes, or until just firm to the touch. Remove from the oven, lift off the crisped dark skin with a small knife, and serve up on 2 warmed plates. Pass the sauce separately.

To make the sauce, place the lemon juice and water in a small pan and heat gently until slightly syrupy and reduced by about two-thirds. Lower the heat to a mere thread and whisk in the butter, bit by bit, until thoroughly amalgamated and the texture has turned creamy. Season, adding a final squeeze of lemon juice, and serve warm.

QUAIL

These dear little birds seem to have a raw deal in gastronomic circles. I can't think why, for when carefully prepared a brace of quails can be quite delicious and most worthwhile. It goes without saying that it is important that the quails should be of fine pedigree rather than scrawny creatures intensively reared in a big shed somewhere near Sheffield. For, I am ashamed to say, we have never, in Britain, quite managed to match the French in rearing fat and succulent quails.

There is, however, a revolution well under way here just now, with small pockets of poultry-breeding excellence popping up in almost every county in the land. But, without wishing to pour cold water over such enterprise, it can only have been the growing influx of Continental poultry over the last ten years or so that has prompted such admirable innovation. Once something such as the renowned *poulet de Bresse* or even the everyday (in France, that is) *poulet des Landes*, with its distinctive black legs, had been tasted, it was clear that something had to be done. All power to those plucky people who took stock, possessed a modicum of taste, and simply cared about such things.

Although immense pleasure can be gained by roasting such diminutive seasonal birds as grouse, partridge, pheasant, and snipe, this enjoyment is a brief and costly one for most of us. Granted, the depth of flavor of a quail is nothing compared to that of a musky pheasant, but at least there is something in the former that causes one to think that this is as near to a game bird as one is likely to get – on a regular basis, at least. And to be frank, I would rather eat a good French-reared quail than a British pheasant these days; the former is often left to hang and mature for longer than the latter, having a great deal more succulence, to boot.

The very first dish of quails I learned to cook was a French one: *cailles sur canapés*. My, was it a rich recipe! Two small squares of white bread were first spread with a rich liver paste that included foie gras, then fried in butter on their underside until crisp and set aside. The seasoned birds were then set upon a bed of sliced mushrooms (common or garden button jobs rather than unnecessarily exotic wild ones; although some fresh ceps would be wonderful here, come to think of it, but you get my drift), smeared with butter, and left to roast until both components became as a well-browned one.

Once cooked, a slug of cognac was poured over them, set alight, and allowed to mingle with the buttery juices from both quail and mushrooms. This simplest of preparations produced all the lubrication that was necessary, negating the fabrication of a sauce, as such, in an instant. Each quail was then perched atop its crouton with the wet and wonderful mushrooms spooned around. A sprightly bunch of watercress completed the assembly as a singular garnish. Anything more would have been superfluous. For once, a true meal in itself. Here it is.

ROAST QUAILS WITH MUSHROOMS

I have now purposely named this dish as prosaically as possible. I like doing this. At Bibendum we do a dish called mushrooms on toast, and it costs about £12. This often raises a few eyebrows, but when the guest is informed that the dish involves a slice of toasted brioche with a generous quantity of fresh morels cooked in cream poured over it they raise their chin and go, "Ah, I see." These quails are a bit like that: just a little more than their name implies.

They are ever so good eaten with a refreshing watercress salad mixed with fresh orange segments and then dressed with a little seasoning, a tiny amount of finely chopped shallots, a splash of sherry vinegar (particularly good with the oranges), and some very fine olive oil indeed. I don't think you need anything else here, really.

Serves 2

4–5 tbsp softened butter
¾ cup sliced button mushrooms
4 quails
salt and pepper
lemon juice
2 very thick, square slices of white bread (cut from a perfectly ordinary loaf,
one day old), crusts removed
2 tbsp soft, smooth homemade (or very good store-bought) poultry liver pâté
2 tbsp cognac or Armagnac

Preheat the oven to 425°F.

Butter an oval oven dish. Fill with the mushrooms. Thinly smear the quails all over with butter and season. Place on top of the mushrooms *breast* side down. Squeeze just a little lemon juice over them (they are going to have some more later) and place in the oven. Roast for 10 minutes.

Meanwhile, cut the 2 slices of bread in half and spread thickly with pâté. Remove the quails from the oven, turn them over, and squeeze over a little more lemon juice. Roast for a further 15 minutes, or thereabouts, or until crisp-skinned and golden. Lift them out onto a warm plate. Switch off the oven and leave the door ajar. Place a small colander over a small frying pan and tip in the mushrooms. Leave to drain for 5 minutes. Tip the mushrooms back into the oven dish and put the quails back on top. Put back in the oven with the door remaining ajar.

Gently heat the buttery juices over a medium heat and place the bread croûtes in the pan, bread-side down. Quietly fry them until their bottoms are golden brown, as you might do for breakfast fried bread. Lift out and place on a sheet of paper towel. Put on a plate and keep warm in the oven. At the same time, retrieve the quails and mushrooms from the oven and place directly over a high flame. Once the mushrooms are sizzling well underneath, spoon the cognac or Armagnac over the quails and ignite (stand back!). Switch off the heat.

Once the flames have died down, place 2 croûtes on each of 2 hot plates and place a quail upon each. Spoon the mushrooms alongside.

ROAST QUAILS WITH SAGE AND WHITE WINE

Just a little less simple-sounding than the previous recipe, but, in this case, what you read is what you get. Delicious, all the same.

Serves 2

a little olive oil
4 plump quails
salt and pepper
4 tbsp softened butter, plus a little more if necessary
10–12 sage leaves
1 small glass of white wine
a squeeze of lemon juice

Preheat the oven to 400°F.

Put some olive oil in the palm of one hand and fondle each quail all over with greasy paws. Season liberally; apart from anything else, the oil helps the seasoning to stick. Divide the butter onto the breasts of the quails and put into a solid baking dish that will also sit upon a naked flame. Place in the oven to roast for about 25–30 minutes, basting occasionally; they should emerge golden and crisp-skinned. Lift from the roasting dish, switch off the oven, and put the birds to keep warm in the waning oven heat, with the door left ajar.

Set the buttery juices over a moderate heat and once they begin to froth, add the sage leaves (add more butter here if you think you need to) and fry until lightly crisp and curling. Sprinkle them with a little salt. Lift them out with a slotted spoon and put with the quails. Drain off about two-thirds of the fat, heat once more, and reintroduce the quails to the pan, including all exuded juices and tipping out any that have collected in the quails' cavities (temporarily keep the sage leaves in the oven). Pour in the glass of wine, allowing it to bubble and seethe, quickly spooning it over the quails as it does so. Continuing in this fashion, turn the heat down and reduce the winey juices until they begin to coat the quails. Add a little lemon juice, reintroduce the sage to the dish, and serve all at once.

POT-ROAST QUAILS WITH PANCETTA, MARSALA, AND POTATOES

I once enjoyed eating a version of this while in Sicily and actually in the seaside town of Marsala itself – but let's say that the description "seaside" is pushing it a bit. However, that aside and the fact that the hotel we were staying in was one of the most dire and drab it has ever been my misfortune to experience, I did eat really quite well.

Serves 2

12 small new potatoes
⅔–¾ cup light chicken stock
3 oz Italian pancetta, in the piece
1 tbsp olive oil
salt and pepper
4 quails
1 small onion, peeled and chopped
2 cloves garlic, peeled and chopped
1 tbsp cognac
1 small glass of Marsala
a squeeze of lemon juice

Preheat the oven to 300°F.

Cook the potatoes until almost tender in the chicken stock. Lift out using a slotted spoon, cool, and peel off their skins. Put to one side. Reduce the chicken stock by half. Cut the pancetta into large cubes (about ½ in). Heat the olive oil in a heavy-based, cast-iron lidded pot and fry the pancetta until it turns a good color. Remove to a plate and set aside. Season the quails gently, and turn them through the fat in the pot until golden all over. Put on a plate and set aside. Now add the onion and garlic to the pot and fry gently until lightly colored.

Reintroduce the pancetta and quails, add the cognac and Marsala, and bring to a boil. (Ignite the alcohols if you wish, but it doesn't matter if you don't.) Pour in the reduced stock and add the potatoes, pushing them below the liquid. Squeeze over a little lemon juice. Put the lid on and braise in the oven for 40–50 minutes, by which time the quails will be very tender indeed and the braising liquid dark and intensely savory. Once again, I think the dish is complete as it stands.

RASPBERRIES

A raspberry does not get much better than when lightly frosted with sugar and drowned in very cold cream. I don't think I am that far away from the truth with this gluttonous thought, do you? My good friend and superior wine merchant Mr. Bill Baker, an aficionado of the very best untreated Cornish clotted cream, ventures down another route. His particular passion is to share a half-pint pot of that luxurious, lactic suspension with no more than say a dozen – maybe even a baker's dozen – perfect top-of-the-season berries, each dipped into sugar once then totally hidden by a veritable duvet of said clottings. So is it both the cream *and* the sugar that allows the raspberry to taste so good? Now don't be so daft, of course it is.

As far as I am concerned, any person who chooses, quite freely, to eat a bowl of freshly picked raspberries all on their own (the raspberries, that is, not the person), in close proximity to a fridge with good cream in it and with easy access to an open bag of white sugar and a spoon, is either a vegan, a difficult vegetarian (they know who they are), partaking of a strict diet, very lazy, or just plain silly.

Some years ago now I consumed some of the most delicious raspberries of my life in, of all places, California. And they were eaten with some surprisingly good cream too – which is difficult to find at the best of times anywhere at all in America. No doubt asking someone for a jug of rich, thick cream with your raspberries there today will be met with a similar reaction to the simple request to enjoy a cigarette with a perfectly made Dry Martini, at any public bar in the entire state. Nothing to do with raspberries, I know, just a moment to have a small moan, and also feel sad that I will probably never visit San Francisco again until I give up the weed.

As much as the tenderest fillet steak is at its finest simply fried in best butter, it is also very good when sensitively played around with. So it is with the raspberry. There are soufflés, mousses, meringue fillings, ice creams, sponge cakes, shortcakes, and sauces, all of which are intelligent things to do to the little scarlet berry. The last, that sauce, languished elegantly in Britain under the name *coulis* for the whole of the 1980s before shyly petering out around the middle of the 1990s. And as is the way of such things it was felt that the description had become a cliché and therefore intolerable to the fashionable chef.

Coulis had always seemed such a harmless little French word to me, neatly bridging the gap between *sauce* and *puree*—two words which, at least, in culinary terms, are set in stone. I mean, a *coulis de framboises* is, unquestionably, a more rational description than *jus* Granny Smith, *jus* tarragon, or *jus* clove, of which all three examples are clearly plain batty.

RASPBERRY CLAFOUTIS

Although the name here is certainly correct, this particular version bears no relation to those often rather mundane examples one finds in countless patisseries and simple cafes and bistros all over France. Some might say that this is as it should be and that they are nothing more or less than a relative of our very own batter pudding. And that's just fine. I sort of like these too. Let's just say that this one is in a different league. Not better. Just different. How about swish?

Serves 4

1 vanilla bean, split lengthways
1 cup whipping cream
a tiny pinch of salt
scant 2 tbsp softened butter
9 oz raspberries
1 egg
2 egg yolks
⅓ cup sugar
1 tsp potato flour (*fécule de pommes de terre*)
a little sifted confectioners' sugar
a tiny glass of raspberry eau de vie (optional)

Serve with

lightly sweetened whipped cream

Preheat the oven to 350°F.

Put the vanilla bean into a pan and heat together with the whipping cream and salt. When the cream is just about to come to the boil, switch off the heat, and whisk carefully, just so as to dislodge most of the vanilla seeds from the bean into the cream. Cover and leave to infuse for 30 minutes or so. Remove the bean, wipe dry, and store in granulated sugar for further use.

Take 4 shallow ovenproof dishes – or 1 large one if you like – and smear with the butter. Arrange the raspberries evenly in the dishes, or dish. Beat together the egg and egg yolks, sugar, and potato flour. Incorporate the cream and gently whisk together. Carefully pour over the raspberries so that they are not dislodged. Place the dishes (or dish) in a roasting pan. Fill the pan with water at least halfway up the sides of the dishes and then sift a little confectioners' sugar over their surface. Carefully slide into the oven and bake for 20–25 minutes until slightly puffed, a little wobbly still, and lightly gilded. (If using one large dish, increase the cooking time by 10 minutes or so.)

Switch off the oven and open the door. Leave like this for 5 minutes before removing the clafoutis. Take out of the roasting pan, allow to cool to lukewarm, sprinkle with the eau de vie if using and, if you like, a little more sifted confectioners' sugar. Eat with lightly sweetened whipped cream.

LINZER TORTE

I think I am right in saying that the *Linzer torte* originates in Austria, and, specifically, from the northern port of Linz, which lies on the Danube. I first came across a recipe for this thirty-odd years ago, in one of those old *Cordon Bleu* magazines (one of my most reliable sources for all sorts of forgotten, very good recipes). I always wanted to make it but never did. Until recently, that is. It is truly delicious. The best jam tart you will ever eat.

Serves 4

For the pastry

2 cups all-purpose flour
a pinch of salt
⅔ cup very cold butter, cut into chunks
¾ cup sifted confectioners' sugar
½ tsp ground cinnamon
grated rind of 1 small lemon
⅓ cup sifted ground almonds
1 egg
1 egg yolk

For the raspberry filling

1 pint fresh raspberries
2–3 tbsp granulated sugar
1 jar excellent raspberry jam
a little beaten egg

Serve with clotted or whipped cream

Preheat the oven to 350°F. Place a flat baking sheet in there too.

Place the first 7 ingredients in the bowl of a food processor. Pulse-process until the ingredients resemble coarse bread crumbs. Tip into a roomy bowl. Beat the egg an egg yolk together and add them, by degrees, to the mixture, deftly blending them in with a table knife until the makings of a rich yellow dough begin to come together. Gather up the dough in your hands and briefly knead until compact. Flatten out slightly, place in a plastic bag, and put in the fridge for 30 minutes.

Put the raspberries in a stainless-steel or enameled saucepan and sprinkle over the sugar. (If the raspberries are very sweet, adjust the sugar accordingly.) Put over a very gentle heat to allow the raspberry juices to flow. Once they are doing that freely, turn up the heat and boil fast for 3–4 minutes. Leave to cool in the pan. Melt the jam in a small pan and pass through a sieve into another pan. Keep somewhere warm.

Roll out the pastry to twice the thickness of a silver dollar. Butter a deep tart pan (anything between 8 in and 10 in diameter) and line it with the pastry. Cut off the overhang and crimp the edges; use the discarded overhang for making the traditional lattice pattern that goes over the top. Pour the raspberries into the tart shell. Roll out the spare pastry thinly and cut into 6 strips ½ in wide. Drape across the raspberries in a crisscross fashion and press their ends into the pastry rim. Brush with a little beaten egg. Bake the "torte" in the oven for 30–40 minutes, covering with a sheet of foil if the pastry is browning too quickly. Remove and leave to cool completely, before glazing the surface with copious amounts of the jam so that it almost forms a seal upon the surface. Put somewhere very cool (not the fridge) to set fully. Extremely good eaten with clotted cream for tea.

RASPBERRY DACQUOISE

This is similar to the raspberry and hazelnut meringue cake that I gave you in my book *Gammon and Spinach*. It is a less dense cake than that one – and less nutty-tasting too, which I actually prefer. If you want to make the experience even more luxurious, why not make a fresh raspberry ice cream to serve alongside?

Serves 4

For the meringue cakes

4 large egg whites
a pinch of cream of tartar
a pinch of salt
¾ cup plus 2 tbsp sugar
1 tsp pure almond extract
4 oz ground almonds, sifted

For the raspberry filling

1¼ cups cream
1 tbsp sugar
12 oz raspberries
confectioners' sugar

Butter and flour 2 loose-bottomed cake pans 8 in in diameter and line the base of each with a circle of baking parchment. Preheat the oven to 375°F.

Whisk the egg whites with the cream of tartar and salt until soft-peak stage, then add the sugar 1 tbsp at a time, continuing to whisk until glossy and stiff. Now beat in the almond extract and then fold in the ground almonds. Fill the prepared pans with the meringue mixture and smooth the tops with a metal spoon dipped in hot water. Bake for about 35–40 minutes until the top is pale golden and crisp. Remove and allow to cool for a few minutes before removing from the pans. (They do tend to sink a little, so don't worry.) Turn out onto a cooling rack and remove the parchment while still warm.

Once the cakes are completely cold, whip the cream with the sugar until just holding peaks. Spread onto the surface of one of the cakes and then evenly pile on the raspberries. Carefully press the other cake on top and sift confectioners' sugar over the surface. Leave to settle for at least an hour, as it will then be easier to cut.

RHUBARB

The scent of an early, forced English strawberry may tempt and tease the impatient palate, but the taste in the mouth now seems bereft of any flavor whatsoever and the premature interior texture all woolly and white. Even the (until recently) respected English asparagus grower has now jumped onto the early-produced bandwagon. By unnaturally forcing the terminally shy East Anglian shoot up out of artificially warmed loam into the muted radiance of a plastic tunnel, thereby removing its world-class individual character in the time it takes to pocket a handful of fifty-pound notes (need I say more?), counterfeit asparagus may now be seen stacked upon the pristine shelves of, say, Fortnum and Mason around about mid-April. To me, this seems quite absurd.

Early-forced, bright pink rhubarb, however, is another matter entirely. It knocks every single one of my many prejudices over predetermining the natural harvest of native produce into a cocked hat. Now, why is this so? I mean, it's really rather irritating. It makes me sound such a fool!

The very sight of those long and spindly, slightly limp sticks of bright pink rhubarb that appear towards the end of each and every Lincolnshire January corrodes my integrity in an instant. I blush. I purchase. I crumble. So I go straight home and *make* rhubarb crumble. Compared with main-crop rhubarb, this early, forced stuff is, confusingly, the very best of the season. It's all the wrong way around, dammit!

As the absence of daylight ensures that the Belgian endive (witloof) and Dutch or German asparagus both remain ghostly white as they grow, so the very same blackout procedure gives spooky old rhubarb its pink glow, its early tenderness, and its intense flavor, while also rendering its triffid-like crinkly leaves a sickly yellow. (The leaves, strictly speaking, are the rhubarb "plant"; rhubarb itself is simply its stalk.) And, to further enshroud rhubarb in every manner of mystery and Stygian gloom, those crinkly leaves are reckoned to be hideously poisonous.

Frankly, late-season stalks of rhubarb — fat and stringy monsters, mostly all green and with just a faint remembrance of pink — are not one of my favorite things to cook and eat however much attention is paid to them. Once you have finally made the decision that you are now fed up to the back teeth with making endless bowls of rhubarb fool — which, however carefully you sweeten, stew, puree, and sieve, continues to turn out the color and texture of Brown Windsor soup — you can relax and allow all your plants to go to seed.

This benevolent betrayal, however, can produce some of the most bizarre and striking table decorations you will ever see. I first encountered such an example of this aesthetic whimsy as a centrepiece in the middle of the long kitchen table in Terence Conran's house in Berkshire. He had simply forced three of these coarse, bloated stalks into the one large glass vase, and I surmised that, in a moment of exquisite lifestyle, he had both weeded the garden and decorated the dining table. Eat your heart out, Martha Stewart.

RHUBARB AND ALMOND CRUMBLE WITH CUSTARD

This is a very rich crumble, due to the slightly higher content of butter and also because of the richness of the ground almonds. Having said that, it is also one of the most delicious crumble toppings I know.

Serves 4

For the crumble

¾ cup all-purpose flour
¼ cup sugar
½ cup almonds
1 tsp ground ginger
a pinch of salt
½ cup butter, hard from the fridge and cut into small chunks
1½ lb rhubarb, cut up into 1 in lengths
2 tbsp sugar

For the custard

(This recipe will make more than you need. Oh yeah?)
2 cups plus 2 tbsp milk
1 vanilla bean, split lengthways
6 egg yolks
⅓ cup sugar

Put the flour, sugar, almonds, ginger, and salt into the bowl of an electric mixer or food processor. Gently blend these dry ingredients together and then add the butter. Mix as for starting to make pastry, but do not work the mixture too much; the look should be a touch lumpy rather than the usual finer-textured "bread crumb" look.

Preheat the oven to 350°F.

Spread the rhubarb into a suitable baking dish and sprinkle with the sugar. Pile the crumble mixture over the top, but do not pack down; give the dish a sharp rap on the worktop to settle the surface. Briefly drag a fork over the surface to give texture. Put on the middle shelf of the oven and bake for 30–40 minutes until the surface is golden and slightly blistered brown in parts.

To make the custard, heat the milk together with the vanilla bean in a heavy-bottomed saucepan. Remove from the stove and whisk for a few seconds to release the vanilla seeds into the milk. Briefly beat together the egg yolks and sugar and strain the hot milk over, whisking as you go. Return to the saucepan and cook over a very low heat (with a heat-diffuser pad if possible) until limpid and lightly thickened. Some say it should coat the back of a wooden spoon, but I don't go along with this theory; it should be taken further than this, almost until there is the odd simmering blip on the surface. When you think it is ready, give a final vigorous whisk to amalgamate and pour into a warm pitcher.

Note: If you are unlucky enough to split the custard, a blast in a blender will usually rescue it.

RHUBARB FOOL

The most important thing to remember here is not to add any water to the rhubarb as it should simply stew in its own juice. Orange seems to have a remarkably good affinity with rhubarb – as too does ginger. When stewing any fruit do make sure the lid to your chosen vessel is a tight-fitting one.

I prefer not to make a fool too rich. In fact sometimes I think that custard is the ideal binder with the fruit; or a little custard and some cream. But really, for the simplest and most traditional of fools, just cream is the answer for the subtlest taste and texture. Don't blend it in too much and also be careful *how* you fold it in, for fear of the cream separating and becoming buttery.

Serves 4

1½ lb young pink rhubarb
a 2 in piece of fresh ginger, peeled and thickly sliced
grated rind of 2 oranges
10 tbsp sugar
1¼ cups cream, loosely beaten

Serve with

crisp sugar cookies or shortbread

Preheat the oven to 325°F.

Peel any parts of the rhubarb you think are tough and stringy. Cut up into 1 in lengths. Put into a stovetop-to-oven dish with the ginger and put on a low heat. (This is just to get the dish hot for the oven.) Stir the orange rind into the sugar in a bowl until it is thoroughly mixed together and strew evenly over the rhubarb. Put the lid on and place in the oven for 30–45 minutes. Remove from the oven, take off the lid and allow to cool. Remove the lumps of ginger and allow to cool thoroughly.

Now drain the rhubarb through a sieve over a bowl to collect the beautiful pink juice that has exuded. Put the pulp into a food processor and blend for about 30 seconds – the mixture should not be too smooth. Tip into a bowl and put in the fridge. Take the pink syrup and put onto the heat. Simmer until reduced by about two-thirds and allow to cool. Remove the rhubarb puree from the fridge and carefully fold in the cream, together with three-quarters of the reduced syrup so that it becomes swirly (a bit like raspberry ripple ice cream). Spoon into chilled glass dishes and then float the final quarter of syrup on top. It is appropriate to offer suitable crisp sugar cookies or shortbread with fruit fools. (See "Butter and Dripping" chapter: Arnhem Cookies, page 37.)

SUZANNE BURKE'S RHUBARB PIE

When I taxed my American neighbor Suzanne over the ingredients for her pie, she admitted that apart from the rhubarb from a very small plot in her beautiful garden (so small that all she had grown went into the one pie) she had also added a chopped-up Cox's apple – and a very nice addition it was too. I have not, but only because I felt deeply pure and was also able to purchase plenty of rhubarb from the greengrocer for my pie. I think in retrospect, however, that Suzanne's pie had the edge, as her rude and healthy rhubarb was picked only half an hour before being covered in pastry and baked.

Serves 4

12 oz puff pastry (frozen store-bought is just fine)
a scrap of softened butter
1½ lb rhubarb, diagonally sliced into 1 in lengths
½ cup sugar
1 tsp cornstarch (the American secret and a very successful addition)
a little milk
a little sugar

Serve with

cream

Divide the pastry into pieces one-third and two-thirds size. Roll each piece out thinly, the bigger piece to generously line a loose-bottomed tart pan (8 in × 1½ in), the smaller one to cover the top. Leave both sheets of pastry to rest in the fridge for 20 minutes to allow the dough to relax. Preheat the oven to 400°F. Also, slip a flat baking sheet onto the middle shelf of the oven; this helps the base of the pie to evenly cook through.

Butter the pan with the softened butter and line with pastry, allowing a little to overhang. Fondle together the rhubarb, sugar, and cornstarch in a roomy bowl and then tip into the pastry-lined pan. Do not be alarmed at the huge pile of rhubarb, as it will sink down dramatically as the fruit cooks. Brush the edges of the pastry with milk and then gently stretch the pastry lid over the rhubarb, clamping the pastry edges together with your fingertips. Cut off the overhanging pastry sandwich with a small sharp knife and then use the tines of the fork to give the crust a pretty finish. Brush the surface with more milk and sprinkle evenly with sugar. Make two or three small slashes in the middle of the pie and slide into the oven. Bake for 20 minutes and then turn the temperature down to 300°F and cook for a further 40 minutes, or until the pastry has attained the most lovely golden crust, all sparkly with sugar and smelling simply divine. Eat with the best cream you can find, and make sure it's very cold from the fridge.

RICE

I have a confession to make. Well, perhaps it is more of a gentle change of heart than a full-blown owning up. In my first book, *Roast Chicken and Other Stories*, I gave a recipe for *Risotto alla Milanese* where I specified using a particular type of rice most unsuitable for the making of risotto. There is actually nothing wrong with this semi-transparent, pale yellow, pre-fluffed Italian rice. Moreover, it is a useful grain to use when making, say, a kedgeree, a savory pilaf, or even the quite delicious smoked haddock "risotto" from that debut volume. But I would not make a genuine Italian risotto with it now; not now that I have finally learned what the dish is all about.

Quite simply, it is the rice and the way it is looked after by the cook that makes the dish so very, very special. I now use either Carnaroli or Violane Nano, or simply Arborio when no other information is given on the package. All three grains are white, hard, and stubby and require a firm hand and practiced timing to make them behave in just the right way; something to consider when learning to make a true risotto.

Here are a few words that I wrote in the *Independent,* in April 1999:

> I was recently informed – and on very good authority indeed – that our best beloved and most influential of all Italian cookery writers, Marcella Hazan, regularly uses stock [bouillon] cubes when making an everyday Venetian risotto. Why yes, of course, a superlative *brodo* (broth) is going to enhance the taste but it is the understanding of how rice behaves as you cook the thing that is the secret to the feel of the grains in the mouth. Great risotto is first and foremost a textural pleasure. Then, soon after the pure taste of good rice has been enjoyed simply for itself (often shamefully

forgotten in the rush for novelty), a thoughtful, secondary flavor may be introduced. This is, essentially, an embellishment. In fact, I see it as more of a seasonal treat. The rice is all.

But possibly the most important insight from stirrings from the Veneto was the *hugely* important friction that must occur when agitating the rice as the hot liquid is introduced to it. For it is during this time that the outer coating of each grain has a chance to release its all-important starch. This cannot occur all on its own; well, it can, but only partially. Which is why if you do not stir the risotto with the tempo of a semi-whirling dervish most of that essential creaminess remains in the rice, when it should, most deliciously, have helped the thing become a whole: creamy and starchy, yet loose and fondant all at once. Those of you who, like me, have been disappointed with risotto that once spooned out from pan to plate is sort of just rice and juice may now be assured that it has probably been lazily stirred.

Conversely, the cooking of the fragrant and more well-behaved Indian basmati rice is really quite simple when compared with the Italian stuff, but there are rules here too. I am forever enthralled by how these two grains of rice perform so differently as they cook. How a grain of basmati rice is imbued with so much flavor as it grows is, for me, a minor miracle. For those who get as excited as I do over such things, is not the waft from a freshly cooked basmati pilaf one of the most exquisite of all culinary smells? If only more designer stoves were actually used for cooking such things rather than idly reheating a carton of Marks & Spencer saffron rice, the British domestic kitchen might, once more, begin to smell very nice indeed.

ARMENIAN LAMB PILAF

This dish was inspired by a funny old recipe from the 1970s *Cordon Bleu* magazine series. Since I cooked this Armenian lamb once – or sometimes even twice – a week for a period of almost three years in Pembrokeshire hotels (1973–75), it is not surprising that it has since settled in my memory somewhat. Whether it is actually authentic to the cooking of Armenia is moot—perhaps in the same way that chicken tikka masala has anything at all to do with the cooking of the Indian subcontinent. Be that as it may, I have always looked upon Armenian lamb as nothing more than a mildly spiced meat stew. Once incorporated into this pilaf however, I feel it has now truly blossomed.

Serves 4

¾ lb eggplant, peeled and cut into small cubes
salt
⅔ lb diced lamb (shoulder, for preference)
5 tbsp olive oil
7 oz onions, peeled and coarsely chopped
2 mild green chillies, seeded and chopped
a 14 oz can of chopped tomatoes
2 tsp ground cumin seed
1 tsp ground allspice
1 cup basmati rice, well washed and drained
1½ cups well-flavored stock
a generous pinch of saffron threads, steeped in 2 tbsp boiling water
3 cloves garlic, peeled and finely chopped
2 oz shelled and skinned pistachio nuts
2 oz currants
a handful of fresh cilantro leaves, chopped

Put the eggplant in a colander and sprinkle with 1 tsp salt. Place over a plate and leave to drain for 30 minutes. Using a cast-iron casserole dish (preferably one that has a lid), fry the meat in 2 tbsp of the olive oil until evenly browned, then remove to a plate. Add another spoonful of oil and fry the onions until golden, then add the chillies and tomatoes. Stir together and return the lamb to the pot. Cover, and cook very gently for 30 minutes, stirring from time to time.

Preheat the oven to 350°F.

Rinse and drain the eggplant, dry well in a dish towel, and gently fry in 2 tbsp of olive oil, together with the cumin and allspice, until softened. Tip into the lamb mixture and add the rice. Stir everything together over a low heat until well combined. Now pour in the stock and steeped saffron threads and check for salt. Add the garlic, pistachios, and currants and stir in well. Bring up to a simmer, cover and bake in the oven for 15 minutes. Remove, leave the lid on, and allow to stand for 10 minutes.

Remove the lid, fork the rice to fluff it up, and cover with a folded dish towel. (This allows excess steam to be absorbed.) Finally, stir in the cilantro and serve up onto very hot plates, as pilaf quickly cools.

RISOTTO WITH PEA SHOOTS

Curiously, I first made this particular risotto in the kitchen of a house in Sydney, Australia, using an electric wok. Although one can purchase pea shoots with the greatest of ease in that sunny city, in London it is best to head for Chinatown whenever the need arises. Once again I am indebted here to Marcella Hazan for explaining exactly what happens to a grain of rice when you hit it a lot with a wooden spoon.

Serves 4

10½ tbsp butter
5¼ cups light chicken stock
(you may, of course, use bouillon cubes!), of which you may not need all
1 large onion, peeled and finely chopped
4 very thin slices bacon, finely sliced into thin strips
1⅓ cups Carnaroli rice
1 lb pea shoots, roughly chopped
salt and white pepper
1 tbsp chopped mint
5 tbsp freshly grated Parmesan, plus a
little more, if liked, handed at the time of serving

Melt 7 tbsp of the butter in a heavy-bottomed pot. (I should also say here that the pot should not be too wide, as the narrower and higher-sided the vessel the more intense and compact the stirring will be.) Have the stock sitting close by, at a low simmer. Add the onion and bacon to the butter and cook slowly, until both are soft and translucent. Tip in the rice and turn up the heat. Stir the rice around with the onion until glistened by the butter before adding the first ladle of hot stock.

This will immediately cause a satisfying seethe, whereupon the stock will almost immediately be absorbed by the rice as you vigorously stir. Now add the pea shoots and stir in. Once the pea shoots have thoroughly wilted, add the second ladle of stock, and continue to stir energetically until this too has been absorbed. As you repeat this process, each additional ladle of stock will take longer to be absorbed as the rice finds its work more arduous, its starchy coating being continually eroded by the efficiency of your sturdy spoon. Do also ensure that you keep the heat up high under the risotto during the whole process.

Soon after two-thirds of the stock has been incorporated, it is time to have the odd nibble at a grain of rice. Along with checking on pasta, this is clearly the obvious way to find out when rice is on the way to being ready. Once the texture of the rice is almost firm to the teeth – or almost *al dente* (which never means, under any circumstances, "still a little chalky in the middle") – now is the time to add the last ladle of stock.

Once that last ladleful has been added and incorporated, stir in the remaining 3½ tbsp of butter and the mint. Check for seasoning. Switch off the heat and tightly cover the pan. Leave the risotto alone for 5 minutes now, to allow the rice to enjoy a final, quiet swell. For a last-minute, fail-safe indication that the rice is cooked, eat a bit once more after this; the swollen grains should now give nicely to the bite, sort of fudgy yet melting. Reheat the risotto briefly, and vigorously stir it for the last time. As you so do, sprinkle in the Parmesan and incorporate fully, until the whole mass is sleek and glossy. Serve straight from the pan, and with not a little pride.

SPANISH GIBLET RICE POT

Hopefully, it should now be trickling through to us Brits that not every single Spanish rice dish is made up of bright yellow grains, a dice of green and red pepper, peas, pink shrimp, and the requisite peeking cluster of black mussel shells. OK, there might be a bit of squid lurking about in there too, but really, we'd rather imagine this as neat rings, nicely battered and deep-fried. Some bright spark will, naturally, soon be pronouncing that the Spaniards are actually far better at cooking rice dishes than any number of those northern Italian risotto stirrers. (They say – and who exactly are "they," pray? – that Spanish cooking is soon to be the next big thing.) Of course, this is absolute piffle, for each tradition is remarkable in its own right. And as all we Britishers have to offer is a nice rice pudding (which, no doubt, has its origins in India anyway), who am I to judge? But what I do find absolutely fascinating is that the closest comparison to the following Spanish recipe is one of those savory rice pots that I occasionally eat at Poons, in the West End of London, one of my favorite Chinese restaurants.

Serves 2, substantially

1 tsp saffron threads
1 cup plus 2 tbsp *passata* (unseasoned tomato sauce)
olive oil
4 oz chicken or duck livers
4 oz chicken or duck gizzards

3½ oz chicken or duck hearts
3½ oz chicken or duck necks
salt and pepper
2 good slugs of dry sherry
6 cloves garlic, peeled and thickly sliced
1 tsp dried chilli flakes
2 small sprigs of fresh rosemary
2 bay leaves
a 14 oz can of cooked chickpeas, drained and rinsed
1⅔ cups light chicken stock
9 oz Spanish rice (the brand called Calasparra is the finest)

Preheat the oven to 350°F.

First of all, soak the saffron threads in a couple of tablespoons of hot water. Pour the *passata* into a small heavy-bottomed saucepan, and reduce over a gentle heat until thick and viscous.

Now if you happen to possess one of those well-seasoned, traditional terracotta *cazuelas,* all well and good. If not, then a solid-based, shallow cast-iron pan, Le Creuset for instance, would be just ideal. Heat 2 tbsp of olive oil and gently begin to color the giblets. It matters not one jot in which order you do them, but only one sort at a time, please. Make sure that they are all as dry as possible and do not salt them. Simply, each item needs only a few minutes in the oil until all surfaces are sealed and lightly burnished. As you finish each batch, remove to a dish and only then sprinkle with a little salt and pepper. Add extra olive oil when you think it necessary. Once all this is finished, rinse out the pot with a slug of sherry, making sure you scrape all the crusty bits off the bottom with a whisk or spoon. Tip this over the dish of giblets. Wipe the pot dry and add yet another generous splash of olive oil. Allow it to warm up.

Now add the garlic. Cook gently until it turns golden and is crisp and a bit sticky. Tip in the chilli flakes, rosemary, and bay leaves and stir around as they briefly sizzle. Now stand back and pour in the second slug of sherry, which will splutter, then tip in the chickpeas. Stir them in, add the stock, steeped saffron, and giblets. Bring to a simmer, check for seasoning, and stir in the rice. Put in the oven, uncovered, for 40–50 minutes or so, until the top is golden and the rice underneath cooked through. Leave to stand, covered with a dish towel for 10 minutes, before eating. A meal in itself.

ROQUEFORT

I adore the taste of Roquefort. And, furthermore, I don't care what anyone says, it is also the finest blue cheese in the world. Period. Stilton? No contest as far as I am concerned. *La fourme d'Ambert?* Can be absolutely delicious, but it has to be in excellent shape. Mountain Gorgonzola? At best, a close second. No, for me, Roquefort tramples all other blue cheeses under its smelly feet.

I once had the great pleasure of visiting the caves where Roquefort is made. A whole mountain conveniently collapsed so that this extraordinary cheese could come to be. Thousands of years ago Mont Cambalou, in the Aveyron region of southern France ('twixt the Auvergne and Languedoc regions), was, as a result of one monumental landmass slip, suddenly left high and dry. The mountain itself – a magisterially beautiful loaf of a rock which catches the morning sun in the most dramatic way – is some 1¼ miles long by about 1,000 feet wide and as much again deep. And then the French, in their inimitable way, decided to build the little village of Roquefort-sur-Soulzon against its majestic walls, after discovering the curious phenomenon that lay within the belly of the rock.

Legend has it that a lonely shepherd, after enjoying his lunch of fresh ewe's milk cheese and bread in the cool of a cave within the Cambalou montain, left part of this frugal meal behind. Some months later, returning to the same cave for similar light refreshment, he happened upon his discarded leftovers: a bit of moldy bread and some equally moldy cheese. But what mold was in that cheese! For that old lump of bread had transferred its natural bacteria upon the fermented curd, turning its interior into something quite, quite different – and indescribably delicious. Whether this tale is true or not, it charmingly illustrates the story of how Roquefort accidentally came into being.

Roquefort is still, to this day, made from unpasteurized sheep's milk and has its own appellation *contrôlée*. Milk may only be collected from designated regional areas as well as from some farms on the island of Corsica. I became childishly happy wandering around the caves themselves, but when the adventure was further enhanced by witnessing the manufacture of possibly the most complex and fascinating cheese in the world, it caused me to turn all humble and worthless, as well as despairing over how glibly we all take such gastronomic miracles for granted.

In its simplest form, Roquefort eaten with a little unsalted butter spread on a tearing from a properly baked French baguette is as good as good food gets. I find a deeply scented glass of red Rhône an indispensable accompaniment to this. I do not, however, go along with the modish tipple of a glass of chilled sweet white wine, such as a richly fragrant Sauternes – though I seem to be in the minority here amongst most of my wine-drinking chums. Controversially, a fine slice of Roquefort eaten with a perfect ripe pear (as we well know, a difficult thing in itself) is a very fine thing indeed. Choose the cheese called Papillon (there are around about a dozen producers in Roquefort); it may well be the most expensive – no Roquefort is cheap – but this one really is the very best you can buy.

ROQUEFORT MOUSSE

I first made this mousse using leftover blue Stilton. It was unspeakably awful. Though, I guess, as I was aged eighteen at the time and feeling all experimental and such, a mousse made from the remnants of a scooped-out half Stilton presented me with a real challenge. I also deeply respected the firm instructions from my boss at the time, a Mrs. Stirling, to embrace economy and try one's best to never, *ever* throw anything away: *"Surely* you can do something with this, can't you, Simon?" . . . etc., etc. And how very right she was.

Thankfully, the mousse never appeared in the dining room. In fact, if I recall, it ended up as part of a staff lunch. They found it unspeakable too. So much so, that they didn't speak to me for the rest of the day. Hungry waiters, more than most, are very angry folk.

Serves 4

½ a cucumber, peeled, seeded, and grated
salt
4 leaves gelatin
¾ cup cold water
4½ oz Roquefort, crumbled
2½ oz cream cheese
juice of 1 large lemon
2 tbsp finely chopped flat-leaf parsley
1 tbsp finely chopped chives
a few shakes of Tabasco sauce
¾ cup heavy cream

For the watercress salad

2 big handfuls of picked-over sprigs of
the freshest watercress, washed and dried
salt and pepper
juice of ½ lemon
4–5 tbsp fruity olive oil

Serve with

good bread and fine butter

Mix together the cucumber and ½ tsp salt, put into a sieve, and leave to drain for 30 minutes. Soak the gelatin leaves in the cold water until floppy and soft. Force the Roquefort and cream cheese through a sieve into a roomy bowl. (Don't be tempted to use a food processor, as this will instantly remove texture and nuggety bits of blue from the Roquefort.) Put the gelatin leaves and their soaking water into a small pan and heat gently until the gelatin has melted; do *not* boil. Allow to cool until tepid and deftly whisk into the cheeses. Tip the salted cucumber into a dish towel and squeeze out excess liquid. Add this, along with the lemon juice, herbs, a little salt (careful here), and the Tabasco, to the cheese/gelatin mixture. Combine thoroughly and put in the fridge. Leave there to stiffen only to a wobbling consistency rather than fully set; say, 40–50 minutes or so?

Loosely whip the cream by hand until just floppy rather than thick. Remove the cheese mixture from the fridge, give it a quiet whisk to a loose smoothness, and then carefully, but thoroughly, fold in the cream. Finally, check the seasoning. Spoon into a deep serving dish (a family-sized soufflé dish, perhaps?) and smooth the surface. Cover with plastic wrap and return to the fridge for a full set. Put the watercress in a salad bowl, season it, and dress with lemon juice and olive oil, all to your own individual taste. Send both vessels to table with a serving spoon, salad servers, and a basket of good bread and some fine butter.

ROQUEFORT TART

A blissfully rich and savory tart. Heed carefully how important it is to make sure that the blind-baked tart shell is dry and crisp before adding the filling; otherwise you will end up with a soggy bottom – and nobody really wants a soggy bottom, now, do they? This directive applies to almost all open pastry tarts, by the way, both savory and sweet.

Serves 4–5

Pastry made with

¾ cup all-purpose flour
4 tbsp butter, cut into cubes
1 egg yolk
1–2 tbsp iced water
a pinch of salt

For the filling

2–3 tbsp dry bread crumbs
7 oz crumbled Roquefort

6 spring onions, thinly sliced
freshly ground black pepper
2 egg yolks
2 whole eggs
1¼ cups heavy cream

Preheat the oven to 350°F.

Roll out the pastry as thinly as possible, line an 8 in tart or flan pan, and bake blind by lining the uncooked pastry shell with a sheet of foil and filling it with, for instance, some dried haricot beans, then cooking it for about 15–20 minutes, removing it from the oven, transferring the foil and beans to a bowl or pan (for future baking blind), and returning the case to the oven for a further 10 minutes or so, until it is golden, crisp, and well cooked through, particularly the base.

Sprinkle the bread crumbs evenly over the base of the cooked tart shell. Distribute the Roquefort and spring onions over the bread crumbs and season with the pepper. Whisk together the egg yolks, eggs, and cream, and spoon carefully over the cheese and onions, as evenly as possible. Slide into the oven and bake for 30–40 minutes until firm, with the surface of the tart pale golden and lightly puffed up. Remove from the oven and leave for 10 minutes or so; savory tarts taste much better warm than hot.

ROMAINE LETTUCE WITH CREAMED ROQUEFORT, GARLIC CROUTONS, AND FRIED PARSLEY

This substantial salad is a veritable explosion of texture: crisp romaine, crunchy croutons, wispy flakes of frazzled parsley, all muddled about with a loosely creamed, salty blue cheese dressing. Done well, a salad such as this is a far cry from the standard: the shredded American iceberg with "Rokefurt" dressing, which is usually an emulsion of a curious duck-egg-blue hue and is, most probably, entirely based upon a very popular fermented Danish import.

Serves 4

For the creamed Roquefort

3½ oz Roquefort
5 tbsp olive oil
3 tbsp sour cream
2 tbsp sherry vinegar
juice of 1 small onion (chopped fine, put into a damp dish towel, and squeezed)

1 small baguette, rubbed with a clove of garlic and cut into chunky cubes
3–4 tbsp olive oil

For the salad

oil, for frying
1 small bunch of curly parsley, stalks removed
salt
2 romaine lettuces, or more, most outer leaves removed (make soup with these)
2 oz Roquefort, crumbled
a little extra olive oil
freshly ground black pepper

Preheat the oven to 400°F.

Blend briefly the first 5 ingredients for the creamed Roquefort in a blender, until smooth. Add a little warm water if the mixture becomes too thick. Do not overwork the cream, as it splits easily. Set aside in a small bowl. Put the bread cubes on a baking sheet, drizzle with the olive oil, and bake in the oven until crisp and golden.

Heat the frying oil (about 2½ cups, or use a deep-fryer if you have one) in a deep, solid-bottomed pan and, using a thermometer, heat to a temperature of 360°F. Make sure the parsley is *very* dry, and drop into the oil. Fry for about 10–15 seconds. Much spluttering will ensue, so stand back. Lift out the parsley – which should be dark green and crisp – and place on some absorbent paper towel. Sprinkle lightly with salt whilst still warm.

Arrange the romaine leaves randomly on 4 white plates and spoon over the creamed dressing. Strew with the croutons then the parsley and drop a few extra pieces of crumbled Roquefort here and there. Finally drizzle a little olive oil on each serving and grind over some black pepper.

SALT

I simply don't understand this recent thing with salt. Oh, I am sure that expert dietitians will tell me that too much salt in my diet is very bad indeed, but whereas experts such as these (surely most worthy and good people) are perfectly happy to consume a bowl of bland brown rice and broccoli to accompany a vigorously trimmed, unseasoned, grilled pork chop, I, unsurprisingly, am not. Salt, to the serious cook, is essential. To be told that I was never to use salt in cooking ever again would remove the very essence of the joy of eating. I might as well give it all up and secure a job selling ties at Harrods.

I will always remember being quite shocked once by a casual remark made to me by some very regular customers of Bibendum, on the subject of salt. This couple deeply love all things gastronomic, the husband being particularly fond of collecting, carefully storing, and then drinking extremely fine wine. In fact, for all the years that Bibendum has been open (fourteen), as well as for a couple of years before that at the Hilaire Restaurant, in the Old Brompton Road (where the husband and I first met), I have happily allowed this passionate oenophile and gourmet to bring wine from his own cellar to drink with food served by us.

But so it was when kindly invited to their home for supper, several years ago now, and while helping to grill some chicken to go with some fine Bordeaux (I think it may well have been La Conseillante '61), the discussion turned to salt. Thinking back, I guess it was just as I was about to fully dredge the tender fowl's greased skin with a healthy handful of scrunchy sea salt . . .

"We've cut back on the salt lately," muttered he.

"Oh, really?" I said, stifling a groan.

227

"Oh, yes. It's really not good to use too much salt."

"Oh, really," I repeated, becoming mildly irritable over this surprising piffle.

"We have both found that food tastes much cleaner and more pure without the addition of salt. And, you know, it is much, much better for your system."

"Erm . . . could you watch the chicken for a bit while I go into the garden for a quick smoke?"

Now I understand that cigarette smoke is difficult for the terminally intolerant, hence the required exit to the backyard. "No salt!" I inwardly shrieked. "No bloody salt! I mean, how can they not want to season food when those delicious wines are themselves so immaculately 'seasoned'? Do they find my food too salty when they come to Bibendum of a Saturday lunchtime?"

How is it possible not to use salt at home, but to then eat properly seasoned food when eating out? And why do quite irrational thoughts such as this, quite suddenly, affect the most rational of folk? I certainly don't remember the *cost* of salt rocketing at the time, which may have been relevant here and was a tiny thought that lingered with me for just a moment, as I fondled the sweet peas and exhaled the smoke from my delicious Marlboro Light.

DUCK CONFIT

Confit is always best made from the legs of a bird. Although this is not essential, I nevertheless find that the more muscular the structure the better behaved it is when intentionally overcooked. Breast meat simply becomes stringy and is far better off cooked either with its original carcass – i.e., roasted on the bone – or removed raw from the bone altogether and either grilled or fried. Duck or goose fat can be purchased in jars or cans from good food shops, but if you are frequent duck or goose roasters then you may well have – should have – some already saved up.

Serves 4

4 tbsp good-quality salt (Maldon or French *sel gris,* if you can get it)
4 tsp sugar
6–7 sprigs of fresh thyme
2 bay leaves
10 black peppercorns
a generous grating of nutmeg
4 fatty duck legs
about 2⅓–3 cups duck or goose fat, depending on the size of your cooking pot
6–8 cloves garlic, unpeeled and bruised

Grind together the first 6 ingredients to a fine powder. Pour half of it into a shallow dish and place the duck legs flesh side down upon this. Sprinkle over the rest, cover with plastic wrap, and put in the fridge, or a cool place, for about 18–24 hours, turning the legs over once, halfway through the process.

Preheat the oven to 275°F.

Melt the fat in a solid cast-iron pot over a low heat. Rinse the duck legs under running water and slide into the fat together with the garlic. Bring the fat up to a gentle simmer and then place in the oven. Cook for about 2 hours, or until a metal skewer shows so little resistance to the meat that it might almost not be there.

Allow to cool and store in a suitable pot or simply the dish you cooked the confit in, but do make sure that the meat is completely covered by fat. Keep in the fridge for at least 3–4 weeks, attempting (I usually fail miserably) not to eat them before then, as they benefit hugely from this storage period. You may, of course, leave them longer than this – anything up to 3–4 months, in fact.

BAKED SALT COD WITH MILK AND PARSLEY

This sublime, intensely savory baked stew appeals to me in exactly the same way as a rich and sweet English rice pudding. I once ate a version of this in northern Italy, and so good was it I promptly requested a second helping. Although initially the waiter's face was a picture of surprise he soon smiled once he realized quite how much I had also enjoyed it; a mad Englishman, maybe, but always a very appreciative one.

Serves 4

2 lb (approx.) dried salt cod
1¼ cups milk
2 bay leaves
3 pieces of pithless lemon zest
2–3 small dried hot chillies, crumbled
1 small bunch flat-leaf parsley (stalks removed, chopped, and reserved)
¾ cup extra-virgin olive oil
2 onions, thinly sliced
1 tbsp flour
4 tbsp butter
4 cloves garlic, thinly sliced
very little salt and only if necessary
a large handful of fresh white bread crumbs

First soak the salt cod overnight in cold water, changing the water several times.

Bring the milk to a simmer with the bay leaves, lemon zest, chillies, and the parsley stalks. Put a lid on and allow to infuse. Put the salt cod in a pan of fresh cold water and very slowly bring up to a simmer. Just as the water is beginning to tremble, immediately drain into a colander. Tip onto a plate and allow to cool for 10 minutes. Scrupulously remove all traces of bone and skin while also separating the cod flesh into flakes. Place in a bowl and set aside.

Preheat the oven to 300°F.

Gently warm the olive oil in a roomy pan and add the onions. Stew ever so gently without allowing the onions to color in any way whatsoever. Once they have become extremely tender sift in the flour and carefully stir until dissolved in the oil. Strain the flavored milk over and, stirring, bring up to a simmer. Stir in the flakes of salt cod and quietly simmer together for 10 minutes, until lightly thickened but remaining oily. (*Note:* Do not expect the milk and oil to homogenize fully.) Coarsely chop half of the parsley leaves and stir in. Heat the butter in a small pan and gently fry the garlic until lightly colored. Remove the garlic with a slotted spoon and also stir in. Check for salt. Turn into a lightly buttered shallow oven dish which is also suitable for the table, and spoon the garlic-flavored butter over the surface. Mix the remaining parsley with the bread crumbs, strew over the surface, and then bake in the oven for 45 minutes to 1 hour, or until a gorgeous golden crust has formed and the dish is quietly bubbling all around the edge.

ANCHOVY EGGS

I have always been extremely fond of a tasty eggy first course. In fact, one of my earliest successes in my mother's kitchen was the dish that soon became known as Simon's Eggs. Its true name was *Oeufs Mollets à l'Indienne* – soft-boiled eggs in curried mayonnaise. They were placed upon a bed of dressed rice salad that had bits in, carefully coated with the curried mayonnaise and a thin strip of bottled pimento draped across each one. My teenage "signature dish," no less, and let me tell you, by the time I had cooked it for almost every single dinner party that my parents held during several school holidays, I felt that I had got it pretty well perfect. Not surprisingly, it soon became known as Simon's Eggs Yet Again.

Serves 6, as a first course

6 large eggs, boiled for exactly 6 minutes, and shelled
¼ cup cream or curd cheese
5–6 tbsp mayonnaise
10 best-quality large Spanish anchovy fillets
(the brand Ortiz is a very good one)
a few shakes of Tabasco
salt, if necessary
2 cartons of mustard cress, their tips rinsed
under a cold tap whilst still in their cartons
a squeeze of lemon juice
12 large capers, patted dry with paper towel
paprika

Halve the eggs lengthways, remove the yolks, and put them in a sieve placed over a bowl. Together with the cheese, push them through the sieve using the back of a spoon. Add 2–3 tbsp mayonnaise but only to loosen to a workable paste. Finely chop 4 of the anchovies and stir in, together with a few shakes of Tabasco to taste. Only add salt if you think it necessary. Using a teaspoon, refill the halved egg whites with the mixture, fashioning them as neatly as possible into little domes.

Snip off tufts of cress using a pair of scissors and arrange onto 6 individual plates or 1 single oval platter. Display the eggs attractively over the cress, curved sides down (do I really have to say that?). Loosen the remaining mayonnaise with lemon juice to taste and use it to sparingly coat the eggs. Split the remaining 6 anchovies lengthways, drape one half across each egg, and dot the center with a caper. Lightly sprinkle with paprika and serve.

SCAMPI

A round the time I was five years old, my elder brother Jeremy was sent off to a small but formative preparatory school in the small and entirely engaging town of Arnside, in Westmorland, as it was then known. Miles away to the average Lancastrian family in the latter part of the 1950s, as a journey north of Lancaster to the English Lakes was then seen as a major undertaking.

It seemed to take forever to drive from Bury to Arnside in those days, even though the very first stretch of motorway built in the country (somewhere between Preston and Carnforth) eventually enabled Dad's Ford Zodiac to veritably *slash* the journey by . . . ooh . . . by at least fifteen minutes, I guess. To me, at the time, it seemed interminable. "Are we there yet?" You know, that sort of carry-on. But sometimes, on the journey home, as a treat and usually at the end of one of Jeremy's terms, we would stop at this groovy place called the Five Barred Gate, several hundred yards off the very exciting Motorway Exit Number 3.

Whether one might have called this a "roadhouse" at the time was of no importance to me (though I guess that an establishment sporting garish lighting, red paper napkins, individual foil-wrapped packets of butter, a warbling Hammond organ, and a ferociously busy bar trade of a Friday night, might, I suppose, have fitted that particular nomenclature to a T). What I most definitely recall, however, is that while Dad appeared entirely happy to swing the wheel of the Ford through a swift 90 degrees at the merest idea of a busy Friday-night bar that sold bottles of Bass, I, egging Mum on from the backseat to agree with him, could only think of scampi in the basket.

It was, you see, at the groovy Five Barred Gate that I first ate fried scampi. It did not take me long to realize that these golden and crunchy fishy things were quite the most wonderful thing I had yet put into my ever-open mouth. They also came with something called "tartare sauce" — which, as I thought at the time, seemed like salad dressing with crunchy green bits in it. (For a short while I remained convinced that these green bits were chopped peas.) We didn't have Delia's capers in our pantry at home then, but, I assume, neither did she, circa 1959.

Now I would imagine that in those formative years of mine (no, the celebrated chef of the Five Barred Gate did *not* inspire me to cater) any restaurant kitchen might even have dipped fresh, fleshy whole shrimp into flour, beaten egg, and bread crumbs all by themselves, flung them into hot oil, and dropped a crusty pile of them into one of the very first hand-woven baskets ever to grace the tables of north Lancashire. Fresh Dublin Bay prawns, after all, were fished in plenty in nearby Morecambe and Flookburgh and were clearly destined for the burgeoning basket market. Those dear little decayed containers may have been seen as a whimsical weave at the time, but their contents would very soon become a travesty, for it was not so very long before all those French and Spanish trucks arrived and simply took them all away.

So, *comme d'habitude,* we have only ourselves to blame for the surreptitious onslaught of the misshaped orange fish crouton. I mean, why did no one notice! It changed its shape from a distinctive comma to an ovoid full stop, became all damp inside, and — surprise, surprise — entirely ceased to taste of shellfish. Allegedly, it had also become the fashion to make breaded scampi from re-formed pieces of (then, completely unknown) monkfish flesh.

I mean, it's a gas, isn't it? Everyone now looks upon monkfish as the fish of the moment. But to request that a freshly breaded langoustine tail be deep-fried to perfection? "Nah, I'd rather roast a nice fillet of monkfish with pesto and pancetta, mate." The curious and rather sad thing is that although pesto may be one of those nice green Italian sauces, it will never, in all my lifetime, fully eclipse the memory of that first taste of salad cream with chopped peas in it.

SCAMPI PROVENÇALE

The jovial Welshman who occasionally delivered items of frozen produce to me and my first little restaurant on the Pembrokeshire coast, circa 1975, remained forever convinced that I should most definitely try some of his company's newest lines: "Simon, bach, these ready-made gourmet meals are vayry, vayry pop-poola just now. Fab-boolus, in point o' fact. How about a nice scampiprovenkarl?" My reply was always the same: "Sounds lovely, Ken. Fancy a beer? And then, you know, I really must be getting on . . ."

Serves 2

10 jumbo fresh shrimp, preferably alive
(in place of Dublin Bay prawns or langoustines)
1 glass dry white wine
1 bay leaf
2 pieces of lemon zest
salt and pepper
4 small ripe tomatoes, cored, skinned, and chopped
2 tbsp olive oil
2 cloves garlic, finely chopped
1 tbsp chopped parsley
a squeeze of lemon juice

Bring a large pan of salted water to the boil. Plunge the shrimp into it, stir them around once, and then leave submerged for no more than 1 minute. Immediately drain in a colander and quickly rinse with cold water. Detach the head and claw part from the tail with your fingers (there is a natural division here which also applies to lobsters) and then remove the shell from around the tail meat, so resulting in a neat and tidy, pale pink, slightly undercooked tail. Deftly run a small sharp knife along the outside curve of each tail to find whether there is a thin, dark, intestinal tract. If this is visible, remove it in one piece. If it is not, forget it; the tract is clean. Put the tails on a plate and keep cool in the fridge. Add the tail shells to the head and claw parts and return all of them to the empty pan in which you have previously boiled the shrimp.

Lightly crush the shells using the end of a rolling pin or similar. Place the pan over a moderate heat and add the wine, bay leaf, lemon zest, and very little seasoning. Cover the contents with cold water and bring up to a simmer. As the liquid begins to shudder up to this point it will be noticeable that a generous amount of filthy scum has formed on the surface. Deftly lift this off with a large spoon and then gently cook the shells for 30–40 minutes. Drain the result in a colander suspended over another pan. Discard the shells and strain the resultant juice left beneath into a saucepan, using a fine sieve.

Add the tomatoes to this liquid, and allow them to simmer gently until, finally, they have reduced to a semi-thick sauce. Put to one side. Now take a frying pan and briskly fry the scampi tails in the olive oil until lightly gilded all over. Throw in the garlic, letting it color a little as you stir it around, and then tip in the fishy tomato sauce and parsley. Reheat, sharpen with lemon juice, and correct the seasoning if necessary.

SCAMPI AND FENNEL SALAD

A sprightly little number, this one. It utilizes one of the most extraordinarily pleasing lotions it has ever been my joy to discover, first coming to my attention in the pages of *An Omelette and a Glass of Wine,* by Elizabeth David ("A Jill Norman Book," published by Robert Hale, and possibly the most informative and enchanting collection of her writings ever assembled), where it is prosaically referred to as no more than a "sauce for boiled lobster" (not by E.D., but from her source). The affinity of this unique dressing with the two main ingredients here is a matchless one.

Serves 2

For the dressing

2 small shallots, peeled and finely chopped
1 tsp freshly chopped tarragon leaves
2 tbsp freshly chopped parsley
salt and pepper
1 tsp Dijon mustard
24–30 drops soy sauce
approx 6 tbsp fruity, extra-virgin olive oil
juice of 1 small lemon
2 tsp Pernod

For the salad

1 small, very fresh fennel bulb, trimmed and thinly sliced
sea salt and pepper
a squeeze of lemon juice
1 tbsp extra-virgin olive oil
10 jumbo fresh shrimp, preferably alive
(also known as Dublin Bay prawns
and langoustines)

Mix the shallots, herbs, seasoning, mustard, and soy sauce together in a small bowl. Then whisk all together thoroughly and add the oil in a thin stream as if making a vinaigrette. Stir in the lemon juice and Pernod. Set aside for at least 30 minutes to allow the flavors to meld and develop.

Lay out the fennel in a large shallow dish so that it is almost in a single layer. Season and sprinkle over the lemon juice. Leave to macerate in a cool place for about 1 hour. Stir together briefly with the olive oil and then lay it out once more. *Note:* If there were any sprightly fronds of green attached to the fennel bulbs, save them, chop them up, and additionally sprinkle over the surface. You may now arrange the fennel upon 2 plates.

Referring to the previous recipe, deal with the shrimp in exactly the same way until you have removed the tails from their shells and any intestinal tracts. Discard all shells and then briefly, as before, gild the tails in a frying pan in hot olive oil and with a little seasoning. Place 5 shrimp on each plate of fennel and judiciously spoon some of the dressing over each serving. Eat at once.

CREAMED SCAMPI WITH SAFFRON PILAF

If I were ever asked to pinpoint the first occasion when the statement "I need to eat because I am hungry" would be replaced (the very next day, as it happened) by "I want to eat because I think it will be absolutely delicious," I would have to offer up the dining room of L'Hostellerie Lechat, in the pretty Norman fishing port of Honfleur, almost thirty years ago. It was also the very last two nights that I ever spent with my parents as the remaining teenager on the family holiday, so it is poignantly memorable for that too.

At dinner on the first evening my mother chose a little copper pot of seafood – *Fruits de mer à la Normande* – cooked in cream and white wine. Firstly, without question, it was one of the *best-looking* things I had ever seen on a dining-room table but, secondly, once I had suggested to Mum that she might allow me to taste a morsel of it, I just knew, immediately, that here was one of the most exquisite tastes of my short life so far. I spent the rest of that night and all of the following day just thinking about having one of those little copper pans all to myself at dinner that night.

Although I have never ventured back to L'Hostellerie Lechat since (perhaps no bad thing, for it may now be quite terrible), I will always remember that dish and how, quite clearly, it confirmed for me once and for all that my future was to be dedicated to the pursuit of eating and cooking in all their finest possible forms. So, here is my interpretation of that seminal dish, only in this case it is shrimp that are the only *"fruit."*

Serves 2

10 jumbo fresh shrimp, preferably alive
(in place of Dublin Bay prawns or langoustines)
2–3 tbsp olive oil
salt and pepper
3 tbsp cognac
½ a 750 ml bottle dry white wine or dry cider
4 tbsp butter
1 small onion, peeled and finely chopped
2 cloves garlic, crushed
2 tomatoes, peeled and chopped
⅔ cup whipping cream
a little chopped fresh tarragon
a pinch of cayenne pepper
a squeeze of lemon juice

Serve with

saffron pilaf (page 238)

To deal with the shrimp, follow the first paragraph of instructions in the recipe for Scampi Provençale (page 234). Crush the shells in the pan using the end of a rolling pin and then lubricate with the olive oil and seasoning. Gently fry the shells in the oil until they begin to color a little. Add the cognac (ignite with a match if you so desire, but this is not necessary) and the wine or cider and *just* cover with water. Simmer for 30 minutes. Strain through a colander and leave to drain for 10 minutes.

Using another pan, melt the butter and fry the onion until pale golden. Add the garlic and tomatoes and stew until soft. Add the drained shrimp-shell liquor and then simmer, uncovered, for 30 minutes, removing any scum that may form in the process with a large spoon or ladle. Strain through a fine sieve into another pan, pressing down on the solids using the back of a ladle.

What you now have is a strongly flavored fishy broth. This needs reducing down to a quarter or less of its original volume, until syrupy and intense. Once again, remove any scum that forms during this reduction. Pour in the cream, bring to a boil, and then simmer very gently until unctuous and the consistency of thickish custard. Check the seasoning and add the tarragon and cayenne pepper. Stir in the lemon juice. Reintroduce the shrimp tails, very gently reheat, and serve with the saffron pilaf (on the following page).

SAFFRON PILAF

2 cups basmati rice
4 tbsp butter
1 medium onion, peeled and finely chopped
a generous pinch of saffron threads
3 cups light chicken or fish stock
2 small bay leaves
salt and pepper

Preheat the oven to 350°F.

Wash the rice thoroughly in a sieve and drain well. Melt the butter in a heavy-bottomed cast-iron or other metal casserole dish with a tight-fitting lid and fry the onion until pale golden. Add the saffron and rice and stir gently over a low heat, until well coated with the butter. Pour in the stock and bring to a boil, stirring occasionally, and slip in the bay leaves. Season. Put on the lid and place in the oven for 20 minutes. Lift out, *don't* remove the lid, and leave for 5 minutes before removing it. Tip out into a hot serving dish and fluff up with a fork.

SKATE

"Skate is the new monkfish" some exquisitely trite cooking witterer penned not so long ago. Oh, just go away, I thought. One might as well say "Beef is the new lamb," such is the lunacy of all pointless comparisons. In other European countries each and every ingredient is simply regarded as either available or not, fresh or seen better days (consequently sold off cheap), suitable for the seasonal meal in mind, good value or more expensive than usual, or, rarely, something that the purchaser likes or dislikes. The idea that skate might suddenly have overtaken monkfish as a more fashionable fish for a Tuesday supper would be seriously considered as the ravings of a deviant.

Any novices about to embark upon the excitement of cooking and choosing essential purchases must be ever so thrilled when encountering their first skate wing. For that flappy wing of skate surely resembles no other recognizable piece of fish that might surround it on the fishmonger's slab. Well, I suppose mackerel looks nothing at all like turbot and hake resembles not one jot a sardine, but assuming that you are familiar with a pink and slimy wing of the freshest skate, you surely get my drift here. Apart from anything else I don't know of any other fish we regularly eat that actually has "wings"; well, all right, we eat its fins.

A tenuous comparison could be the succulent flesh that the Chinese prise from the dried fins of a shark, which, when displayed as thin gelatinous strands within a bowl of authentic "superior shark's fin soup," reminds one that – fin or wing – the cartilage structure of each has been designed in exactly the same way. Interesting comparisons apart and with chopsticks laid to one side, it occurs to me that to gently prise the hot and steamy flesh away from the cartilage of a freshly steamed

239

skate wing must surely be one of the nicest things ever to do with a clean fork.

Along with filleted fish enclosed in crisp batter and deep-fried, thin slices of roasted spring lamb with freshly made mint sauce, or a thigh of good chicken smothered by tarragon cream sauce, a taut wing of steamed and skinned skate lubricated by nutty browned butter, vinegar, capers, and parsley rates very high indeed amongst some of the finest dishes ever created. As one of a band of many curious chefs in the early 1980s I was occasionally moved to play around with skate from time to time: filleting it from raw, curling it into rolls, stuffing it with nonsense, dressing it up, slicing it into neat "circlets" (no, surely I did not!), while glibly missing the whole point all along the way. Skate wing becomes something quite else when it's unnecessarily fettled with in advance of a source of heat, in exactly the same way that an over-neatly trimmed loin of lamb behaves when bereft of its essential bone to cuddle against as it cooks. Both are rendered, in a moment of perceived technical advancement, weak and spineless.

SKATE WITH BLACK BUTTER

Whatever anyone might say, this way with skate is as good as it gets. The following two recipes are not in any way poor relations, it's just that the combination of skate, capers, and toasty-flavored butter (*beurre noir,* black butter, is not actually black, by any means, or burned for that matter) is to fish dishes as Connolly leather is to the interior of a Rolls-Royce: a unique fit.

Serves 2

1 onion, sliced
2 sticks celery, washed and sliced
1 bay leaf
3 tbsp red wine vinegar
salt
a few peppercorns
2 skate wings, preferably with skin still attached
4–6 tbsp butter
1 tbsp large capers (not those tiny wee ones or wholly inappropriate Italian salted ones)
1 demitasse spoon of chopped parsley

Serve with

plain boiled potatoes

Put approx. 1 quart of water in a large pan and add to it the first 6 ingredients. Boil together for 20 minutes. Slip in the 2 wings of skate and bring to a gentle simmer. Poach for 10 minutes. Lift out with a spatula, drain for a few seconds, and put on a large plate. Using a small knife, deftly peel back the dark skin (including any "thorns" that protrude from just beneath the skin) and then transfer each wing to a heated serving plate. Melt the butter in a small pan and quietly cook until toasty-smelling and pale golden brown in color. Add the capers – which will splutter – together with a little of their pickling vinegar, or, if you prefer the end result not to be over-capered, substitute a little more red wine vinegar. Swirl together, tip in the parsley, and spoon over the fish. Plainly boiled potatoes, surely? *Note:* As far as I am concerned, it is not necessary to remove the tender white skin from underneath the wing.

STEAMED SKATE WITH SAUCE VIERGE

As in the previous recipe, I do think skate is a meal for two. I'm not sure why, it just seems to suit a quiet supper. As I also mentioned previously – and if you know your fish-store man very well – try and persuade him to let you have the skate with its skin intact. If not, don't worry, the dish will still be fine. Just compare the difference, though, if you have a chance to cook it this way. This sauce is everyone's favorite just now, including as it does tomatoes, basil, fruity olive oil, and a little garlic; it's a dressing really, rather than a sauce.

Serves 2

For the *sauce vierge*

2 very ripe tomatoes, skinned, seeded, and chopped
1 demitasse spoon red wine vinegar
salt and pepper
1 small garlic clove, peeled and thinly sliced
2 spring onions, trimmed and finely chopped
3–4 sprigs of basil, leaves only, torn into pieces
5 tbsp finest extra-virgin olive oil

For the skate

1 onion, sliced
2 sticks celery, washed and sliced
1 bay leaf
3 tbsp white wine vinegar
salt
a few peppercorns
2 skate wings, skin attached

First make the sauce. Mix together the tomatoes, vinegar, salt and pepper, garlic, and spring onions. Leave to macerate for 30 minutes. Stir in the basil and olive oil.

While the sauce ingredients are macerating, repeat exactly the preparation and cooking instructions for the skate from the previous recipe. As before, place each piece of fish on a warmed plate, then spoon over the *sauce vierge*.

SALAD OF WARM SKATE WITH NEW POTATOES

The combination of strands of softly cooked skate flesh and slices of waxy potatoes is a deeply pleasing one. No explanation needed here, it simply is; think damp fish and chips, but not explicitly so.

Serves 2

10½ oz new potatoes, unpeeled

For the dressing

1 tbsp smooth Dijon mustard
1 tbsp sherry vinegar
salt and pepper
a little lukewarm water
½–⅔ cup peanut oil

For the skate

1 onion, sliced
2 sticks celery, washed and sliced
1 bay leaf
3 tbsp white wine vinegar
salt
a few peppercorns
1 large skate wing, if possible, unskinned
1 tbsp finely chopped spring onions
chopped parsley

Put the potatoes in a steamer, salt them, and set the water boiling. When evenly cooked through, drain and leave until you are *just* able to handle them, then peel. (Peeling potatoes while still hot is easier and they will accept and absorb the dressing more easily.) Put back into the steamer and leave to keep warm in its residual heat.

To make the dressing, put the mustard, vinegar, seasoning, and a couple of tablespoons of the water in a blender or food processor. Process until smooth and then start adding the oil in a thin stream. When the consistency has become creamy have a taste. If you think it is too thick, add a little more water; the look should be that of thin mayonnaise. Put to one side.

Poach the skate wing as in Skate with Black Butter, page 241. Remove both the black *and* the white skin this time and remove the flesh with a knife, easing it carefully off either side of its flimsy cartilage, in strands. Transfer to a hot plate and loosely cover with foil – or something or other.

Thinly slice the potatoes into a warmed, shallow serving dish, sprinkle over the spring onions, and spoon over just enough dressing to coat them. Stir together. Distribute the skate strands over the potatoes, lubricate with a little more dressing, and sprinkle with much parsley.

SUET

When asked questions about traditional British cooking, I am often stumped as to what it really is these days; that tiresome moniker "Modern British" seems to refer to nothing more than something in a sticky *jus* surrounded by bits of vegetable garnish and served in huge, deep soup plates. We have our roasts, beef in particular, but we are clearly not the only cooks who do this to a joint of meat. And the delicious stodge that is Yorkshire pudding? Think of the French *gougère*, or the pile of steaming polenta that is the Italian foil for a roast or game stew. Mind you, I wouldn't be at all surprised if one day soon some bright spark decides to "wittily" serve up a plate of roast beef with horseradish polenta. Time will surely tell.

But there is one particular ingredient that will forever be part of traditional British cooking, and that is suet. Apart from being one of the most original forms of lubrication used in cooking, this crumbly white animal fat is also extremely easy to work with. A large packet of Atora suet will constantly be found in my fridge, quietly concealed in one of the door compartments; sometimes there are more than one as, along with Worcestershire sauce, Tabasco, ketchup, and cans of Heinz tomato soup, a packet of suet is, more often than not, thrown into the shopping basket as a "just in case." I don't actually know a more perfectly useful product than a colorful packet of Atora suet, but the real thing is quite another matter.

Freshly grated or chopped suet, extracted from either beef or veal, is the Super League stuff. And if it is taken from around the kidney, then this is the crème de la crème. As with many traditions that we are increasingly deprived of, such as chicken giblets, bones, unpasteurized cheeses, etc., it would not surprise me if a perfectly harmless lump of suet soon becomes a lost luxury. I mean, in a similar vein, how many butchers do *you* know who still have a regular stock of those nice packets of beef dripping, elegantly packed into folded "cups" of creamy-colored wax paper?

Apart from anything else, suet pastry is one of the easier pastries to make and also performs correctly every single time. There's no rubbing in (rubbing in, in fact, often spells disaster with a suet crust), no eggs to add, and no worries over whether the ratio of fat to flour is right for the recipe in question, as it is almost always half the weight of fat to flour—and always self-rising, to boot. Along with many others of my age group it is the memory of suet puddings in the school canteen of the 1950s and '60s that now sits heavy in the mind – and sat heavy in the tum too. However, the steamed jam roly-poly pudding I used to look forward to once a week at Bury Grammar School, Lancashire, remains one of the finest gastronomic memories of my life. And I enjoyed it even more when they let me have the skin off the top of the custard too. "Dead man's leg with skin, please?" I used to squeak.

Note: Always make sure that the initial 20 minutes' steaming of all suet puddings is executed at a full, rolling boil. This first blast makes for a lighter pudding, exciting the rising agents in the dough immediately. The remaining time may be taken at a more leisurely pace.

STEAMED PORK, BACON, AND LEEK PUDDING

If I might say, a deliciously savory turn on the original beef version. Although I guess I came upon this idea in a moment of culinary diversion, I feel sure that the dish would feel very much at home served up in the Lincolnshire wolds, or as far north as Tyne and Wear, where the growing of leeks is looked upon with both reverence and great respect.

You will need a pudding bowl with a capacity of approximately 1 quart.

Serves 4–5

For the pastry

3 cups self-rising flour
7 oz shredded suet
salt and pepper
cold water, to mix

For the filling

9 oz meaty belly pork, cut into ¾ in chunks
4½ oz pork shoulder, cut into ¾ in chunks
2 oz lean bacon, minced
1 pork kidney, minced
2 large leeks, trimmed of most of the green parts, thickly sliced and washed
several sage leaves, chopped
salt and freshly ground white pepper
2 tbsp medium sherry
a little flour
½ cup water

Mix together the flour, suet, and seasoning in a roomy bowl. Add just enough water to mix to a cohesive mass: not too sticky, not too dry. Knead for a few minutes until supple. Flatten a little and leave to relax while you prepare the filling.

Put all the ingredients for the filling apart from the flour and water into another bowl and mulch together with your hands. Lay the meat out flat in a shallow pan and dust the surface with a fine but thorough sprinkling of flour. Gather up and return to the bowl, add the water, and briefly mulch once more.

Generously butter the pudding bowl. Roll out two-thirds of the pastry quite thinly and line the bowl with it, allowing a little to overhang the rim. Pack in the filling, lightly pressing it down. Roll out the remaining pastry to form a lid. Dampen the edge of the pastry overhanging the bowl, lay the pastry lid over, and clamp the two together with your fingers. Trim off the excess and cut 2 small holes in the center of the lid. Cover with a sheet of buttered, pleated wax paper and then with a sheet of foil. Tie with string to secure. Steam the pudding for 2–2½ hours – or even as long as 3; it will not affect the final result.

SWIRLY MINCEMEAT SUET PUDDING WITH BRANDY SAUCE

I have always had trouble with my roly-poly puddings when cooked as a long log affair; whether steamed or baked, they always seem to spread out and go all flat and dull-looking. However, prepared in this way, not only does everything behave very well indeed, restricted within the confines of a pudding bowl, but it also looks very pretty indeed when turned out.

You will need a pudding bowl with a capacity of approximately 1 quart.

Serves 4

For the mincemeat suet pudding

2 cups self-rising flour
4½ oz suet
a pinch of salt
cold water, to mix
a 14 oz jar of mincemeat, or, of course, homemade
2 tbsp softened butter
1–2 tbsp soft brown sugar

For the brandy sauce

1½ cups milk
3 tbsp butter
3 tbsp flour
a tiny pinch of salt
2–3 tbsp sugar, to taste
2–3 tbsp cognac, or rum, if you prefer
2½ tbsp cream

Mix together the flour, suet, and salt in a roomy bowl. Add just enough water to mix to a cohesive mass: not too sticky, not too dry. Knead for a few minutes until supple. Flatten a little and leave to relax for 10 minutes. On a floured surface, roll the pastry out fairly thinly (about 12 in square). Spread with the mincemeat, leaving a gap of about ¾ in around the edges. Roll up neatly, but not too tightly.

Generously grease the inside of the bowl with the butter. Sprinkle the sugar all over the butter, pressing the residue that falls to the bottom against the sides; all the butter must be well coated with sugar. Now cut the roly-poly into sections, about ½–¾ in thick. Arrange 3 in the bottom of the bowl, more up the sides, pressing them well against the butter–sugar mixture, and the remaining slices in the middle (these do not matter so much, as they won't show in the final assembly, but try to make the final ones lie flat). Cover with buttered wax paper, then foil, and tie with string around the bowl. Steam for 2–2½ hours, or as long as 3.

Meanwhile, make the sauce. Put the milk into a pan and heat through until hot but not boiling. Meanwhile, in a heavy-bottomed saucepan, melt the butter, but do not allow it to froth. Stir in the flour until well blended. Cook over a very gentle heat for 2 or 3 minutes. Now carefully pour in the milk, whisking all the time. Allow to come up to a gentle simmer and stir for a few minutes with a wooden spoon until smooth and lightly thickened. Add the salt, sugar, and cognac or rum. Let the sauce cook very gently, ideally on one of those diffuser pads, for several minutes. Stir occasionally. Pour in the cream, gently reheat, and give it a final whisk.

To serve, carefully run a knife around the edge of the pudding and turn out onto a warmed serving dish. Hand the sauce separately.

SUSSEX POND PUDDING

Surely one of the most unusual of all English steamed puddings. Not surprisingly, also very, very delicious. I have made individual ones, using large dariole molds (the ones for making caramel custards, with sloping sides), but here you have to chop the lemon into small pieces and slightly up the quantity. Quite good made with oranges too – or a mixture of the two, perhaps?

You will need a pudding bowl with a capacity of approximately 1 quart.

Serves 4

1½ cups self-rising flour
3½ oz shredded suet
a pinch of salt
a little cold milk, to mix
½ cup very cold butter, cut into small pieces
⅔ cup soft brown sugar
1 large unwaxed lemon

Mix together the flour, suet, and salt in a roomy bowl. Add just enough milk to mix to a cohesive mass: not too sticky, not too dry. Knead for a few minutes until supple. Flatten a little and leave to relax for 10 minutes.

Generously butter the pudding bowl. Roll out two-thirds of the pastry quite thinly and line the basin with it, allowing a little to overhang the rim. In a bowl, tumble together the butter and sugar with a fork. Place about half of it in the pastry-lined bowl. Using a sharp meat skewer, puncture the lemon all over. Push it down into the butter and sugar, arranging it vertically. Cover with the remaining butter and sugar.

Roll out the remaining pastry to form a lid. Dampen the edge of the pastry overhanging the bowl, lay the pastry lid over, and clamp the two together with your fingers. Trim off the excess and cut 2 small holes in the center of the lid. Cover with a sheet of buttered, pleated wax paper and then with a sheet of foil. Tie with string to secure. Steam the pudding for 3 hours, or even as long as 4; as in the previous recipes, this will not affect the final result in the least.

TARRAGON

"There's bags of tarragon growing in the garden," said Tessa brightly. "Help yourself to as much as you want. You'll never use it all, it just goes on and on and on!" Tessa was right. There *was* a forest of something green and spiky growing out there but, unfortunately, it was the rampant bush known as Russian tarragon, which tastes of bugger all.

Tessa Facey, from whom I rented my first little restaurant (five tables and just me in the kitchen – heaven!) in Pembrokeshire during the mid-1970s, was a keen if erratic gardener: she bored easily – and, perhaps, she still does. But she remains a cracking dame and is now living on the island of Minorca. I recall her zucchini patch was very prolific in Wales too, so maybe she will grow enough for the whole of the Mahon market during her long summers there.

As I recall, I paid Tessa 10 pence per pound for her Pembrokeshire zucchini. These were so fresh – as they surely would be when picked twenty minutes before the first customers walked through the door – that all they needed, once cut into half-inch pieces, was one minute's immersion in fiercely boiling water, a big knob of butter added, and a grind of pepper. She kept chickens and ducks too, of which one of the latter waddled under a wheel of my Renault 4 one morning – and inadvertently I squashed the poor drake. Mind you, once plucked and roasted he was absolutely delicious with apple sauce and peas, although just a little trickier than usual to carve . . .

The only tarragon to use is French tarragon. That stuff known as Russian must surely be related, but you might as well roll it up and smoke it for all the pleasure it will afford you. For the terminally persnickety, which is certainly no crime when it comes to culinary matters, you should bring back tarragon plants in an airplane, as

Michel Roux does each year, from the south of France. As soon as he arrives back in Bray, where is his pride and joy, his Waterside Inn, he plants it in his *jardin potager* and smiles: "Eet is sur murch better from zee 'omeland, particular when grurn een Provence!" (I just happened to be on the same flight as he one year when he was doing this very thing. He had a trunk full of garlic packed into the hold too. I had duty-free smokes and gin.)

In my first place of work, in Lancashire, we had to order tarragon from London. It would arrive with other choice items from a company called Benoist: bottled truffles, *jambon* de Bayonne, dried morels and cèpes, and walnut oil too, as I recall. But there, tucked among all these, there was always a little brown paper bag with a couple of bunches of fresh tarragon in it. Well, it *was* 1972, when it was either parsley or nothing or you grew your own herbs at home.

Our garden apple mint, which was so prolific that it invaded the adjacent field, was the only other herb I knew as a child, but I knew it very well indeed, as it always seemed to be me who was sent to pick it for new potatoes all summer long. How evocative it is, don't you think, that smell of mint boiling with new potatoes? Tarragon to me then was nothing more than dusty green flakes in a jar.

TARRAGON AND MUSTARD BUTTER FOR STEAK AND LAMB

Any grilled food cries out for all manner of spiced and savory compound butters. When I see it slowly melting over the charred surfaces of grilled meat it promotes a dribbling of saliva like no other cooked food. A fine mustard is a must with steak at any time, naturally, but in the following recipe I believe the one to use is one of those coarsely ground seed mustards. The French manufacturers Maille make a most individual compound labeled "Moutarde Fins Gourmets." This is extraordinarily good, and never having been a big fan of most seed mustards I remain quite amazed to find how much I really like this one. But then, it is smoother than others yet also possesses the required potency.

Makes about 5 oz (generous ½ cup) of savory butter

generous ½ cup best unsalted butter, softened to room temperature
1 small clove garlic, chopped
4–5 sprigs of tarragon, leaves only, chopped
1 tbsp seed mustard
½ tsp mustard powder
½ tsp salt
freshly ground black pepper
1 tsp tarragon vinegar

Put all the ingredients into the bowl of an electric mixer (or a food processor using the plastic blade) and beat together until smooth and homogenized. Dampen a sheet of wax paper and spoon the butter onto it in a rough log shape. Roll up into a tighter log, twisting the ends to form a sort of Christmas cracker. Then roll this up tight using a sheet of strong kitchen foil, once again twisting the ends. Put to chill in the fridge— or freezer, if you wish to simply have it to hand when you need it. If so, return to the fridge to soften slightly before slicing off thick discs to garnish grilled meats, and further not forgetting to remove their little paper and foil collars before sending the finished dish to table.

POTTED SHRIMP WITH TARRAGON

Similar to other potted shrimps, but with the added savor of an intensely shellfish-infused butter gained from the discarded shrimp carcasses.

Serves 6

¾ cup plus 2 tbsp best-quality unsalted butter, melted
1 lb cooked shrimp, whole, in shell

(these are freely available in supermarkets and have been previously frozen,
but their quality is just fine here)
1 tbsp Pernod
salt
the leaves from 4–5 sprigs of tarragon, chopped
¼–½ tsp cayenne pepper
a generous scraping of nutmeg
juice of ½ a lemon

Serve with

mustard cress
1 lemon
toast

Put the butter to melt in a large pan. De-head the shrimp then peel the tails. Put the peeled tails in a bowl and refrigerate. Place all the shells and heads in the pan with the butter. Stew gently, over a low heat, stirring occasionally, for 15 minutes. Tip the whole lot into a sieve suspended over a bowl and leave to drip for 5 minutes. Then press the contents of the sieve (all those aromatic shrimp heads and shells) with the back of a ladle, pushing and shoving every scrap of essence out of them into the buttery residue beneath. Discard the exhausted debris.

Now, decant approximately half of that buttery residue into a large frying pan. When hot but not frothing too much, tip in the shrimp and stir around until heated through. Add the Pernod and set it alight with a match. Once the modest flames have subsided, sprinkle with a little salt, add the tarragon and spices, and squeeze in the lemon juice. Stir around once more and remove from the heat.

Now take 6 ramekins and divide the buttery shrimp between them, making sure you give an equal amount of buttery liquid to the collection of shrimp in each pot, and keeping some butter back. Gently press them down with the back of a spoon so that all are as submerged as possible. Place in the fridge to cool.

Once they have just set, spoon the remaining shrimp-flavored butter over their surfaces, to seal. Put back in the fridge for a final set. To serve, run a small sharp knife around the insides of the pots and tip out onto individual plates. (*Note:* There may be an unattractive leakage of muddy shrimp juices here. Don't fret. Simply wipe them away with paper towel and re-plate.) Decorate with a bundle of mustard cress, a wedge or two of lemon, and have some hot toast to pass around the table.

CHICKEN TERRINE WITH TARRAGON

I came across a picture of this deceptively simple-looking terrine in a spiral-bound recipe book-cum-diary while spending quality time in Sydney, Australia, three years ago now. It transpires that it was, in fact, a collection of recipes and philosophies pertaining to a restaurant called *ecco*, in Brisbane. Coincidentally, it had also been the recipient of the Australian Gourmet Traveller Restaurant of the Year award the previous year (1997), when my friend Rick Stein had been the guest judge. As he is a man I know to be blessed with rare good taste and precise judgment, it seemed natural to promptly purchase a copy of this flimsy volume. And how glad I am that I did, for I treasure my *ecco* cookbook.

Philip Johnson (chef/proprietor of *ecco*) asks that you first remove the skin from the chicken and use it to line the terrine mold before packing the chicken morsels within it. This really does make a difference and is only a slightly tedious task; well, at least consider it. Here is a brief description of the process.

Start by cutting away the skin with the bird placed upside down (breast resting on chopping board), making a lengthy initial incision along its backbone. As you start to cut the skin away, it will soon begin to separate itself from the flesh quite naturally, slipping away from the pink meat as you explore beneath the skin and work your way around the contours of the bird. (The skin is far more resistant to the occasional rupture than you might imagine.) Before you realize where you are, you will be left with a huge rectangular flap of chicken skin.

Note: I have slightly adapted the original recipe, substituting tarragon for basil – which is, after all, an assured longtime bedfellow of a fine chook. Now, read on . . .

Serves 6–8

1 free-range chicken with giblets
(approximate weight 5½ lb)
the leaves from at least 8–9 sprigs of bushy tarragon, chopped
1¾ oz peeled garlic cloves (new season's whenever possible)
the grated zest of 1 large lemon
1½ tbsp sea salt
1 tsp freshly ground white pepper
a few scrapings of nutmeg

Serve with

hot buttered toast
cornichons (optional)

Remove the skin of the chicken with your favorite small, sharp knife, as described above. Once you have the flat piece of chicken skin, place it on a work surface, the familiar side of the chicken skin facedown, and trim off any fatty or unnecessary bits.

Preheat the oven to 350°F.

Remove all the flesh from breast, thigh, and drumstick and cut into ¾ in pieces. Put into a roomy bowl and mix in the tarragon, garlic, lemon zest, salt, pepper, and nutmeg. Use your hands here, mulching everything together, until all seems well blended. Pile this muddle into the middle of the chicken skin, fold over the flaps to form a loose parcel, and then fit neatly into a suitably sized terrine mold or a dish that you use to make pâtés in.

Put the terrine dish in a deep pan and fill the pan with boiling water from the kettle until it reaches three-quarters of the way up the sides of the terrine dish (a bain-marie). Cover with a lid or foil and bake for 1 hour and 20 minutes on the middle shelf of the oven. (*Note:* The skin and contents will naturally do their own thing as they cook: the skin will shrink back, the meat will contract, juices and fat will exude and coagulate. This is meant to be.)

Once cooked, remove the terrine dish from the bain-marie, pour off the water, and return the terrine to the empty pan. Leave to cool and settle for 15 minutes. Compress the surface of the terrine with a board or lid, weighted down with something such as a couple of family-sized cans of baked beans, for about 1 hour. Fat and juices will well up during this time, maybe even flooding over the lip of the dish; it is important to collect these and reintroduce them into the dish. Now seal the terrine dish with plastic wrap and put in the fridge for at least 12 hours to cool and set.

To serve, slice the chicken terrine thickly, directly from the dish, making sure that you use careful sawing motions as you cut, so as not to tear the pressed chicken meat as you go. Present on pristine white plates, for preference. Eat with hot buttered toast and, perhaps, a few crisp and aromatic cornichons.

TONGUE

One of the most successful dinner parties I remember cooking was for four friends, two of whom are Jewish. Now it was not for that reason alone that I decided to boil together an ox tongue and a nice slab of fatty brisket, it was food that I just knew would appeal to anyone who enjoys good food. "Each and everyone seated around my table will enjoy this sumptuous feast tonight," I said to myself with much confidence, as I watched the meats gradually begin to sink beneath the water in my big copper boiling pan.

Apart from anything else, boiling meats such as these (I should say simmer, really, as you don't ever want to boil the very devil out of them) is one of the easiest of operations, especially when doing it all on your own. Apart from anything else, it is also really quite difficult to overcook these joints. Moreover, you can even cook them the day before, until the point where they possibly need a further half an hour to reheat and simmer until tender right through when pierced with a thin skewer. All that is then necessary is to leave them immersed in their cooking liquor and kept hot over the merest flicker of a flame, preferably with one of those heat-diffuser pads underneath to keep things stable.

I am also particularly partial to a poached veal tongue. These are not so easy to come by, more's the pity. I have always thought it strange that however much veal we import from Holland their tongues rarely manage the journey here; I reckon they all go to France, Belgium, and Italy, where such a delicacy is, how shall we say, lapped up? But we have always liked a nice bit of *salt* tongue – and cold sliced ox tongue, in particular, which remains delicious but safe, in the best British tradition. So why, pray, do we not wish to eat delicious and tender *un*-salted tongue?

Maybe it is because it doesn't look very appetizing once cooked, all gray and wet. But if, like me, you are fond of such a thing and live in or near London, then the ever wonderful Selfridges Food Halls should be able to furnish you with a nice fresh calf's tongue. In fact all veal products on sale at this estimable store are some of the very best I have ever seen. They even do a nice line in calf's tails.

Apart from the following recipe for calf's tongue with *sauce charcutière,* I also enjoy boiled tongue with a simple *sauce ravigote.* This is a loosely thick vinaigrette made with vinegar, mustard, tarragon, parsley, chopped capers, chopped raw onion, and bound with a light salad oil such as sunflower or a good vegetable oil – *never* olive oil. The oil here is used simply to carry the sauce, not to flavor it. Moreover, I am heartily sick and tired these days of being served such a sauce made with olive oil. And this surely informs me that here is a chef who might well have been told how to put the sauce together but has never actually eaten it himself anywhere else (like maybe in France, yeah?); or actually does not know how to eat properly at all and possibly never bothers to; or thinks that all oil for use as a kitchen condiment, lubricator, or as part of an emulsification process can only be made from olives. A rotten trend, to be sure.

Note: These days, both salted and fresh tongues usually arrive in a plastic pouch, swimming in briny pink or natural juices. Before attempting any of the following recipes, first cut the bag open and rinse the tongue well in tepid water. Pat dry and place in a roomy pot. Cover with cold water and slowly bring to a gentle simmer. Once the surface of the water is covered with a light layer of scum, and small bubbles are breaking through, lift out the tongue with a slotted spoon and rinse under a cold running tap. Chuck out the water, clean out the pot, and only then begin the recipe.

BRAISED OX TONGUE WITH CAPER SAUCE

A more substantial version of the traditional English caper sauce here, by virtue of the fact that the tongue has been richly braised. Do not be tempted to use those tiny Italian capers that have been packed in salt. Some bewildered folk are now of the opinion that no other capers will do. (I blame the obsessive River Café girls for this belief.) Nor do I think the similarly midget-sized ones in vinegar are suitable here either. So *please* will you use those old-fashioned big and blowsy ones that are also packed in vinegar but actually possess the most pronounced flavor of all, particularly for this dish? I have nothing against the tiny ones – whether salted or vinegared. They are simply the wrong ones to use for this caper sauce.

Serves 4–6

6 tbsp butter
2 onions, chopped
2 carrots, chopped
3 sticks celery, chopped
3½ oz sliced button mushrooms
4 peeled tomatoes, chopped
7 tbsp tarragon vinegar
¾ cup white wine
¾ cup strong, well-jellied beef stock
thyme, bay, parsley stalks
1 ox tongue, pre-prepared (see note on page 258)

For the caper sauce

2 tbsp flour
the braising liquor
1–2 tbsp of vinegar (decanted from the jar of capers), to taste
salt and white pepper
1 demitasse spoon smooth Dijon mustard
1 tsp red-currant jelly
5 tbsp heavy cream
1 tbsp capers, squeezed of excess vinegar
1 tbsp chopped parsley

Serve with

mashed potatoes

Preheat the oven to 275°F.

Melt the butter in a roomy, lidded cast-iron pot. Add the vegetables and stew gently, covered, for 20 minutes, or until lightly colored. Add the vinegar, turn up the heat, and reduce the vinegar to nothing, stirring frequently; the result should be a sort of sticky mess. Add the wine and stock and stir in the herbs. Bring up to a simmer and bury the tongue in this aromatic braising liquid. Turn it through the mixture a few times and then cover with a sheet of wax paper, cut to fit the interior of the pot. Press it down lightly and put on the lid. Cook in the oven for at least 2 hours, turning the tongue over from time to time. The tongue is cooked when a skewer pushed right through the thickest part shows no resistance.

Once the tongue is fully cooked, remove to a dish, scrape off any bits of clinging vegetable or herb, and leave to cool. Once cool enough to handle, carefully peel off its skin and discard it. Return to the dish, cover with foil, and keep warm in the oven. Strain the braising liquor through a fine sieve into a bowl and leave to settle for 10 minutes. Discard the solids. Spoon off the fat that has collected on the liquor's surface and add 2 tablespoons of it to a small pan. Pour away the remainder.

Add the flour to the fat and cook over a low heat, stirring, for a couple of minutes until lightly colored. Stir in the braising liquor slowly, until all is lightly thickened and very smooth (use a whisk as an aid, if you like). Add the vinegar, seasoning, mustard, and red-currant jelly. Allow to simmer gently for 10 minutes. Whisk in the cream, add the capers, and stir in the parsley. Simmer once more for a couple of minutes and spoon over the tongue, which should be served cut into thick, juicy slices. Mashed potatoes? Of course.

Note: Should you think that there is too little of the braising liquor to give the correct consistency to the sauce, simply add a little water or more wine.

POACHED CALF'S TONGUES, SAUCE CHARCUTIÈRE

Presumably, this traditional French sauce is so named because it goes so very well with most cuts of meat from the *charcutier,* the local French pork butcher and master of all things to do with *jambon, saucissons, fromage de tête, museau et les pieds, les queues et les oreilles de porc, et quelques choses d'autres . . .* Prosaically, however, this piquant and intensely savory lotion is most often served up with nothing more than a grilled pork chop. Nothing wrong with that at all, of course, but it is also very nice indeed, although not exactly *propre,* when served with these tongues.

Serves 4–5

2 fresh calf's tongues, pre-prepared (see note at close of introduction, page 258)
1 quart light veal or chicken stock
a few pieces of cleaved veal knuckle bone or the same of calf's foot
4–5 carrots, peeled and cut in half lengthways

4–5 small onions, peeled and each stuck with 1 clove
4–5 beautiful sticks celery, peeled and cut in half
3 bay leaves

For the sauce

a 14 oz can of chopped tomatoes
3 strips of pithless lemon zest
5 juniper berries, bruised
2 bay leaves
4 shallots, finely chopped
3 tbsp butter
5 tbsp red wine vinegar
1 tbsp flour
1 small glass of white wine
2 cups plus 2 tbsp of the hot poaching stock
several cornichons, diagonally sliced
1 tsp each chopped tarragon, parsley, and chives
salt and freshly ground white pepper

Put the tongues into a roomy pot, and add the stock and the pieces of veal bone or calf's foot. Simmer gently for 40 minutes, removing any resultant scum as it forms on the surface. After this time, add the vegetables and bay leaves. Simmer for a further 35–45 minutes. To check whether the tongue is cooked, insert a skewer through the thickest part of the meat; if there is no resistance, the tongue is done. (Depending on its size, a calf's tongue can sometimes take a further half hour.) Keep hot with the vegetables, in the stock, until ready to serve.

To make the sauce, first put the tomatoes, lemon zest, juniper berries, and bay leaves into a small stainless-steel pan and allow to simmer away quietly for 20 minutes or so, until reduced by about two-thirds and very thick. Push through a sieve into a bowl and set aside.

In another small pan, fry the shallots in the butter until pale golden. Add the vinegar and reduce until all but disappeared. Stir in the flour and allow all to gently cook, stirring constantly, until the paste is straw-colored. Whisk in the wine until smooth and then pour in the hot stock, taken from the attendant pot of tongues. Stir in the sieved tomatoes, bring up to a simmer, and quietly allow to cook for 10 minutes more, while also skimming off any scum which forms on the surface in the meantime. Finally, introduce the cornichons and herbs and correct the seasoning.

To serve, skin the tongues and cut into thickish slices. Lay out on a heated platter and surround with the vegetables. Pour the hot sauce into a heated sauce boat and pass separately.

COLD OX TONGUE WITH EGGS "AU VERT"

The following recipe is inspired by the dish *anguilles au vert* (green eels), where rich sections of eel are set among a mess of chopped egg, green herbs, sorrel, watercress, etc., which once left to cool gels wonderfully around the fish. Here, however, the sauce for the eggs is, perhaps, more akin to the Italian salsa verde. Well, to be honest, it is exactly that. *Vert? Verde?* At least, they are both green! And, quite frankly, I happen to think it is an inspired assembly.

Serves 4–6

1 salt ox tongue, pre-prepared (see note on page 258)

3 large carrots, chopped

3 onions, peeled and stuck with 4 cloves each

6 sticks celery, peeled and chopped

3 bay leaves

2–3 sprigs of thyme

8 peppercorns

For the eggs *"au vert"*

a bunch of flat-leafed parsley, leaves only

10 large basil leaves

15 mint leaves

2 cloves garlic, peeled and crushed

1 tbsp Dijon mustard

6 anchovy fillets, chopped

1 tbsp capers, drained and squeezed of excess vinegar

⅔ cup extra-virgin olive oil

a little salt and much pepper

6 hard-boiled eggs, shelled and cut in half lengthways

Serve with

boiled new potatoes

Put the tongue in a roomy pot and cover with water to a depth of about 2 in. Simmer gently for 1 hour, removing any resultant scum as it forms on the surface. After this hour, add the vegetables, herbs, and peppercorns and simmer for a further hour. To check whether the tongue is cooked, insert a skewer through the thickest part; if there is no resistance, the tongue is done. Allow to cool completely in the cooking liquor before removing the skin. Wrap in foil or film and keep cool.

Meanwhile, begin to prepare the eggs. Put the herbs, garlic, mustard, anchovies, and capers into a food processor with a few tablespoons of the oil. Process for a few minutes and, with the machine still running, add the rest of the oil in a thin stream until very green and thick, yet spoonable. Season with any necessary salt and pepper. Arrange the halves of egg flat side down on a small oval plate, and carefully spoon the sauce over each one, so covering it entirely. Thinly slice the tongue onto another oval platter, overlapping the slices for prettiness, and send to table with the eggs. A bowl of scrupulously scraped new potatoes, boiled with a little mint and then lightly lubricated with olive oil, would be absolutely delicious here too.

TRUFFLES

The very first Perigord black truffle I ever put in my mouth I ate with sweetened whipped cream. Not a perfect match of flavors, I have to admit. But when you are a sixteen-year-old completely obsessed with cooking and eating (the order is interchangeable) and blessed with three weeks of paid school-holiday work in a tip-top French restaurant six miles from home, sneakily snaffling one's first truffle employs a similar mentality to rapidly smoking three No. 6 cigarettes behind the school bike sheds before throwing up all over Martineau.

In retrospect, I guess that I simply saw each misdemeanor as demonstrating a real need to experience the unknown; not exactly a crime as such, more part of a learning curve that wished to relish each and every extreme of the oral spectrum, vomit excepted. Although I am reluctant to say that, at the time, the smoke might just have had the edge on the costly truffle.

All blame lay with Dorothy, however, the straight-talking, hardworking, non-French waitress in the virtually 100 percent French personnel of La Normandie Restaurant et Bar, Birtle, near Bury in Lancashire, who inadvertently gave the game away. Just when I thought that exactly the right moment had presented itself to me to shove a whole Perigord black truffle (it *was* only a very small one) into my temporarily apprenticed, eager maw – I was precisely arranging a stratum of truffle up and down the length of a terrine of quail at the time – Dorothy also chose to present my pinched and pursed lips with a generous spoonful of freshly whipped *crème Chantilly,* a rare part of her dining-room *mise en place* performed in the kitchen.

"Taste that for the sugar will you, Simon love. I've got a bugger of a cold tonight!" trilled Dorothy, thickly. "Mmmgnumunk . . . yeah, OK," I mumbled, trying urgently to differentiate between the flavor of lactic vanilla and bosky tuber. "*Alors, mon petit chou*" (the French at their most endearing: "my little cabbage boy"), hollered Chef Champeau. "Zee black trooffle wiz zee whipp-ed cream, *c'est bon*? Eez eet a new dish for zee *table d'hôte*?"

I continued to blush for the rest of the day, but was eventually forgiven with a teasing, knowing grin from departing Chef, as if to say, "At least when I did it at your age, I managed to get away with it . . ." The enduring legacy, however, of my wicked deed is that I learned very early on how important it is to allow the Perigord black truffle to fraternize and hobnob with sympathetic partners, thereby allowing its unique scents and flavors to marry and blossom. The single raw *Tuber melanosporum* crunched by the teeth is a deeply disappointing experience – with or without the addition of "whipp-ed cream." Even consuming it with a small degree of honesty will not improve matters.

COOKING TRUFFLES

I bought rather a lot of truffles in the year of the millennium. They came direct to me from France, specifically from the undisputed truffle king, M. Peybère, in Cahors. We did the deal in the Connaught Hotel, where Peybère stays every year as the guest of Michel Bourdin (who buys enough to last him all year!), who has been chef of the Connaught for as long as I can remember.

These particular truffles were of stupendously good quality, and so perfumed were they that their waning, heady odor permeated the inside of my motor car for several days to come – even though they had only made the short journey from Mayfair to Shepherd's Bush.

Preparing a dish using fresh truffles is clearly the finest way in which to use them. However, I also take enormous pleasure in bottling them up, and over the years have devised a slightly unorthodox method of preserving them that is both easy and offers the most pleasing results to the home cook.

Most commercially bottled truffles are cooked with very little liquid indeed. Now then, as far as I am concerned the thing that is almost more important than the truffle itself, once preserved, is the juice in which it has been cooked. So I make lots of it. This then has endless uses in sauces, dressings, elegant little soups and consommés, and as part of a marinade for pâtés, everyday terrines, and – if you are up to it – a sumptuous terrine of fresh foie gras. This is the way to go about it.

For 5 oz fresh black truffles, you will need:

1 small Ball jar for each truffle
½ cup good-quality white wine
2 tbsp Madeira
2 tbsp dry sherry
1 tbsp cognac
1 tsp sea salt
a few grinds of white pepper
1 tsp sugar
½ cup bottled still water

Wash the jars thoroughly in very hot water, together with their rubber seals. Leave to dry. Put all the ingredients except the truffles and the water into a stainless-steel or enameled pan and bring to a boil. Once it comes to the boil, stand back and ignite the liquid with a match. Allow the flame to burn itself out and then add the water. Divide this mixture between the jars and pop a truffle into each one. Attach the rubber seal to the lid and clamp or screw shut.

Place a thick fold of newspaper (about half a tabloid) in the bottom of a large pan and place the jars upon it. Fill with cold water up to just below the wire clip. Gently bring up to a simmer and cook slowly for 40 minutes; the water should just be bubbling around the jars. Switch the heat off and leave the truffles to cool completely in the water. Lift out and place in the fridge, where they will keep well for at least 4 months, if not longer.

Important: The truffles *must* be kept in the fridge at all times, as this particular preserving method is not 100 percent foolproof, unlike commercially preserved truffles that can stand varying degrees of ambient temperature. However, the result is ten times better.

GRATIN OF POTATOES WITH BLACK TRUFFLE

This is the moment to use your carefully preserved truffles to their best advantage. A treat for serving with 2 small roast partridges, for that candlelit supper you keep meaning to have.

Serves 2

1 small clove garlic, bruised
1 cup whipping cream
salt and pepper
3–4 tbsp truffle juice (the preserving liquid)
11 oz medium-sized potatoes, peeled and thinly sliced
1 black truffle, thinly sliced

Preheat the oven to 350°F.

Put the garlic, cream, and a little seasoning into a small saucepan and gently bring to a simmer. Reduce by about a quarter and strain through a sieve into a bowl. Stir in the truffle juice and put to one side. Butter the base of a small oval gratin dish and lay in half the potatoes, neatly overlapping. Cover with the truffle slices, pour over half the garlic-seasoned cream, and then finish with the remaining potatoes, overlapping, so that they look pretty. Spoon over the rest of the cream and allow to settle for a minute or two. Cover with foil and bake for 25 minutes. Remove the foil and cook for a further 15–20 minutes, or until pale golden and tender right through when prodded with a fork. Allow the heat to wane for 5 minutes or so before eating.

BAKED EGGS WITH FRESH BLACK TRUFFLE

Here is one of the very nicest ways of using fresh black truffles.

Serves 2

2 free-range and very fresh eggs
a fresh black truffle
a cut clove of garlic
butter
4 tbsp heavy cream

Perfume the eggs with the truffle in a sealed container in the fridge for a minimum of 2 days.

Preheat the oven to 350°F.

Rub 2 cocotte dishes (ramekins) with the garlic and smear with butter. Place 2 slices of truffle in the bottom of each dish, add 1 tbsp of cream, and then break an egg over it. Season and spoon over another tablespoon of cream. Slip 2 more slices of truffle into the cream and set a tiny sliver of butter on the surface.

Bake for between 7 and 10 minutes in a bain-marie in the oven. Poke them with a tentative finger the first time you go about it, just to be sure that the white has set sufficiently beneath. You should be able to see when the yolk is perfect, sporting its strangely lilac-blue, opaque skin through the gently bubbling cream – an immediate indication to those of you who are familiar with the frying and basting of a very fresh, orange-yolked egg.

VINEGAR

May I just say here, for the record, that I regard true balsamic vinegar (using artisanal and traditional methods) as one of the most remarkable of all culinary condiments ever created. There now, that's that one out of the way. But there are other vinegars. Real vinegars. Vinegars that are not black, sweet, sticky, or even very rare.

As a kiddy, I used to sip Sarson's malt vinegar directly from the bottle. I loved the smell of it almost as much as I craved the heady hit of petrol when Dad filled the tank of the old Ford Zodiac. Although those groovy gases that emanated from the Esso nozzle eventually palled (and I should jolly well think so too!), the inhalation of all types of vinegar, from good to indifferent, has never ceased to titillate my nostrils.

The fact that I now have the choice to use only good wine-based vinegar in my cooking has caused me to discriminate somewhat. Even so, malt vinegar is still the one and only vinegar to splatter over a damp, scrunched-paper serving of fish and chips. And, as you very well know, this assembly always tastes best when eaten in the car – and with all the windows firmly closed, of course. Seeing a stationary car with steamed-up windows parked outside a fish-and-chips place on a wet British winter's night never fails to twitch my tummy juices.

I once made the huge mistake of collecting some fish and chips from my local emporium and rejecting the in-house offer of salt and vinegar, preferring to add my own once home only a few streets away (they stay crunchier that way). Horror of horrors! I quickly discovered that I only had a bottle of white wine vinegar in the cupboard. So it had to be that, as the thought of eating them without any sort of vinegar at all was inconceivable.

The sorry result turned out to be quite the filthiest combination imaginable. So much so that I only managed to finish half of it, flinging the mismatched mess into the trash with rage. I mean, right is right and wrong is wrong, which is why I have become incensed with the way that *aceto balsamico* – and that's not the artisanal product – is now used as an everyday seasoning, sloshed over anything and everything. I bet you someone, somewhere, has already stained their cod and chips with it. The saddest outcome of all, however, is that it will probably have been *enjoyed*.

In a serious kitchen, a bottle of good wine vinegar can perform some of the cleverest tricks of cooking. Apart from that all-important acidity lurking in the background of a simple vinaigrette, fine vinegar is also one of the essential players in the making of a proper *gazpacho Andaluz* – and the vinegar should be made from sherry to be truly authentic.

White wine vinegar, briefly reduced to a smear in a small pan with shallots, is the base of a classic *beurre blanc,* perhaps the most elusive and most seductive of all French sauces. Similarly, the traditional *poulet au vinaigre* greatly relies upon gentle evaporation of the aromas of a good red wine vinegar as it simmers around the joints of a farm chicken, its eventual essence, together with poultry juices, neatly emulsifying with some added butter to form a sauce of the utmost piquancy.

It was with great excitement that I purchased my very first bottle of sherry vinegar that had been boosted with a generous slug of the legendary PX sherry. This is an abbreviation of Pedro Ximenez, the sherry that looks and pours like gravy browning yet laves the tongue with the very essence of the deepest, sweetest sherry imaginable. And I just know that once word gets around, the Italians will be blending old *balsamico* with their very best *aceto di vino rosso* in retaliation. I'll look forward to that, especially as I was part of the initial discussions at Sánchez Romate, Jerez de la Frontera, when this exquisite sweet sherry vinegar was about to become a reality. No doubt someone will then organize a comparative tasting . . . heaven forfend!

EGGPLANT WITH SWEET SHERRY VINEGAR, GARLIC, AND MINT

This mildly fiery dish is, for me, best eaten at room temperature. It is just bang on for vegetarians, but it is also excellent when served alongside barbecued food that has been given a noteworthy marinade that involves Asian spicing. Lamb cutlets seem quite clearly the first choice here, but a cheaper cut of meat such as a thick slice of belly pork is also notable and should not be overlooked. If you like grilled tuna (which I don't very much), then a nice thick steak of it cooked rare would be the ideal choice of fish to eat with this eggplant.

Serves 4

1 lb eggplant, peeled and cut into large cubes
1 tbsp salt
2–3 tbsp vegetable oil
3 tbsp sweet sherry vinegar
2 tbsp finely shredded spring onions
½ tsp dried chilli flakes
1 tbsp freshly chopped mint

Sprinkle the eggplant with the salt and then mix together with your hands in a colander. Leave to drain for 40 minutes and then rinse in a sink of cold water. Drain, tip onto a clean dish towel, and carefully pat dry.

Heat the oil until smoking in a nonstick frying pan. Fry the eggplant briskly, tossing it about energetically until well colored on all sides. Tip into a serving dish. Trickle over the vinegar and stir in the spring onions, chilli, and mint.

Note: You may, if you like, leave the skin on the eggplant simply because you like the look of it. However, I have for some time now been of the opinion that this does nothing whatsoever for the taste of cooked eggplant. In Sicily, for instance, it is virtually impossible to find an unpeeled eggplant even though those that they grow and use most frequently (the large and bulbous lilac- and white-colored ones) sport the thinnest of skins. Taste and texture are, after all, all.

VINEGAR REDUCTION FOR THE MAKING OF BÉARNAISE SAUCE

Makes about 5 tbsp

1 cup plus 4 tbsp tarragon vinegar
5 shallots, peeled and chopped
2 tbsp dried tarragon
salt and pepper

Using a stainless-steel or enameled saucepan (if you use aluminium the reduction will react with it, producing a nasty metal taint to its taste, and will also be in danger of turning out a sort of muddy gray color), heat together the vinegar, shallots, and tarragon until the liquid has reduced by three-quarters. Remove from the heat, cool for a few moments, and then pass through a very fine sieve into a bowl, pressing hard upon the debris with the back of a small ladle so that every last drop has been extracted. Decant into a small screw-top bottle or jar and store in the fridge.

This is one of the most useful things to have to hand when the fancy takes one to whip up a quick Béarnaise sauce. Once 3 egg yolks have been whisked with a splash of water over a low heat until thick, and the butter has been melted and deftly incorporated (scum on top removed, only a trickle or so of the milky residue beneath used to loosen the sauce if need be) off the heat, using the same whisk, then all that is further necessary is to sharpen the sauce to taste with a little of the concentrated reduction, stir in some freshly chopped tarragon leaves, season, and, if you think it needs it, add a tiny squeeze of lemon juice.

So there you have it. And it is also worth remembering that Béarnaise sauce is for eating not only with a grilled steak – however matchless a vehicle that might be – but also with a cutlet of grilled or poached wild salmon, turbot or halibut, grilled lamb chops, poached chicken (especially fine, considering how perfect a herb tarragon is with chicken), or a poached egg sat upon a large, freshly cooked artichoke heart and coated with the sauce (artichokes are similarly delighted when associated with an emulsion of egg and butter).

Asparagus? Purple-sprouting broccoli? A baked potato? French fries? Most certainly fries; one of the finest bar snacks never to have been fully exploited is surely a bowl of crisp, fat, and salty fries with a small – no, make that a large – bowl of Béarnaise sauce on the side in which to dip them.

SIMPLE FRIED CALF'S LIVER WITH AGED BALSAMIC VINEGAR

As pure as cooking can get. I adore this dish and it is one I prepare often for myself at home alone – and, for once, the most useful and correct fashion in which to upend that bottle of traditional balsamic vinegar. But I do wish to stress quite how important it is to invest in one of those small bottles that have at least 35–40 years of age to them. Be warned, it will come in at quite a hefty price, but only a little is necessary to anoint the liver, so it should last quite a long time, and it keeps almost indefinitely in a dark cupboard.

Serves 2

6 tbsp butter
2 thin slices of calf's liver, all nervous tissue removed
1 peeled and bruised clove of garlic
aged balsamic vinegar (the more syrupy it is, the better)
sea salt and freshly ground black pepper
a squeeze of lemon juice

Serve with

very smooth mashed potatoes

In a large frying pan melt 4 tbsp of the butter until just beginning to foam.

Lay the slices of liver in the butter and, keeping the heat moderate, fry on both sides for 1–2 minutes until lightly singed and golden brown around the edges – the very model appearance, don't you think? Remove the liver to 2 warmed plates. Tip away the used butter, wipe out the pan, and add the remaining 2 tbsp of fresh butter. Heat gently with the garlic clove for a moment just enough to flavor the butter, lightly browning it and also the garlic. Discard the garlic and spoon the butter over each slice of liver. Trickle balsamic vinegar over each slice and spread it around with the back of a spoon. Season with salt and grind over some pepper. Finally, squeeze over the tiniest amount of lemon juice to finish. Very smooth mashed potatoes here, I think.

Recipe Index

275

Index